Girly Drinks

Also by Mallory O'Meara

The Lady from the Black Lagoon

Girly Drinks

A WORLD HISTORY *of* WOMEN *and* ALCOHOL

MALLORY O'MEARA

HANOVER
SQUARE
PRESS

**HANOVER
SQUARE
PRESS™**

Recycling programs
for this product may
not exist in your area.

ISBN-13: 978-1-335-28240-8

Girly Drinks: A World History of Women and Alcohol

This edition published by arrangement with Harlequin Books S.A.

Hanover Square Press
22 Adelaide St. West, 40th Floor
Toronto, Ontario M5H 4E3, Canada
HanoverSqPress.com
BookClubbish.com

Printed in Italy by Grafica Veneta

For Lauren,
who, upon hearing me complain that
there wasn't a written history of women drinking,
told me to write it.

CONTENTS

Don't try me nobody, cause you will never win
I'll fight the army, navy, just me an' my gin

—Bessie Smith

"…it went straight down into my stomach like a sword swallowers'
sword and made me feel powerful and godlike."

—Sylvia Plath

"Comfortable shoes and a strong drink —
what more could a girl need?"

—Woman wearing a green dress in the bathroom of the
Strange Brew Tavern, Manchester, New Hampshire, 2013

INTRODUCTION

Skinny margaritas. Appletinis. Cosmos. Drinks flavored like cake or whipped cream. Drinks *featuring* cake or whipped cream. Bright red maraschino cherries and pastel umbrellas. You know, girly drinks. Drinks for girls.

These are the drinks you snicker at when you hear someone order them at the bar. You feel embarrassed about choosing them off the menu. They might even be your guilty pleasure. Beer and scotch, those are real drinks. They're respectable drinks. Why? Well, they're men's drinks.

Hang on a minute.

Who decided that drinking was a gendered act? When did certain kinds of alcohol first become *respectable*? Where in the world did this happen? Why did this happen? *How* did this happen?

Human beings have been imbibing for thousands and thousands of years. When did we start roping off certain types of booze with a pink frilly ribbon and condemning them as *girly drinks*? And why is marking a drink feminine a bad thing in the first place?

The truth is, all drinks are girly drinks. Not just because women have been drinking since alcohol was invented, but because they've been making and serving it since the beginning, too.

I love having a drink. I suspect that if you picked up this book, you do, too.

Like many people, my first exposure to alcohol—I'm talking real exposure, without your parents around—was a lukewarm can of Natural Ice handed to me at a party in someone's garage when I was a teenager. I thought then, just like I would think now, that it was pretty gross.

But I didn't want anyone to know that I thought it was gross. I wanted to be *cool*. I didn't want to be some loser girl who couldn't handle a beer. Because that's what beer was to me: a guy thing. Girls couldn't handle drinks made for guys. Eventually, the nastiness of Natural Ice, which I would still describe as tasting like a sweaty gym sock that rotted in a gutter, convinced me that I needed to try something else if I wanted to drink at all. I couldn't handle real drinks. I needed a girly drink.

So began my teenage dalliances with such alcoholic atrocities as Smirnoff Ice, Mike's Hard Lemonade and Mad Dog 20/20 (blue flavor, please). Of course, teenagers aren't drinking for the flavor, they're drinking whatever they can convince someone's older brother to buy for them. When I was a teenager, boys got cheap, gruesome beer and us girls got cloyingly sweet, fizzy drinks.

Once I finally hit legal drinking age, I decided my tastes needed to mature. That's when I got acquainted with the drink that accompanied me through many parties and bad dates in my early twenties: the vodka soda with lime. I saw people drinking cocktails, but I never experimented. I didn't want to be embarrassed if I ordered something stronger than I could take. Whiskey and scotch were for dudes. I didn't want to flaunt my girliness by ordering a frozen margarita or daiquiri, either. And I was too sheepish to admit that I didn't know the difference between types of wine besides *red* or *white*. So vodka and I, we became pals.

Then, I moved to New York City, and I met my best friend, Lauren. She is a cocktail enthusiast, and the first time we ever hung out, she took me to a craft cocktail bar. I had absolutely no idea what I wanted to drink. As an alcohol ignoramus, the menu was overwhelming to me, so I picked something at random. When the glass appeared in front of me, I was enchanted. The dark and smoky rum concoction was delicious, but more importantly, it was interesting. There was talent in the making of it; there was alchemy. I was hooked. I had never put much thought into what I was drinking or all the different flavors that were possible. Alcohol had always been a means to an end. Holding that delicate coupe glass and savoring flavors that weren't just *sugar* and *red 40*, I realized that it could be so much more.

A couple of years later, I moved to Los Angeles. As a housewarming present, Lauren bought me a home bartending set: a shaker, a bar spoon, a mixing glass, the works. She also bought me a book on cocktails. For the first time in my life, I realized you could get nerdy about alcohol.

My eyes were opened to the science and history behind cocktails and drinking. I was overcome with curiosity. No longer just eager to taste craft drinks, I wanted to learn about them. The history of alcohol and drinking is an amalgamation of anthropology, chemistry, sociology, culinary history, economics, politics and science. I started reading all the books I could, in between shaking up cocktail recipes from them.

The first disappointment came when I noticed that the authors of these books were mostly men. The second disappointment came when I noticed that the subjects of these books were mostly men. If there was any women's history in there, it was typically relegated to a measly single paragraph. One book briefly mentioned how Prohibition was the first time in American history that women were allowed to drink in bars, since the bars during that time were all illegal speakeasies and all sorts of social rules were upended. *Damn!* I thought. *That's what I want to know about!*

I wanted an entire book made up of these scattered paragraphs, these snippets of women's history. But I couldn't find one. I asked my best friend, the same booze guru who started me on my cocktail journey. She agreed: the book I wanted didn't exist. There was one book about female whiskey distillers who worked during Prohibition, but even that was written by a male author. There were some wonderful recipe books and industry memoirs written by women, but no histories.

So I started researching. I wanted to collect all of those snippets, and I wanted to uncover new ones. I wanted to know what and where and how women were drinking, all over the world, across every era. I wanted to find out if drinking had always been a gendered act. Where did the concept of a girly drink even start?

It was soon clear that women's roles in alcohol history didn't start with those female whiskey distillers who worked during Prohibition. There have been female distillers, yes, but also female brewers, bartenders and, most importantly, drinkers in every part of the world since alcohol was first created. They have always been there, not just alongside men but usually one step ahead of them. From the ancient women who brewed beer and worshipped drunken goddesses, to the original makers of Japanese saké, to the widows who revolutionized the world of champagne, to Russian bootlegging grandmothers, to the luminaries who invented and inspired cocktail classics, to the innovators—both behind the bar and ordering from it—that are the vanguard of the current craft-alcohol renaissance, women have been crucial to nearly every era of alcohol and drinking culture. In this book, I set out to tell their story.

To do so, I'll be focusing on fifteen different stories. Fifteen different women, in different time periods, in different parts of the world. Each one will help me guide you through her time period. Some, like Cleopatra and Catherine the Great, you might already be familiar with. Others, like Sunny Sund and Gertrude Lythgoe, purposely avoided the spotlight while they were alive and thus have stayed relatively unknown. All of them will illuminate certain facets of what it was like through the ages for a woman who wanted to have a drink.

During my research, it was impossible not to notice how strong the correlation was between a culture that allowed women to drink and a culture that gave women their freedoms. In this book, you'll learn about women drinking, but also about when and why they couldn't. Patriarchal oppression and misogynistic societal expectations play the biggest roles in a culture's drinking habits. The double standard that drinking women face is deeply rooted in male anxieties about control and their fear of women acting like people, not property.

If you want to know how a society treats its women, all you have to do is look into the bottom of a glass.

For thousands of years, raising a toast as a woman was a subversive act. In many places all over the world, it still is. But if they get paid less, withstand more pain and have to fight against more oppression, aren't women more deserving of a goddamn drink?

1

DRUNKEN MONKEYS AND
DISCOVERING ALCOHOL

The Dawn of Time

Before there was bourbon, before there was beer, before there was wine, there was bad fruit.

The very first girly drink was not served in a cup or a glass or a tankard. It was served, slightly rotten, on the forest floor. One of our ancestors, an early precursor to Homo sapiens, picked a piece of overripe, fermented fruit off the ground and had herself a delicious snack. See, being attracted to alcohol is not a new thing. We can trace our boozy origins back millions of years to our primate ancestors.

An attraction to alcohol isn't new, but it turns out, it might be quite important. There's a theory, originally proposed by Dr. Robert Dudley of the University of California, Berkeley, called the drunken monkey hypothesis. Dr. Dudley believes that human attraction to alcohol may have originated with our more hirsute forebears and their dependence on fermented fruit as a food source. Fermentation occurs naturally in overripe fruit, which has a high sugar content. Yeasts eat that sugar and leave behind ethanol (among other things), which is the chemical backbone for the type of alcohol we drink. There are other kinds of alcohol—chemically speaking—but ethanol is the type used in beverages, toiletries and pharmaceuticals.

If you've ever used one of those food-tracking apps, you know that alcohol has a high calorie content. This is annoying if you're trying to lose weight, but if you were a primate trying to survive a few million years ago, it was extremely convenient. Dr. Dudley posits that early primates evolved a genetically based behavioral attraction to the molecule. And they didn't even have karaoke back then.

Ten million years ago, alongside big physiological changes like becoming bipedal, something shifted in our ability to process ethanol. A single point mutation in our genes increased our capability of metabolizing it twentyfold, a result consistent with greater dietary exposure to it. What does all that mean? Our ancestors came out of the trees, strolled around the forest floor and found a bounty of fallen fruit which had been fermenting on the ground instead of waiting to be picked fresh from the branches. This fermenting fruit had a higher calorie content and gave off a slightly different smell. Our hairy great-to-the-nth-degree-grandmothers had an advantage if they were attracted to it. One ounce of pure ethanol—less than a shot—contains 224 calories. More calories with less work! For these primal women, it was a huge boon. They needed those calories to run from predators, an experience I pay fifty dollars a month at my local gym to simulate.

The long and short of it is that there was a big evolutionary advantage to being attracted to ethanol before any of our ancestors realized the psychoactive effects it could have. There was no way they could eat enough fermented fruit to get a buzz. All that came much later.

Before we get there, though, let's take a moment to figure out what exactly booze is. Ethanol, in its pure state, is not something you want to mix in a cocktail. It would be even worse to drink than Everclear. It's colorless and highly volatile, just like many Everclear-fueled frat parties. Yet ethanol is the chemical backbone of all alcoholic beverages. Combine with ingredients like water, flavor-producing chemical compounds and sugar, and you've got something actually tasty to drink, like beer, wine or whiskey.

Alcohol is a depressant, which means that it inhibits the workings of the central nervous system. It's also biphasic, so its effects on the drinker vary depending on the quantity consumed. Small doses of it, the definition of which differs from person to person, can generate a sense of euphoria, diminish inhibitions and foster an uncharacteristic desire to dance in public. Large doses can slow brain activity, impair motor function, slur your speech and make you drowsy. In huge doses, it is fatal.

When alcohol gets metabolized by your body, it's broken down into more toxic and annoying substances like acetaldehyde and acetic acid, which can cause headaches, nausea, lethargy, heightened sensitivity to loud noises and a craving for home fries. (When our lady-ape ancestors were chomping down on that fruit, they weren't consuming enough to get a hangover.)

Now, let's say goodbye to our fermented-fruit-eating ancestors. Nothing changed in the world of booze for a long time, so we can safely fast-forward a few hundred thousand years.

Alcohol wasn't invented as much as it was discovered. No one really knows for sure exactly when, how or by whom, since there is no clear record of a *Eureka!* moment. The best guess is that it was probably by accident. When you leave certain types of food sitting out—things like fruit or grains or honey—yeast starts to gather. That yeast, like all living things, is hungry. When it starts eating the sugars in that fruit you've left in an open container outside of your hut, the process of fermentation begins. Maybe the container then gets rained on. After a few days of fermenting, the fruit slop you forgot about is alcoholic fruit slop. Boom! You've got alcohol. At some point, brave folks started drinking this accidental booze and thought it wasn't half bad.

We don't have a record of when exactly people discovered alcohol, but we do have evidence of when our ancestors started to drink. Even at the very start of things, women were equally as important to drinking culture as men. One of the earliest known depictions of a person drinking is an approximately 25,000-year-old carving, chiseled into a cliff at Laussel in the Dordogne region of France. This carving depicts a nude woman, with one hand on her belly[1] and holding what looks like a drinking horn in the other. Some male historians posit that it is not a drinking horn but rather some kind of musical instrument that the woman is holding incorrectly. Imagine being so staunch in your belief that women aren't drinkers that you think someone would take the time to immortalize a picture of the world's worst hornblower into the side of a cliff. Either way, she's called the Venus of Laussel, she's great, and she is very likely the earliest surviving artistic representation of drinking.

AZOOR PHOTO/ALAMY STOCK PHOTO

The Venus of Laussel in all her glory.

---

1   Many historians assume she is pregnant, but wow, how rude.

In that drinking horn was likely mead, which is just fermented honey (essentially honey wine).[2] The word *mead* is older than any other word associated with alcohol, and it was probably the first kind of alcohol ever made. Early humans might have found a beehive in the hollow of a tree that had filled with rainwater and decided to try the liquid inside. This crude mead would have tasted like honey and gotten the drinker slightly buzzed.

Finding boozy fruits and accidental alcohol is one thing, but eventually, things got more organized. The earliest evidence we have of the deliberate preparation of booze is from around 8000 BCE. After humans settled down and took up agriculture, they finally had the resources to intentionally make alcohol. By resources, I mean dedicated containers in which to replicate the process they had been taking advantage of for thousands of years (mixing water with honey, fruit or grains to form a liquid that could become alcoholic) and, now that they were no longer nomadic, the time to wait and let things ferment. Pottery from a grave in Northern China held residue that, when chemically analyzed, became proof that humans were converting some of their food to alcohol around 7000 BCE.

Things really got cooking (well, fermenting) in Mesopotamia, where humans eventually started to grow crops specifically to turn them into alcohol. Evidence of this first appears in what's known today as the Fertile Crescent, an area of land between the Tigris and Euphrates Rivers.

Life as a woman was pretty good in ancient Mesopotamia. It wasn't a feminist utopia, but in most aspects of life, women usually had fairly equal status to men. Culturally, a woman's role was primarily as a wife and mother, but women also engaged in trade and business. From selling goods to food production, there were lots of female vendors and businesswomen on the streets. Ladies could also gain power as priestesses. There was

---

2 Mead came first, so we should probably call wine *grape mead*, but it doesn't sound as nice.

no stigma around women doing sex work. Girls attended school (the same ones boys went to, run by priests or scribes) if they were royal or rich enough.

The industry where women ruled, though, was brewing. Women were in control of the production and distribution of both beer and wine, two very important goods. Beer, at the very beginning of its history, was a girl thing.

Between 6000 and 5000 BCE, the small agricultural settlements around the Fertile Crescent grew into villages and towns and cities. Culture rapidly developed in Mesopotamia, especially in Sumer, the region at the conflux of the Tigris and Euphrates (located in what is now Iraq). Sumer is the earliest known civilization, and it was active between about 4500 and 1900 BCE. Writing, art and brewing all blossomed there. There's evidence that writing itself was invented to record and quantify the beer-making process. Once the Mesopotamians started developing crops to turn into booze, they needed a system to keep track of things. Maybe I should have dedicated this book to beer, the first alcoholic beverage with a historical record.

The principal city of Sumer was Uruk. In Uruk, they really liked beer. Everyone drank it. Men, women, children, the elderly.[3] Hold on a minute, though. What is beer?

Beer is, in the simplest terms, any alcoholic beverage made from the brewing and fermentation of grain. Just like wine can be made with any kind of fruit, you can make beer with different kinds of cereal grains. Most beers today are brewed with barley—malted barley specifically. What the heck is malt? It's grain that has been germinated and roasted. You can flavor the beer with stuff like herbs if you want, but that's basically it. Beer was one of the staple foodstuffs in early civilization for people of any class because it was a rather nourishing beverage. It was

---

3 Before you wonder how anyone got anything done back then, know that Sumerian beer had a much lower alcohol percentage than the beers of today.

high in calories and carbohydrates for energy and contained small amounts of some vitamins and minerals like calcium and vitamin B6.

Since everyone drank beer (called *kash*), the women of Uruk brewed on a massive scale in order to produce enough of it. They made at least eight different styles of brew from barley, eight from wheat and three more from mixes of different grains. The Fertile Crescent wasn't just where civilization and agriculture began, it was also where the business of large-scale alcohol production kicked off. This industry became a major force that shaped the world's trade and economy—all fueled by the labor of women.

As the arts blossomed, they reflected the role of alcohol in society. Art from this time shows that booze became more than simply a part of everyone's diet. Drinking started to figure significantly into culture and religion. Along with the biological imperatives associated with alcohol, its universal allure includes religious and social imperatives, as well. Surviving artifacts show that while beer was ubiquitous in everyday Mesopotamian society, it was also a key religious offering. In the ancient world, consumption of alcohol became a principal way to communicate with dead ancestors, gods, goddesses and spirits of all sorts.

When Mesopotamians wanted to celebrate beer itself, they did not dedicate their toasts to a god but rather a goddess. Her name was Ninkasi.

Ninkasi was a Sumerian deity, the goddess who ruled over beer. This divine being knew how to party. It was believed that beer was imbued with the spirit of Ninkasi herself. The elated buzz you feel after a few beers? (Or if you're a lightweight drinker like me, halfway through your first glass?) That was thought to be the essence of Ninkasi.[4]

She knew how to party, but Ninkasi also knew how to work.

---

4   Her name translates to *the lady who fills the mouth*. For the Mesopotamians, drinking beer was literally imbibing the divine.

She ruled over the art of brewing, as well. Since beer was considered to be Ninkasi's gift to humanity, it was brewed in temples as part of religious ceremonies. The first large-scale brewers in Sumer were the priestesses of Ninkasi. Women who worked at the temples were paid in beer, about two liters at a time.

The most important legacy of Ninkasi is a hymn about her, sung by the women brewing the beer. The hymn was simultaneously a love letter to Ninkasi, a celebration of beer and a detailed guide containing instructions for every stage of the brewing process. Most people in Mesopotamia were not literate, so a catchy song was the best way for folks to remember and share the recipe for beer. Besides the brewers, people worshipping Ninkasi during festivals and religious rituals (and likely happily buzzed folks drinking their daily beers) sang the hymn. Here is part of the hymn, translated by Miguel Civil:

...

Ninkasi, you are the one who soaks the malt in a jar...
You are the one who spreads the cooked mash on large reed mats...
Ninkasi, you are the one who pours out the beer of the collector vat,
It is [like] the onrush of Tigris and Euphrates.

The women began the brewing process by making twice-baked barley bread, known as *bappir*. They broke the bappir up into pieces and mixed it with honey and dates. This delicious-sounding mixture was then soaked with water and put into a container to ferment. Once the fermentation process was over, the thick liquid was poured into a collector vat. Jars were then filled from these vats. The pouring of the beer being described as "the onrush of Tigris and Euphrates" means that it was thought to bring life to those who drank it.

The world's earliest known poet was a woman named Enheduanna. Born around 2286 BCE, she was a high priestess in the Sumerian city of Ur. Enheduanna wrote frequently about the city's drinking habits and the religious rituals that involved toasting to the gods and goddesses. On clay tablets—or at least the forty-two that survived—she wrote hymns in praise of all the gods and temples in Sumer, creating the world's first literary collection. Enheduanna's work is the first signed piece of literature in all of history. She was also the first writer of any gender to use *I* in poetry and personally identify herself. Enheduanna probably celebrated all these literary accomplishments like many writers do today—with a toast.

So both writing and poetry were created by beer-drinking women. They weren't just shaping the way alcohol was made, women were shaping the way it became part of our culture.

Religious rituals aside, Mesopotamian women also drank because they liked to. Everyone drank, and there was no stigma around it. (Unless you couldn't hold your booze. It wasn't Ninkasi's fault if you were a lightweight—that was all on you.) Alcohol was praised for its painkilling, relaxing and euphoric effects, which eased the difficulty of just about everything. Ancient Mesopotamians were encouraged to drink, especially the elderly, in order to make themselves feel better. For women, it maybe helped them forget the fact that they rarely lived past their forties (while men had a longer life expectancy by about a decade).

Sumerian queen Puabi, who lived sometime between 2600 and 2300 BCE, was buried with a silver jar that held her daily six liters of beer (as opposed to the one liter that common women received), along with all her drinking apparatuses such as cups, straws, jugs and fluted bowls. Even the straws were made of silver and gold. When her tomb was excavated, the skeletons of at least fifty attendants were discovered, the unfortunates who were expected to serve beer to the queen in the afterlife.[5]

Why would Queen Puabi need a straw to drink with? Well,

---

5 Evidence suggests that these people were either poisoned or poisoned themselves in order to follow the queen into the afterlife.

women were still refining the way beer was made. It was usually unfiltered, so to avoid a mouthful of grit, beer was consumed through a straw. In fact, straws were invented to drink beer with. Somehow, this still sounds less disgusting than drinking a can of Natural Ice.

On the other end of the class spectrum, women were also serving beer, along with brewing and drinking it. The taverns in Sumer were female-owned and -operated. This is one of the roots of the long-held idea that hospitality is women's work. These bar owners were of a low economic and social status and catered to the men and often the sex workers who frequented their establishments. However, it's believed that they had full legal and economic equality with men, as far as commercial activities go. Providing beer to people was just as important as providing bread. This also means the first bartender someone told their troubles to was a woman.

The importance of beer in Mesopotamia set a key economic standard, one that stuck even when social drinking habits began to change. Alcohol production and sales have, since the beginning of civilization, played a huge part in domestic economies all over the globe. It is a labor-intensive industry, and that labor was predominantly performed by women. A female labor force shaped trade in the ancient world.

The foundations of alcohol craft and culture were laid by female hands. The first known depiction of drinking was of a woman, and the first alcohol-related deity was a goddess. Thousands of years before Christians drank the wine of the Eucharist, thousands of years before Dionysus was worshipped with wine in Greece, Ninkasi was honored with beer by the Sumerian women who brewed and drank it. Her dominion over all aspects of alcohol is a symbol of how influential women have been.

And she wasn't alone. Over in Egypt during the same time period, Ninkasi had a sister. In spirit, anyway.

Hathor was known as *the drunken goddess*, and she really liked beer. She was the goddess of the sky, women, fertility, love and, most importantly, drinking. Every year, there was a festival to honor her, known as The Drunkenness of Hathor. The party started at the beginning of the yearly flooding of the Nile. It celebrated the myth that Hathor had gone on a rampage to destroy all of humanity in one of her alternative forms, the lioness-goddess Sekmet. The sun god Ra distracted her by filling the fields with red beer (to look like an enticing pool of blood). She drank a whole lot of it, and in her contented, drunken state, completely forgot to destroy mankind. Very relatable.

The origins of drinking in Egypt are very similar to its origins in Mesopotamia. The ancient Egyptians were avid beer drinkers. Their beer was known as *hek*, and brewing was a sacred activity, a divine secret imparted from the goddess Isis. There was a lesser goddess named Menqet, who was the deity of beer making. She was closely associated with Hathor. Naturally, the two would be pals.

At first, hek was made on a small scale by women in their homes. The process started with barley bread crumbled into jars. The bread was then covered in water and allowed to ferment. Afterward, the liquid inside was drained off, strained and drunk.

Hek became a diet staple and soon needed to be made on a large scale. The oldest known brewery in the world—the ruins of it, anyway—is in Egypt. It was operating around 3400 BCE, and women did the brewing there, too. (Depending on the size of the operation, enslaved men sometimes assisted.) The brewery was capable of producing up to three hundred gallons a day. The beer was about 5% ABV,[6] the strength of an average beer today. Workers were rationed about a gallon and a third of it every day. Illustrations from ancient Egyptian art show working-class women brewing—topless and up to their elbows in beer. What a dream.

---

6   This stands for *alcohol by volume*, the standard measurement of how much alcohol is in an alcoholic beverage. Most beers are about 5% ABV, while wine is usually around 13%. Most liquors are around 40%.

WORLD HISTORY ARCHIVE/ALAMY STOCK PHOTO

Ancient Egyptian woman brewing beer.

Most of what is known about the lives of ancient Egyptians concerns how the upper echelons of society lived. We don't have as much information about the daily lives of those topless peasant women making beer. But we do know that women in ancient Egypt liked to drink, and they also liked to get men drunk. Drinking and sexuality were closely linked. There was an affluent Egyptian woman named Chratiankh (birth and death dates unknown) whose tomb inscription read *I was a mistress of drunkenness, one who loved a good day, who looked forward to [having sex] every day, anointed with myrrh and perfumed with lotus scent.* This is all we know about Chratiankh, but what else is there to know? Be the Chratiankh you wish to see in the world.

Another thing the Mesopotamians and Egyptians had in common was exuberantly celebrating their boozy goddesses. Women of all economic classes loved the festival of Hathor. They would dress to the nines in their finest clothes, jewelry, makeup and fresh garlands, descend on the temple dedicated to Hathor and drink. There was a lot of binge-drinking and a lot of vomiting, and there was no shame in either. Gendered disapproval of drunkenness did not exist yet. An ancient tomb painting depicts a woman saying, "Give me eighteen cups of wine; I want to drive to drunkenness; my throat is as dry as straw." Entire communities, people of all genders, attended festivals for Ninkasi and Hathor. The parties would last for two to three weeks at a time. There was music and feasting, dancing and plays, orgies and lots and lots of drinking.

Ancient Egyptian painting of people drinking beer with a straw.

In Egypt during this period, beer was for the working class. We know those working-class women were drinking what they were brewing. But the higher classes wanted wine. Wine was the drink of the elite. Wine meant privilege. That's what the wealthy women of Egypt were toasting to Hathor with. It was much harder to acquire than beer during this time, making it a more expensive, more extravagant drink. Because red wine looks so similar to blood, it was also used in religious ceremonies. It wasn't long before there was such a demand for it that Egyptians began to produce their own wines, both red and white varieties.

Mesopotamians were making wine in 3000 BCE, but it was first produced way back in the Neolithic period, sometime between 9000 and 4000 BCE. (I know we're talking huge amounts of time here, but this is the best historians have to go on. I'll go deeper into wine in the next chapter.) As far as we know, things kicked off in the Zagros Mountains, roughly where Armenia and Northern Iran are now. Residue found in jars from this period shows that people were intentionally fermenting grape juice. The ruins of the oldest known winery are found here, from roughly 4100 BCE.

There was one more important similarity between Mesopotamian women and Egyptian women: their freedom. There were no economic restrictions on women during this time in Egypt. They could own property and businesses and had many of the same legal rights as men. Things were pretty great for drinking women during this time.

Then, the two cultures drastically diverged.

A Babylonian king named Hammurabi was determined to conquer and unite all of Mesopotamia. After he succeeded, around 1754 BCE he created a code, a list of two hundred and eighty-two rules that regulated things like commercial interactions and punishments for various crimes. The code built a justice system on the concept of an eye for an eye, which became foundational. A lot of folks believe (because it's taught in

American schools) that it was a positive turning point for civilization. But it was bad news for women. The Code of Hammurabi essentially established the patriarchy and literally set in stone the idea that women are the property of men.[7]

To supposedly *protect* women, his code took away many of their rights and made them, in the eyes of the law, the possessions of either their fathers or husbands. It forbade arbitrary ill treatment of women, but the code sanctioned ill treatment of women that was deemed *deserved*. Women were forbidden from commercial activities outside the household. The code also gave men power over women's bodies, along with power over their sexual and reproductive rights. After the Code of Hammurabi was adopted throughout Mesopotamia, women's lives were increasingly controlled, and their rights curtailed. This was a devastating blow to women's economic and sexual freedoms. (One we still haven't recovered from, thousands of years later.)

Women lost control of the brewing industry as their status declined across the land. All over Mesopotamia, brewing operations were taken over by men. Things only went downhill from there.

In this post–Code of Hammurabi Mesopotamia, good girls and so-called godly women didn't go into taverns. One of the two hundred and eighty-two laws dictated that if a priestess entered a tavern to drink, she could be *burned to death*. Priestesses who were previously responsible for the production of and culture around beer were now not allowed to make it, let alone drink it.

This was it: this was the moment. The very beginning of the gendering of alcohol.

Not only was there now a moral stigma attached to a woman drinking, for some types of women, there were legal consequences. Deadly ones.

Up until this point, the people in control of making and serv-

---

7   It was chiseled into a massive piece of stone that looks like a giant penis. You truly cannot make this stuff up.

ing alcohol were women. Even the deities that were worshipped for and with alcohol were female. But now booze, just like nearly every other aspect of society, was a man's world. The Code of Hammurabi made a drinking woman a bad woman, a corrupt woman, a disreputable woman. It tore an entire industry, one crucial to Mesopotamia's economy, culture and religion, out of women's hands and left them with nothing.

The influence Hammurabi's code had on civilization would help take down one of the most powerful women this world has ever seen.

2

CLEOPATRA AND HER INIMITABLE LIVER

The Ancient World

Cleopatra was not only the most famous woman of the ancient world, she was also the most infamous and still is to this day. Some regard her as a powerful ruler, a feminist icon or a political force. Many more consider her a shameless hussy or an evil seductress. Regardless of what you think of her, thousands of years after her death, you know who Cleopatra is.

Her seat of power was Egypt, a kingdom she ruled for twenty-one years, from about 50 BCE to 30 BCE. At the height of her reign, this woman controlled the entire eastern Mediterranean coast. She was the last great Egyptian ruler, one of the only two women in the ancient world who governed alone. During her rule, Cleopatra had more prestige and wealth than anyone else in the Mediterranean.

Today, what Cleopatra is most well-known for is her fabled sex appeal. Right now, you're probably thinking about Elizabeth Taylor, slinking around marble columns wearing a long white linen dress and enough black eyeliner to make a raccoon blush.

You're remembering myths about her seductions and legends about her death. Sneaking to see Julius Caesar wrapped up in a rug, enchanting Mark Antony, dying by suicide via snakebite.

Cleopatra occupied a dangerous position in the ancient world, a position that is still dangerous in modern society: a powerful woman. Roman leaders launched a smear campaign against her, and its enduring success stained the image the world had of Cleopatra. Instead of brilliant and powerful, she was cast as evil, lustful and wild. Part of the reason for this concocted infamy is that Cleopatra was a woman who liked to drink.

To many, Cleopatra embodies the spirit and aesthetic of ancient Egypt. But she was actually born in Alexandria, a largely Greek city. Greece is another country whose ancient culture is closely associated with drinking. Togas and grape vines immediately call to mind a wine-fueled, Dionysian party. Swap out the wine for a keg of cheap beer and you can still see these symbols of drinking culture today at any terrible frat party.

Unfortunately, the Dionysian revelries didn't include everyone. When Greek culture was formed, around 9000 BCE, it absorbed the ideas about women drinking that Hammurabi had brought to nearby Mesopotamia.

The ancient Greeks were all about wine. To them, wine was the embodiment of civilization and refinement. If you were drinking wine, all was well in the world. That is, if you were a guy. Women were discouraged from drinking and just about anything else.

If you went to an American school, you probably grew up thinking that ancient Greece was the birthplace of democracy and that it was a wonderful place to live. They had all those fun myths about gods and monsters and Mount Olympus! So many influential philosophers and thinkers and inventors lived during that time! Everyone was quaffing wine and wearing togas and coming up with new ideas!

Ancient Greece was actually a really shitty place to be.

The democracy born during this time gave freedom to a small group of people. Ancient Greece ran on slavery. Even if you weren't an enslaved person, participation in democracy was only open to men. Women were banned from pretty much everything.

Conditions in Greece for women were some of the worst in the ancient world. They were almost totally absent from public life and record. When you learn about ancient Greece in school, it's easy to see all the incredibly cool and powerful female Greek deities like Athena and believe that a culture that worshipped them would afford freedoms to its women. Wrong! Do not confuse the adventures of the female figures of Greek mythology with what was happening in reality. Real-life women were given almost no power and were rarely allowed to participate in anything besides some religious festivals and rituals.

Men in ancient Greece sought to control women, and that absolutely included drinking. A drinking woman is an uninhibited woman, something that Greek men deeply feared. Wine was thought to make women violent and dangerously immoral. Dangerous? Well, dangerous to their husband's or father's estate. If a woman—whose reproductive abilities were considered property—got drunk and had a fling that resulted in the loss of her virginity or in the conception of a child, that was a direct financial blow to the man who controlled her. Misogynist fears like these resulted in myths that depicted an uninhibited woman as a threat to everyone's safety.

The tale of Pandora's box, or even just the phrase, is well-known today. A woman, unable to contain her curiosity, opens a box containing all the evils of the world and unleashes them on humanity. But for thousands of years, the story has been misunderstood. It was translated incorrectly. The story is actually about a jar, not a box. In ancient Greece, a jar was a metaphor for a woman's womb. The Greeks believed that all the evils of the world came from a woman's opened womb...meaning a woman having sex. An unbound, uninhibited, uncontrolled woman was believed to be the source of all the bad in the world. Why would you let a woman have a drink? She might start the apocalypse or something!

The heart of Greek culture was the symposium, an all-male aristocratic ritual that took place in a special, dedicated room. Symposiums were essentially formal, intellectual drinking parties for privileged freemen (a type of person that only made up about a fifth of the population). Wine was required for a symposium. Before it was drunk, the wine had to be mixed with water[8] in a large bowl, because drinking undiluted wine was considered barbaric. No matter where Greek men drank, the wine was diluted. Drinking straight wine back in ancient Greece would be the equivalent of chugging vodka straight from the bottle today. They wouldn't just mix it with fresh water, either. Saltwater was also used frequently, with various other ingredients added to improve the flavor like honey, salt, spices, herbs and oils.

As a beverage that needed saltwater to enhance the taste, you can probably tell that the quality of wine back then wasn't particularly high. The most prized characteristic was sweetness, and wine was assessed on a scale from sour to sweet, essentially on a scale of Terrible to Good. At the time, Greeks had three different kinds of wine: red, white and amber.[9]

There was no stigma for freemen drinking, even when they weren't holding a symposium. For them, there was only a stigma if you were sober. Wine was the drink of a manly man, a soldier, a thinker. You drank wine while you sacked cities and made

---

8 We're talking a lot of water. Equal parts water and wine was considered a strong drink.

9 Amber wine is created when the skins and seeds of red grapes are left in contact with the juice during the wine-making process. The final product has a deep orange hue. Orange wine is actually back in style nowadays!

oaths. Oaths taken that were sealed with wine were considered stronger and had more weight. All important rituals involved drinking wine, since wine ostensibly made men speak the truth. Some orators only practiced while they were drunk.

Eventually, ancient Greek wine drinkers grew snooty about wine. Different types and vintages of wine became a big deal. Since wine drinking was ubiquitous among rich men, they needed a way to distinguish themselves even further. Old wine became a status symbol, right around the fourth century BCE.

Women were not allowed to attend symposiums, unless they were serving in some capacity, whether as dancers, musicians, entertainers or servers of some sort.[10] The heart of Greek culture…and women were barred from it. Forbidding women from drinking didn't just impose control over their bodies but also the influence they held in society. Modesty was demanded of women, and they were required to be veiled in public.

Medical men from the time justified these alcohol-related prejudices with all sorts of bullshit ideas. Never mind not drinking while pregnant, doctors thought that women shouldn't drink when they were making a baby. They believed that women needed to be sober during sex. If not, she would have strange hallucinations in her soul that would be passed on to the fetus. This sort of thinking was actually radically progressive for the time, considering that influential (and misogynist) thinkers like Aristotle believed that women didn't even have souls.

Even the women feeding those babies were given medical reasons not to drink. Wet nurses couldn't have sex, let alone have any wine. It was believed that wanton activities like these lessened their affection for the infants in their care, suppressed the flow of milk and spoiled the milk that did flow. Alcohol

---

10   The sex workers and lovers of the men at the symposiums were allowed to attend and drink, however. Known as *hetaera*, these women sometimes drank diluted wine along with the men, but their position was tenuous. With no rights, their well-being was dependent on the goodwill of the men they attended with.

tainted a woman's spirit as well as her fluids. (The CDC says that moderate alcohol consumption by a breastfeeding mother is not known to be harmful to the infant.) A Greek physician named Soranos thought that if an infant drank the breast milk of a wet nurse who drank wine, they could be affected with symptoms like sluggishness and convulsions or even go into a coma. Being a wet nurse was the most popular occupation for a freewoman in ancient Athens, so these widely held beliefs helped effectively control women's drinking.[11]

In theory, anyway.

There were a lot of Greek women who looked at all these repressive rules and regulations and beliefs and said to themselves, "Screw this, I need a drink."

In most homes, the wine stores were managed by a (usually male) enslaved person. This person had strict orders to deny women access to the wine. But that didn't stop those women from secretly slipping out and surreptitiously visiting the local taverns, called *kapelion*. Kapelion were widespread, and most neighborhoods had their own wine bar. These taverns catered to a more plebeian crowd—even enslaved women were sometimes found drinking there. Underneath the yoke of an oppressive society, many ancient Greek women were dedicated covert drinkers.

Clandestine drinking among Greek women increased whenever there was a war on, during the second half of the fifth century BCE, for example. When many of the men were away at war, women did more of the things they wanted to do that they were discouraged or forbidden from doing.

However, there *was* one special time of year that freewomen were allowed to drink in public.

Dionysus, the ancient Greek god of wine, represented the untamed side of human nature. He embodied carnality, chaos

---

11 Thanks to surviving records, more is known about ancient Athenian women than women in any of the other Greek city-states.

and pleasure. Unsurprisingly in this oppressive society, this god was a favorite among Greek women. He symbolized everything they were not allowed to experience. His female devotees were called maenads, meaning *women who were driven mad*. They were called that by men, but I'd be willing to bet that among themselves, they were called *women who wanted a little freedom for once*.

The only time it was acceptable for a woman to drink was during festivals celebrating Dionysus. When women celebrated these rites, it was said that they *surrendered themselves to Dionysus*. Funny how the lone sanctioned drinking ritual for women involved surrendering themselves to a male figure. Orgies were common during these festivals, so the case might have been that men were okay with women drinking…if it meant there was an expectation of getting laid.

The Greeks' intolerance of drinking women was part of the reason why they had a strong dislike of their neighbors in Etruria (an area that is now central Italy). They believed that Etruscans were degenerates and their women were morally corrupt. Their proof? Women in Etruria drank. They were welcome at Etruscan dinner parties and banquets, which shocked Grecian men. In fact, women often led the toasts. Etruscan women imbibed alongside the men and owned their own personal drinking vessels. They had much more autonomy than their Greek counterparts, able to enjoy some freedom and some wine. An unnamed Greek traveler described the women of Etruria as "terribly bibulous and remarkably beautiful," a description I should have stolen for the subtitle of this book.

Even though Cleopatra was Greek, she was not raised in oppressive Greek culture. She was the last monarch of the Ptolemies, a Greek dynasty that ruled over Egypt for nearly three hundred years.

Born the daughter of the ruling pharaoh Ptolemy XII in 69 BCE, Cleopatra was highly educated and taught by the scholars of the Library of Alexandria. At an early age, she was trained in public speaking. Cleopatra could clearly and concisely deliver her thoughts, something rarely taught to women during this time. She could even do it in multiple languages. The future queen was the first of her line to actually learn how to speak Egyptian, something that came in handy for addressing her nearly one million subjects. And speak to them she did.

While not universal in Egypt, it was much more common for girls to be educated there than in Greece.[12] Along with being able to drink, Egyptian women could make their own marriages, inherit wealth, hold property independently and get divorced. They did not have to submit to their husbands' control.

Another important facet of Cleopatra's ascent to power was the fact that she had so many incredibly powerful women to look up to. These role models were the Egyptian queens who came before her and waged military campaigns, raised fleets, built temples and, of course, drank wine.

Egyptian wine was made from grapes and other fruits like figs, pomegranates and dates.[13] First, the grapes were harvested. Ancient Egyptian female laborers did this alongside both men and children, usually in late summer. These women cut the grapes by hand from the vine and placed them in wicker baskets. Then, those grapes were placed in large vats so they could be stomped on. Believe it or not, stomping around on the grapes was the best way to extract the juice. Using a stone press was effective, but it also crushed the seeds and stems, adding bitterness to the wine. So instead, people stood in these vats and crushed the grapes with their (hopefully clean) bare feet. The juice then flowed

---

12 Upper class girls, that is. Most of what we know about ancient societies consists of knowledge of how the upper classes lived. Enslaved people and the lower classes didn't get to live like this.

13 For the purposes of this book, when I say *wine*, I'm referring to grape wine. Nowadays, that's what we think of when someone offers us wine. As I said in the last chapter, though, you also can make wine from nearly any old fruit.

from the large vats into smaller ones through a drain. Next, it was pressed again, this time by twisting the juice, and whatever solids were left, in a large piece of linen. The juice was collected in a pot beneath the linen. Then, the pot was left to ferment for a while. If left for a few days, the juice became a light wine. If left for a few weeks, the juice became a heavier wine. Either way, the final product was sealed and labeled. Minus the feet-stomping, wine is made in a very similar way today.

From the roots of Greek culture, the empire of Rome began to grow around 500 BCE. Roman civilization co-opted many aspects of Greek civilization, such as their sociological beliefs, their gods and their drinking culture.

Romans also believed that drinking wine straight was barbaric[14] and carried on the practice of diluting it. For them, wine was both a dietary staple and a cultural one, especially for the upper class. Like all things that were important culturally in Rome, wine was only for rich men. Romans also assimilated Greek views on women drinking.

Traits that would be prized in Egyptian women, such as being strong-minded and bold, were reviled in Roman women. In Rome, women who didn't stay sober, contain their opinions and desires, and tamp down their sexuality were abhorred. They were failing to operate within their behavioral limits.

During Rome's early years, before Greek influence took hold, drinking by pretty much anyone was frowned upon. It was a dry empire. In fact, early Romans distrusted alcohol and had

---

14 For the Greeks and Romans, being *barbaric* was about the worst thing you could be. *Bar bar bar* in ancient Greek was their equivalent of *blah blah blah*. Anyone who didn't speak Greek sounded like they were saying *bar bar bar*, and so the term *barbarian* developed. The Germanic tribes to the north were considered the epitome of barbaric. The ancient Greeks knew about beer, but they regarded it as a barbarian drink because it was the preferred beverage of those savage tribes. Beer never became popular in Greece, even among the poor and the enslaved. It was seen as an inferior alcohol for an inferior people.

banned any rites that celebrated Dionysus. For women, it was worse. Women drinking wasn't simply frowned upon, it was completely illegal. It could also get you killed.

One of the legends surrounding Romulus, the first king of Rome, was that he instituted a death penalty for any woman caught drinking. There was a common practice at the time for women to kiss their relatives so that the relatives could sniff their breath and make sure they hadn't had any wine. Women were banned from any association with wine, including pouring religious libations to the gods. Original Roman laws allowed a husband who caught his wife drinking to divorce her. Before he did that, he legally could beat or even kill her. The last divorce on grounds of a drinking wife was granted in 194 BCE.

Within a few decades of Rome's development, however, views began to shift. There was an economic reason behind the change. When Rome became a significant producer of wine, Romans started to think that maybe booze wasn't so bad after all—for the men, anyway—and their drinking culture was born.

By the middle of the first century BCE, drinking wasn't just accepted, it was celebrated. Rome adopted the Greek god Dionysus as their own and called him Bacchus. He got his own formal rites: wild, wine-drinking festivals called Bacchanalia. Like Dionysus in Greece, Bacchus had female followers who participated. What sources say actually happened at these rites ranged from women simply getting drunk and loud...to women getting drunk and loud and then tearing their clothes off and terrorizing the countryside in frenzied groups, intent on murdering or having sex with anyone they saw. It is tough to tell just how outrageous women actually got. Most sources on this subject are male and extremely biased. It's very possible that seeing a group of women drunkenly cavorting in public was so shocking to a Roman man that he thought they were a violent, horny mob.

After Roman attitudes toward drinking relaxed, the convivium was born. It was Rome's version of the Greek symposium. As the country grew its empire and its coffers, Rome fell in love with ostentation. What's more ostentatious than an exclusive drinking party? Almost identical to the symposium, the convivium was an intellectual salon centered around discussion and drinking wine. Wine was served before, during and after the meal. Before drinking culture spread, all-male literary banquets had been common in Rome, and the convivium was a boozy continuation of that practice.

In the wake of shifting attitudes about alcohol, the laws concerning women and alcohol also changed. It was no longer illegal for a woman to drink. One major difference between the symposium and the convivium was that, eventually, women were allowed to join the convivium. Again, the male bias of most of the primary sources we have about Rome makes it difficult to suss out an accurate picture of women's participation in the convivium and other banquets. It seems like the extent of a woman's welcome varied depending on the preference of the host and the particular female guest's social status.

Even though women were allowed to join in the drinking festivities, it didn't mean that they were equal to men. The laws were more lax, but the social constraints were not. Women were expected to drink less than men, to prefer different types of drinks than men and to behave differently when they were drinking. The women who did join in the convivium were also not drinking the wine that the men were. They were drinking something called *passum*, a wine made from raisins. It was a sweeter wine and had a lower alcohol content. Passum was the world's first girly drink.

This was the moment that types of alcohol became gendered. Creating a distinction between *manly drinks* and *girly drinks* was (and is) about control. Access to alcohol and judgment-free intoxication was reserved for men in power. Roman women—and usually upper-class ones at that—were allowed just a taste, a weaker version of the wine that the men drank. Rome adopted the Greek idea that masculinity was linked to the practice of men drinking with other men.

Women joining in screwed everything up.

Roman leader Julius Caesar became Cleopatra's lover when she was twenty-one. That's right, not the other way around. She sought out the relationship and entered it of her own free will—something unheard of in Roman society at the time. Before she got together with Caesar, she was leading Egypt as an absolute monarch, which is absolutely as awesome as it sounds. Cleopatra ascended to the throne alongside her brother when their father, the ruling pharaoh, died in 52 BCE. After an open civil war between the siblings for the throne, Cleopatra came out on top.

She is famously known as the lover of great rulers, but don't be mistaken.[15] Cleopatra was first and foremost one herself. This queen commanded the military, dispensed justice, regulated the economy, negotiated with foreign powers and led the country to prosperity with her brilliant pragmatism. She was whip-smart and commissioned books on medicine, cosmetics, gynecology and systems of measurement. A scholar of her time described Cleopatra as a "sage and a philosopher." With control of both religious and secular bureaucracies, she was more than queen. For Egypt, Cleopatra was simultaneously high priestess, magistrate and merchant in chief. She was a living goddess to her subjects.[16]

Taking Caesar as her lover in 48 BCE was a calculated move on Cleopatra's part and ultimately strategic for both of them. He needed Egypt; she needed Roman power.

Therein was the problem.

---

15 I'd also like to point out that Caesar was famously horny. He didn't drink, which was a rarity in Rome at the time, so sex was his vice. He was known for his many, many lovers.

16 With great political acumen, she styled herself after the goddess Isis, quelling all doubt that she was meant to rule Egypt.

In Rome, female authority was—literally—a completely foreign concept. Women didn't have political rights there. In other less civilized places, maybe. But not in Rome. Seeing Cleopatra as a ruler was impossible for Romans. They could only see her as Caesar's exotic, immoral lover. (Caesar had a wife at this time.)[17]

To add to the bafflement of the Roman public, Cleopatra wasn't conventionally (for the times) attractive. Even though today we imagine her as a kohl-eyed, slinky babe, we actually have no clue what she looked like. But she is probably the most famous woman to be constantly negged by contemporaneous writers. Plutarch described her thus: "...for her actual beauty itself was not remarkable...but the contact of her presence... was irresistible."

Silver coin featuring Cleopatra.

SMITH ARCHIVE/ALAMY STOCK PHOTO

---

17   Monogamy was certainly expected, but it was common for men to transgress.

Caesar was clearly attracted to her, because soon Cleopatra was pregnant with his son. After the birth, she came to visit Caesar in Rome, which didn't go over well with anyone.

The Egyptian queen was the polar opposite of the Roman female ideal. She was a powerful woman, she spoke her mind (Cicero despised her for being "arrogant" and "insolent") and, of course, she liked to drink. Sweet wines from Syria and Ionia were what she preferred, especially when spiced with honey or pomegranate juice. She also flaunted her wealth. Cleopatra came from the Alexandrian court, where *tryphe* reigned supreme. Tryphe was the notion that boundless, luxurious ostentation was the true manifestation of power. Rome in Caesar's time was... not into tryphe. It was absolutely hated. Any man who made a show of tryphe was intensely criticized. A woman doing it? Unthinkable.

Cleopatra brought dangerous influence. A powerful, drinking woman—the horror! Other women might see her and get dangerous ideas!

Roman women were expected to behave above reproach at all times, and a drunken woman does not. When Roman men witnessed women drinking, they were horrified to see that drunken women were just like drunken men. They drank as much and with the same gusto, they were loud and bold, they stayed out late, they wanted to wrestle, they got horny, they threw up. (Hopefully not all at the same time.) In a speech to the Roman Senate condemning Bacchanalian rites and the people who celebrated them, a man named Postumius said, "...a great part of them are women, scarcely distinguishable from males, dancing frenetically, having lost their minds...by drink." Roman men did not want to have to confront women acting like people and not property. They especially didn't want to see their property drunk and running amok.

Drinking women are a challenge to a patriarchal society. In Rome, they were unwelcome to the established dominance of men.

Caesar's relationship with Cleopatra was one of the factors that led to his assassination. To his political enemies, his love for the Egyptian monarch was obvious proof that he didn't have Roman values at heart.

After his death, Cleopatra fled back to Egypt. She ruled alone there for three years, struggling to keep her country independent of Rome.

Back in Rome, everyone was preparing for war. Mark Antony (one of Caesar's generals, supporters and close friends) was trying to rouse the republic to the defense of Caesar's memory to help defeat Caesar's political enemies and stop them from taking over the country. The only problem with his campaign was that Caesar named his great nephew Octavius as his heir, not Mark Antony. And Octavius absolutely hated Cleopatra.

The Egyptian queen watched what was happening in Rome and made her own wartime preparations. She knew supporting Mark Antony was her best bet. If he won out as the leader of Rome, her relations with the empire and her power would be secure. At twenty-eight years old, Cleopatra led a fleet of warships out to sea in support of him.[18]

After the defeat of Caesar's enemies, Mark Antony summoned Cleopatra to visit him, and she refused. (Power move.) The queen finally accepted after his fourth summons, but she demanded that he come to her. He showed up to find her decked out like a goddess on a royal barge, surrounded by the finest food and drink Egypt had to offer. Overwhelmed by her, Mark Antony soon sought to be Cleopatra's lover and, more importantly, her political partner. Like Caesar before him, he saw the economic advantage to allying himself with Egypt. Also like Caesar before him, he was married at the time.

As a way to become a power figure to the Roman people, Mark Antony had styled himself as the living Bacchus. The strategy wasn't a stretch. Mark Antony was a party boy. His tastes for

---

18   A terrible storm caused her to turn back to Alexandria. But still, pretty cool!

entertainment, drinking, feasting and gambling were insatiable. Choosing to have him as her lover meant Cleopatra needed to keep him indulged. The two started their own drinking club with some close friends called the Inimitable Livers.[19] The group met regularly to drink wine, eat, play dice and hunt. There are also legends about them disguising themselves and playing tricks on regular citizens. (Gossip from the time says that the group got up to secret Bacchanalian rites, but there is no proof of that.) Cleopatra even had an amethyst ring engraved with the word *methe*, which was Egyptian for *intoxication*.

She liked to drink, but Cleopatra didn't overindulge. Mark Antony was the sloppy one, constantly getting trashed. For the Egyptian people, it didn't matter either way. Drinking and partying was an accepted activity for either sex. Upon hearing tales of the Inimitable Livers' exploits, the Roman people didn't scorn Mark Antony for drinking. But they did scorn Cleopatra. For men, drinking too much was a pardonable offense. A woman taking open, unashamed pleasure in drinking was unforgivable. Octavius called a celebration a couple threw in Rome "a Dionysiac revel led by an Eastern harlot."

While this was happening, political tensions were rising between Octavius and Mark Antony for control of Rome. After Mark Antony's wife passed away,[20] he married Octavius's sister Octavia in a bid for peace between the two. He continued on as Cleopatra's lover, however.

Cleopatra convinced her lover to return land (what is now Syria, Jordan and Lebanon) that was once ruled by her dynasty to Egyptian control in exchange for money, food, supplies and a fleet to

---

19 What's amazing is this was long before the liver's function was known. Cleopatra had no idea that the liver processes alcohol. In ancient Egypt, the liver was thought of as the life force of the body and sometimes the seat of the soul.

20 His second wife, Fulvia, an incredible woman in her own right. It is said she passed away from a broken heart because of how awful Mark Antony was to her.

support his military campaigns.[21] Bountiful, prosperous Egypt could easily afford the exchange, and she was thrilled to finally be extending her empire. This deal enraged Octavius, who believed that all land should belong to Rome. Instead of blaming Mark Antony for the loss of the territory, he blamed the influence of Cleopatra. After Mark Antony's campaigns failed, Octavius seized the opportunity to take down the couple politically.

Because of Cleopatra's rule, Egypt was thriving and recognized as a nearly equal ally to the great Roman republic. With her smarts and political strategy, she kept Egypt both powerful and, although protected by Rome, still independent of it. In her country, she was seen as a goddess. In Rome, Octavius wanted her to be seen as a wicked, drunken succubus.

Women who chose to drink were easy targets for both moralists and satirists in Rome. Drunken, lustful women were featured as caricatures in comedic plays. In real life, showing signs of intoxication was considered to be embarrassing, even shameful for a woman. It was another way to try to control them. That's what Octavius desperately wanted to do.

He launched a propaganda war, saying that Cleopatra was an evil sorceress, exaggerating tales of her drinking and talking of Mark Antony's "enslavement" to her. Octavius swore "to allow no woman to make herself equal to a man."

Other Roman senators and politicians helped spread the rumors. They declared that Cleopatra was out to destroy Rome, adding fear to the hate. Roman rhetorician Julius Florus claimed that "The Egyptian woman demanded the Roman Empire from the drunken general as the price of her favors...for she so charmed and enthralled not only him but all the rest who had any influence with him that she conceived the hope of ruling even the Romans." The Egyptian queen became the number

---

21   She actually accompanied him on his campaigns for a while until she
     realized she was pregnant with twins.

one enemy of the Roman Empire. Romans saw her as an unnatural creature, an immoral, immodest predator of a woman.

This smear campaign—that Cleopatra was an evil seductress
and a lusty drunk—shaped the way that the world saw her for
thousands of years.

Classical scholar W. W. Tarn said, "Rome, who had never con-
descended to fear any nation or people, did in her time fear two
human beings; one was Hannibal, and the other was a woman."

Roman senators were happy to take up rhetorical arms against
Cleopatra. They were incensed that Mark Antony had invited
her to be involved in his political affairs and especially his military preparation. He sought her wisdom (against the senators'
wishes) in all things war, from securing supplies for his armies
to supervising the creation of a fleet to being involved in military councils. Even those loyal to him were upset by it, advis-
ing him that it hurt his image, just like it had hurt Caesar's. To
them, it was simply not a woman's place. Mark Antony ignored
them and kept Cleopatra by his side.

Faced with such political drama, his marriage to Octavia
failed. When Mark Antony announced his divorce,[22] Octavius
dismissed him as a coruler of Rome and declared a war against
Cleopatra. Octavius knew his loyal Roman troops wouldn't
fight against Mark Antony, but they would fight against her.

The couple was doomed. Octavius's forces defeated them both
at land and at sea. Cleopatra rallied, collecting forces, building
ships, planning attacks, but Mark Antony brooded and sulked.
Without his help, nothing was successful against Octavius.

On the brink of crushing defeat, the couple revived the Inimitable Livers. The drinking club renamed itself as the Partners in
Death. Cleopatra indulged Mark Antony in one last wild fling

---

22 He never actually married Cleopatra. Caesar didn't either. It was illegal for
    Romans to marry a foreigner. Although, we shouldn't assume she would
    have wanted to be married, anyway. And contrary to her reputation, these
    were the only two lovers Cleopatra had over the course of her life.

to hold off despair. Like everything she did, it was a calculated move on her part. She refused to show weakness and wanted to raise everyone's spirits with drinking parties.

After the final defeat in 30 BCE and Mark Antony's suicide[23] immediately afterward, Cleopatra retreated to her mausoleum, determined to burn it to the ground before she was taken alive. When Roman forces broke in, looking to capture both her and her treasure, she killed herself.[24] She was thirty-nine years old.

Octavius had all her likenesses destroyed after her death. She was stripped of her historical and political validity. Most of the Roman writers who filled pages about her had never been in her presence, and tales of her power linked it to beauty, to seduction, to excess. She became a symbol of sensual delight, of sin, known as the Queen of Kings.

Cleopatra was just the goddamn queen.

She was a brilliant philosopher and scholar, a pragmatic military leader and, yes, a drinker. Cleopatra was everything a drinking woman represents to the patriarchy: both male fear and fantasy in one. Men want women uninhibited, but only when they can control them. Men will tolerate a drinking woman only if her inhibition is in service to them.

Cleopatra refused to submit to these constraints. To the bitter end, she fought to keep both her power and her pleasures. She had her wine and drank it, too. Because of this, everything was taken from her. Octavius and his cronies in the Roman Senate

---

23 In a very *Romeo and Juliet* moment, Mark Antony mistakenly believed that Cleopatra killed herself after Octavius's successful invasion of Rome. He threw himself on his sword and then quickly was informed that Cleopatra was actually still alive. His friends brought his bleeding body to her, and he died in her arms.

24 There are a lot of legends surrounding this moment in history, but no one actually knows how she did it. Also, most (male) artistic depictions of her death show her as nude. She was wearing clothes, despite what thousands of years of horny painters would have you think.

could not control Cleopatra, so they destroyed her. Her tomb is now lost beneath the Mediterranean Sea.

Over two thousand years later, society is still uncomfortable with a woman drinking just because she wants to. The roots of Greek and Roman misogyny have not yet been torn up. Their tendrils lurk throughout the pages of this book.

In the wake of Octavius's victory, Egypt became a province of the Roman Empire. The East was seen as a feminine, wild, sensual place that needed to be conquered by the masculine, civilized, intellectual West. Rome was the great military power of the world—built on slavery and suffused with misogyny, classism, xenophobia and racism.

Its might couldn't last forever, though. The world was changing, and so were the drinks.

3

HILDEGARD'S BREWNUNS JUST WANT TO HAVE FUN

The Early Middle Ages

When you think of a bitter, hoppy beer, you probably picture some bearded hipster guy holding it.

Maybe he's leaning on the edge of a bar, explaining craft beers and IPAs to you. Maybe you're making an excuse to go to the bathroom so you can crawl out the window. What you could explain back to him is that his hoppy drink—a big innovation in the world of alcohol—was popularized by a woman. By a nun, in fact.

Hildegard von Bingen is one of the most famous women in Christianity. She's well-known for being a prolific writer and composer, but this brilliant nun was also a beer lover and a feminist troublemaker. Hildegard might have made different wardrobe choices than Cleopatra, but she was just as dedicated a drinker. And even more important to the history of booze. She helped change the course of the entire beer industry.

By the time Hildegard was born in 1098 CE, the Roman Empire had long since split and crumbled. Starting in 376 CE, civil

wars and an invasion of Germanic tribes from the north led to
the collapse of its economic and social structure. In 410, Rome
itself was sacked by the northern tribes. Those beer-drinking
barbarians ended up having the last word.

The uniformity that Rome had enforced across the land was
gone. In the empire's wake grew territories with different languages and cultures, which eventually became what we now
know as England, Wales and Europe. The Western world entered a new era: medieval times.

Unfortunately, it wasn't anything like the themed restaurant.
There were a lot less roasted turkey legs and a lot more open-
air latrines.

See, one thing you have to understand about drinking during the medieval era was that everything was gross. The water
was gross, the wine was gross, the beer was gross. Although the
drink menu was the pits, there was at least one big improvement in drinking culture from the age of Rome: the women
could drink. They had to. Even babies had to drink booze. Most
wines and beers were low quality and tasted bad, but water was
generally unsafe and filled with bacteria. Almost all beverages
were alcoholic. It was a pretty easy choice between that and di-
arrhea. The only people who drank water exclusively were the
poor (the really, really poor) and occasionally monks. Coffee
and tea came from plants that most folks in England or western
Europe hadn't even heard of yet. Milk was not a beverage for
the table. And you can just forget about juice.

Mead and cider were sometimes available, but honey wasn't
plentiful everywhere. Most of the time, what folks drank was
beer. Beer is so nourishing that medieval villagers drank it mostly
for sustenance. Each meal, including breakfast, was accompanied by a weak beer. Hildegard would've drunk beer every day
while she was growing up.

She was born in Böckelheim, Germany, but when she was
still very young, Hildegard was dropped off at a Benedictine

monastery in nearby Disibodenberg by her parents. This was a common practice for families who could afford it. Perhaps they wanted their daughter to get an education or they craved assurance of their place in heaven. In any case, girls given to a monastery or nunnery learned to read and write Latin, the rituals of church service and sometimes more advanced subjects like arithmetic, astronomy and music.

Hildegard lived during a time when one of the only real avenues to any power, authority or autonomy for women was through the Church. During the early Middle Ages in Europe, they mainly fell into one of three categories: virgins, wives and widows. Most women were passed from father to husband. If her husband died, well, hopefully she had a son or her husband's business to support her. However, there was a fourth category with a little more wiggle room: nuns. If a woman married God, she ended up having more freedom than her friends who married a human being.

Compared to other women, many nuns were able to exercise an extraordinary amount of control over their lives. Nunneries emerged around the same time as monasteries, around the year 400 CE. But some monasteries had nuns that lived and worked in separate buildings, places the monks were not allowed to enter. Whether in a nunnery or a monastery, a woman had access to education and a chance at leadership. Nuns typically came from wealthier backgrounds because payment was required for them to enter a nunnery or a monastery. Even God wanted women with a dowry.

From Hildegard's earliest years in the Disibodenberg cloister, she suffered with what she said were visions. She described them as "…great brightness, concentric circles, shooting stars and shining lines resembling the ramparts of a celestial city." Today, many scholars believe these visuals were the precursor to migraines. Judging from her extensive autobiographical writings, it seems likely that her ill health was exactly that: migraines. But to her, and to the other nuns around her in the Benedictine order, they were visions from God himself. At the urging of a monk that she was friends with, Hildegard began to write down the visions she experienced so that others could read them and determine if they were divine. The monks of the order read her writings and declared that yes, her visions were sent from God.

This was the moment when Hildegard's life—and consequently, the beer industry—began to change.

For the women who didn't want to join a nunnery, there was another path to gaining some autonomy: making beer. Only instead of calling it beer, they called it *ale*. (Beer was what drinkers during this time period called ale that had hops added to it. This will be important soon.) Ale was usually made from barley, wheat, oats or a combination of all three. The women who made ale were called *alewives*. Sadly, no, this does not mean they were married to beer. The alewives were also known as *brewsters*. (Words ending in -*ster* meant female.)

Every village had an alewife. In fact, usually several. Most or even all of the brewers in any given medieval village in the Western world were women. Ale was as important to the popular diet as bread. But the flour for grinding and making bread was strictly controlled. Men had a monopoly on it. Nearly every industry was dominated by men.

Brewing, however, was a different story.

Brewing was freely permitted for anyone. All a woman had to do was make the ale, put up a sign and, boom, she had a pop-up alehouse. There were some key pieces of equipment that were needed, mainly a large cauldron, but these were readily available and usually did not prevent even poor women from brewing.

An alewife germinated the ground oats, barley or wheat to make a malt, then mixed it with boiling water. This concoction was left overnight. The next day, she strained it and, depending on her own particular recipe, added yeast and herbs. Alewives added different herbs depending on the region they lived in. The most common flavoring all over was bog myrtle, which is just about as delicious as it sounds. It gave the ale a very bitter, strong taste. Which was sort of the point, since overpowering the taste was the goal. Medieval ale smelled musty and had an astringent flavor. Horseradish was a particularly popular flavoring, if that says anything about how rough medieval ale tasted. Northern European alewives added herbs like juniper, caraway and yarrow. English alewives were partial to rosemary, sycamore sap and ivy. German alewives preferred mint, marjoram, sage and acorns.

The ale was ready to drink in twenty-four hours and needed to be consumed within five days or so. It wasn't great to begin with, and it got worse quickly.[25] One writer of the time described English ale as "abominable in sight and taste." After about a week, it went sour. An alewife could take ale that was about to turn and make it last another day or so with some sweeteners or extra flavorings. Sometimes, when the ale soured, the alewives used it as vinegar in recipes.

In castles or the homes of the rich, wine was the drink of choice. Good wine was available if you could afford it, but depending on the region, it had to be imported by the barrel at great cost. Viticulture never took off in England's climate, so even those living in English castles usually made do with subpar wine that needed to be sweetened or spiced to be more palatable.

Most people, the common folks, patronized the alewives. When the ale was ready to serve, the alewife put out her ale stake—a horizontal stake sticking out above her front door. The stake had a bundle of sticks and twigs tied to the end of it. This was the medieval equivalent of a neon OPEN sign. When the

---

25 It didn't look great, either, but back then glass was rare. Most people couldn't see what they were drinking. Ale was usually drunk out of wooden or sometimes glazed-ceramic mugs. If you were drinking out of a glass, you were probably sipping wine in a castle.

alewife was out of ale, she'd simply take down the stake. Entrepreneurial alewives made their ale stakes long in order to attract more attention, to the point that they sometimes interrupted the flow of traffic in the streets. Eventually, things got so competitive among alewives in London that there was a decree in 1375 stating that ale stakes could be no longer than seven feet.

The ale was served in the alewife's kitchen. Designated taverns and planned-out pubs didn't exist yet. Most women brewed ale for their own home use. Whenever there was enough left over, a woman put out her ale stake and turned her home into an alehouse. That's literally what an alehouse was: ale in a house.

Alewife enticing customers with her gigantic ale stake.

To make it more customer-friendly, an alewife might put out a barrel of beer, along with some tables and stools. Some benches, perhaps. (No bar yet. We have to wait several centuries for that.) The alewife herself ran the operation, serving the neighbors and local laborers who stopped by for a drink after work. Travelers occasionally showed up. This was also where the servants of the nearby castle came to drink; the alehouse was their escape from toiling for the elite. Even teenagers might be customers (no drinking age!).

Aside from the teenagers, folks passed the time like they do in any pub you'd see today. People drank and talked. Sometimes, there was gambling, and occasionally someone got rowdy. But generally, it was just neighbors drinking ale together.

A small percentage of those alehouse patrons were female. Drunkenness in a woman outside the home was considered shocking, so they usually didn't get drunk, but they were there. Neighboring wives might come to buy some ale for their own households. Courting couples went there on dates. It was rare to see a woman drinking alone, but a group of wives or unmarried women occasionally showed up, especially if they had something to celebrate.

But before all this, before the alewife could open her doors, she needed to call the aletaster.

Aletasters were the officials whose job was to judge the quality of the ale and monitor the prices. During this period, Europe and England were ruled by a system known as manorialism. The economic power of rural communities was given to a lord of a local manor. There was a manorial court held yearly, ruled by an all-male governing body. The aletasters for villages were chosen at this annual court. They were usually men, but sometimes women were chosen. This was the only public office that was ever filled by women then, as brewing was the only trade they controlled.

Alewives could be fined by the aletaster for several different violations, such as selling ale that was too weak or serving amounts that were too small. It sounds strict, but being an alewife was actually one of the most unregulated trades. Local governments had a tough time keeping an eye on a business that took place in a kitchen. This made brewing an industry that the lord of the manor did not have a monopoly over.

Alewives could also be fined for selling ale that hadn't been approved by the local aletaster. When a very poor woman was caught selling untasted ale, a plea that selling ale was the only way to feed her children was usually effective in convincing the manorial court to let her go. This happened frequently because so many poor women worked as alewives.

See, that was the important part about the alewives. Theirs was a trade available to even the poorest women, who made up a large portion of the female population. Brewing in the early Middle Ages had a distinct lack of specialization. A woman could brew in her kitchen while doing housework and tending to her kids at the same time. Unmarried women and widows could support themselves by becoming alewives. It was possible to be independent and maybe even eke out a slightly higher standard of living. Brewing was the *only* trade like this. Women working in other trades were usually paid three-fourths or even half of what men were.[26] There was no pay discrepancy in brewing and selling ale because women controlled the trade. For many medieval women, being an alewife was the best option to support themselves or their families.

It was also an important industry. Ale was crucial to everyday life. Everyone drank ale. There was always, always a market for it. It was the only part of the local economy and politics where women had any power.

Medieval women over in Ireland were brewsters, as well. Ireland was never conquered by the Romans, so their commitment to beer was never interrupted by an obsession with wine. Fourth century literature describes over a dozen types of beer that were brewed and enjoyed by the women of Ireland. Around the fifth century, the land eventually did succumb to Roman influence and became a Christian isle.

Christianity had been spreading across Europe for a few hundred years, especially after emperor Theodosius made it the official religion of the Roman Empire in 380. The conversion from paganism to Christianity didn't affect the Irish thirst for beer, though. Several saints and divine figures used it in the miracles they worked, including Saint Brigid. There are a few stories about her turning water into alcohol (Jesus wasn't the only one with that superpower), including one where she turned the

---

26 Wild how far we haven't come, huh?

bathwater of a leper colony into a big tub of red beer. In one legend, when faced with a beer shortage right before Easter, Brigid
prayed over the barrels and made more. Much more—enough
red beer to last through Easter week and beyond. Amen![27]

The saints loved wine, too. Wine was one of the parts of pagan
worship that Christianity adopted in Rome. Communion—
drinking red wine that represented the blood of Christ—as a part
of Christian rites played an especially important role in keeping
viticulture alive in Europe after the fall of the Roman Empire.
The Church's needs influenced the distribution of wine across
the continent along with the social and ideological significance
of the drink. One of the groups that helped keep wine making
alive post–Roman Empire was nuns.

Nuns and monks were vital to the continuation of viticulture
during the early Middle Ages. They were not the sole protec-
tors of the vine (the idea that barbarian tribes totally wiped out
wine making in Europe is a myth), but they certainly played
an important part. Monasteries and abbeys became major wine
producers, mostly because they needed a lot of it. Christian
churches purchased wine for religious use, but the majority of
it wasn't used for Communion. In fact, fifth century Christians
rarely took Communion. Most of the wine was used to entertain travelers and for daily consumption by monks and nuns. In
medieval Europe, it was commonplace for abbeys to have vineyards or breweries that were run by nuns. Sometimes referred to
as brewnuns, these holy drinking women also made what was
known as *small* or weaker beer. Depending on what the abbey
produced (or what was readily available), the nuns had a daily

27   There are still many churches dedicated to Saint Brigid, patron saint of
     poets, blacksmiths and healers. Little is known about her except that she
     lived in the late fifth century, she founded a powerful monastery that ac-
     cepted men and women, and she made really good beer.

allowance of beer or wine. Nuns drank, on average, about a liter and a half of wine or beer a day.

Hildegard certainly never missed her daily beer. In fact, beer was her favorite drink, especially when it was made with hops.

Hops are the little, cone-shaped flowers of the *Humulus lupulus* plant. They're very bitter, and today are primarily used as a flavoring to give beer what we call a *hoppy* taste. Hildegard loved the taste of a well-hopped beer. She also believed that hops imparted beneficial properties to the drinker and the beer itself. Her ideas about hops might have stayed within her convent if it wasn't for an extraordinary series of events.

Hildegard became convinced that her visions gave her a prophetic ability and helped with her creative endeavors, such as composing music. What they certainly did was give her a lot of influence in her monastery. It was tough to argue with the lady that God was sending visions to. By 1136, she was selected to be the leader—the Mother Superior—of her group of Benedictine nuns.

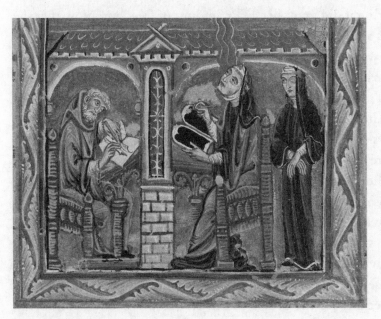

Hildegard receiving a vision.

A few years later, when she was forty-two, Hildegard had an intense vision. She wrote it down, along with some other visions that followed, in a manuscript called *Scivias*. Some of the monks in Disibodenberg read it, and eventually, *Scivias* went all the way up the chain to Pope Eugenius III, who declared it to be of divine origins.[28] Not only that, he declared Hildegard a prophetess of the Church. This title authorized her to preach, a power nearly unheard of for a woman when nuns were encouraged to be silent.

With the pope's endorsement, Hildegard was off to the races. Well, off around Germany. She went on four speaking tours of the country. When she was home, pilgrims traveled from all over to consult with her. In 1148, she received another vision that compelled her to start a new convent near Bingen, an area on the Rhine River. The monastery reluctantly let her go, because who were they to argue with a vision from God?

Her new convent near Bingen didn't have a lot of money, but having it did grant her a fair amount of freedom. Now that she was away from the prying eyes of monks, Hildegard ran things *her* way. Things got pretty wild. For nuns, anyway. It was such a rarity during this time for a woman to have both autonomy and authority. Hildegard took advantage of both.

She allowed her nuns to literally let their hair down on feast days. In medieval Europe, just as in ancient Greece, women were expected to have their hair covered at all times in public. It didn't matter if you were a princess or a nun or a common peasant woman. But Hildegard's nuns had their hair out and flowing. Even the fact that they had hair at all was controversial, since nuns typically had their heads shorn four times a year. Flowing hair out in the open was a look reserved exclusively for those with authority. Silence and humility were female virtues, especially for the brides of Christ, and the Church considered

---

28   Like getting a starred review from the Vatican!

them ways for women to honor God. Any signs of boldness were likened to Eve. Hildegard had some different ideas.[29]

During celebrations, her nuns wore gold crowns and silk clothes. All of this was directly against the rules of Saint Benedict that concerned female dress. When criticized, Hildegard argued that a lot of these rules applied to married women, not to nuns, who occupied a more nebulously defined female space outside of the rules of other women. Nuns—they're not like other girls.

Her nuns still had a typical convent workday. They got about eight hours of sleep every night and were up at dawn. These women dedicated themselves to three to four hours of prayer, four hours of study and eight hours of manual labor daily. Many of these manual labor hours were spent brewing beer, which was an important part of the nuns' diet. They ate mostly vegetables, bread and beer. There are no accounts of the nuns going really wild and getting smashed, but they did drink beer every day.

Settled in her seat of power, Hildegard began writing up a storm. It was such a rarity for a woman in this era to have the ability to write, but more rare to be read by others. Her manuscripts were copied and read widely. Hildegard took advantage of this incredible amount of influence. She flourished as a writer during these years and produced brilliant texts of greatly different types: musical compositions, a vast collection of letters (including correspondence with the pope), poetry and books of science. She is one of the first female doctors[30] and scientists from whom we have surviving works. Hildegard even wrote about the female orgasm. (She was very much in favor.) The positive way she wrote about the cisgender female body and femininity was decidedly different from the condemnatory way male

---

29 Hildegard was extremely liberal for her time, but she was also extremely classist. She believed that classes should not mix and only accepted women from wealthy families (perhaps to help fund her bold convent). She was criticized for this even then.

30 Nuns often acted as midwives and nurses to local women.

Church authorities did. For Hildegard, a woman and her sexuality were not inherently evil or shameful.

One of the most important books was *Physica*, her first scientific book. It's a medical encyclopedia divided into chapters about metals, reptiles, birds, fish, animals, trees, stones, plants and elements. Each entry contains their healing properties, alongside some general information about them. *Physica* is considered to be Germany's first natural history text. Because it contains medical knowledge mixed with ideas about magic and Scripture, it isn't a straight up natural history text. But *Physica* paints a pretty good picture of twelfth century medical practices and folk remedies. It was influential for nearly four hundred years. Much of what Hildegard wrote holds true today, such as the soothing properties of aloe plants and the calming power of chamomile. Some of her ideas are still in use by those who practice alternative medicine.

Hildegard was also correct about many of the botanical powers of the ingredients in beer. She wrote extensively about barley, considering it beneficial for the digestive system, particularly the stomach and intestines. Most importantly for the future of the beer industry, she wrote about her favorite additive. Nearly one thousand years before any bearded man in a bar could praise them, Hildegard helped to teach the world about the benefits of hops.

Many doctors during this period believed in the Hippocratic four humors system of physiology. The body was thought to be made of a balance of four fluids that regulated behavior: the sanguine, choleric, melancholic and phlegmatic humors. Hildegard wrote in *Physica* that hops increased the melancholic in your system (too much of which could give you a melancholy mind). She was the first person to write scientifically about this, and she was correct. Today, we know that hops can relax the nervous system, have a calming, sedative effect and promote sleep.

Hops in beer, however, had a much more important job to do. Hildegard wrote that "...its bitterness inhibits some spoilage in beverages to which it is added, making them last longer."

Again, she was correct. Hildegard was the first person to write scientifically about this, as well. The preservative property of hops was about to become the biggest beer innovation since Ninkasi's hymn.

The status of drinking women in China differed from dynasty to dynasty, but the Tang dynasty was a particularly fortuitous time to be one. Known as the golden age for women, the Tang dynasty began in the year 618 and ended in 907.[31] Women worked as government officials during this time, served as generals in the military and even played polo. There was access to education and social freedom, especially for upper-class women. And they were toasting to the occasion.

Elite, urban women of the Tang dynasty liked to drink as much wine as they could and sing loudly in the local taverns. Even if they weren't drinking, it was fashionable for aristocratic women to apply rouge to their cheeks to make them look flushed with alcohol. Being a drinking woman was not only encouraged, it was *sexy*.

The Tang dynasty was a short but pivotal one. In the previous dynasty, the Sui dynasty, the Northern and Southern regions of China became unified. Tang society followed the traditions of Northern China, which were closely related to the nomadic people of Central Asia and the northern Steppes. These tribes had women involved in politics, warfare and, yes, drinking.

It wasn't a totally free world for women, though. There was a common perception of women as a marketable product. A man could only have one wife but could legally purchase as many concubines as he wanted. There was a robust, competitive market for sex workers. Alcohol was a central feature in Tang social customs, so these women needed to be seasoned drinkers.

Drinking was a part of every feast, every banquet, many meals and lots of important religious rituals. It was a cultural essen-

---

31 Briefly interrupted from 690 to 705, when it was ruled by Wu Zetian, the only female emperor in the history of China.

tial for any event, secular or otherwise. Elites were even buried with their drinking vessels. Courtesans were expected not only to drink but to hold their own in drinking competitions. It was considered a bonus if she knew a slew of drinking games.

Beer existed in China during this time, but the drink of choice for all those aristocratic drinkers was wine. The climate in parts of China, unlike England, was favorable for viticulture. There was millet wine and rice wine, but it was grape wine that was the favorite of one of China's most famous—and beautiful—drinking women.

Yang Guifei is known as one of the Four Great Beauties of China.[32] She was the concubine of the renowned Tang emperor Xuanzong and such a goddamn babe that he was constantly distracted by her. (So distracted that the entire dynasty fell apart.) Like Cleopatra, although she is the subject of many poems, plays and legends, it's not known what exactly Yang Guifei actually looked like. All that we know for sure was that she was fat, with long, dark hair and dark eyes. Her beauty set the standard for fashion. All her outfits and hairstyles were copied by the women of the palace. She had a particular affinity for long, loose fitting robes with high necklines and they became all the rage.[33]

As a skilled courtesan, she was adept at singing, dancing and drinking. She loved lichee fruits[34] and grape wine. Not one for subtlety, Yang Guifei drank it out of a jewel-encrusted glass cup.

Yang Guifei was known as a dazzling, voluptuous woman who loved boozy parties. She was the embodiment of female freedoms during the Tang dynasty and hundreds of years after

---

32 Guifei was not her real last name. Guifei was the highest rank for imperial concubines at the time. Her last name was actually Yuhuan.

33 There is a story that one day, she fell off her horse, causing her massive updo to become disheveled and loose on one side. As the women of the palace saw her ride inside, they all rushed to copy her asymmetrical I-just-fell-off-a-horse look.

34 A lichee is a summer fruit in southeastern Asia. They are small, pink and juicy. Their juice makes for a great cocktail, and there are several lichee-based cocktails that honor the legacy of Yang Guifei.

her death in 756, she was the source of inspiration for *The Tale of Genji*, the world's first novel, written by a woman named Murasaki Shikibu.[35] Unfortunately, women in China wouldn't be a part of the mainstream drinking culture again for a long time after the Tang dynasty ended.

The earliest evidence we have of saké creation is from 4800 BCE in the Yangtze Valley in China, but today it's a type of booze associated with Japan and Japanese cuisine. It is one of the oldest drinks still consumed all over the world. We call saké rice wine, but since it's made from a grain, it's actually more like beer. Like wine or beer, it was originally used in religious rituals. It was made as an offering to different gods and deities, especially in the Shinto religion.

When saké was first brewed in Japan, it was called *kuchikami*, meaning *chewing in the mouth*. Around 300 CE, it was made by chewing rice, chestnuts or millet, then spitting the bolus[36] into a big wooden tub. It was left to ferment there for several days before being consumed.

The first historical Japanese chronicles, known as the Kojiki and Nihongi, tell us that there was a belief that a female deity, a goddess named Konohana Sakuya Hime, created the saké-making process by first chewing mouthfuls of rice herself to ferment them. As saké brewing developed in early Japan, for a long time only women were allowed to make it. The original term for brewer was *toji* (written in Chinese; everything Chinese was popular in Japan at this time), written with characters that meant *lady*.[37] Women were specified as natural-born brewers. Especially young women. Virgin ones, at that.

---

35 This is, like Yang Guifei, a descriptive name and not a personal one. Her real name is unknown.

36 The word for a chewed-up wad of food in your mouth. Use it at your next dinner party!

37 Toji is still used as a term for brewer, but it's now written with different characters. It means *brewmaster* and is associated with men.

Teenage virgin girls were the ones who chewed the rice balls and spit them into the wooden tubs. To make enough for a religious ceremony like a harvest festival, they'd be chewing balls of rice until their jaws ached. These poor girls were considered mediums of the gods, and the booze they produced was called *bijinshu*, or *beautiful women saké*.

This saké was not very alcoholic, and it wasn't even quite a liquid. Filtration was not a part of the process yet, so the final product had the consistency of oatmeal, with partially digested chunks of rice floating in liquid. It was eaten with chopsticks and it was more of a mash than a beverage. Though it seems unappealing, the urge to drink was powerful, and saké gradually spread to the general population for year-round consumption, instead of exclusively for religious purposes.

As Japan moved into the Heian period (starting in 794), women still played the principal role in saké production. Inside the emperor's palace compound was a royal brewery where women made multiple types of saké, including white saké, which was a more refined and liquid version of the original chunky stuff. They also made a black saké, which was flavored with the ashes of aromatic wood. Unfortunately, records of this process no longer exist, so we don't know exactly how many other types of saké these women made or how to brew black saké today.

Royal and upper-class women took part in banquets and drank saké along with the men at feasts and parties. Peasants still made and drank the older version of saké, so it was easy to tell which class a woman belonged to by which type of saké she had. Chunks or no chunks, it was quite common there for women of all classes to drink.

Women in India had their own rice–based alcohol, but there was a lot less chewing involved.

There was *sura*, made with fermented barley or rice flour. *Ki-*

kala was also made with grains, but it was sweeter. *Maireya* was a spiced grape wine. *Medako* was made with water, fermented rice, herbs and spices, honey and grape juice. *Prasanna* was made with flour, spices and the bark and fruit of the *putraka* tree. *Asava* was made with wood apples, sugar and honey, and flavored with spices like cinnamon. *Aristha* was made with water, treacle, honey, butter and pepper. A beer made from rice was widely drunk, and to supplement all this, wine was frequently imported from other countries.

During India's Classical period, which started around 320 CE, alcohol was manufactured and consumed on a large scale. Much of the country was under the rule of the Gupta Empire at this time and some historians refer to this as India's golden age. Scientific, political, artistic and cultural developments flourished in this era. As much as anything can flourish without women, anyway. Women were considered to be inferior to men and were not allowed to own property but were afforded some freedoms. An education in the arts was permitted, and some participated in administrative roles in government. (These freedoms steadily declined over the next thousand years.)

Drinking shops and taverns opened up, and booze was enjoyed en masse at feasts and festivals. Some groups of women drank so much that they couldn't walk straight and had to stumble home together in one big wobbly group. Brahman women (of the highest caste in Hinduism) were prohibited from imbibing, however. There was a belief that a Brahman woman who drank would be deprived of her husband's company in the next world. Worse, she could be reincarnated as a leech or an oyster. Women in all the other caste levels drank, though.

Maireya, the spiced wine, was so popular that Buddhist followers were banned from drinking it. Despite this, it remained a bestseller and was sold in taverns, sweetened and thickened with sugar. There was a belief that drinking gave women a special charm, maireya in particular. It was said to give them a rosy complexion and to make them flirty. After Roman passum, it seems like maireya was the world's next girly drink. It was the rosé of classical India.

The short shelf life of her product was the alewife's biggest problem.

Ale soured so quickly that she needed to sell it or drink it as soon as possible. The shelf life kept ale an extremely local product and kept alewives brewing constantly.

Hildegard's hops solved the problem.

Adding hops prevented the growth of bacteria in the beer, meaning it stayed fresh longer and it could travel. It could even be exported. Adding hops to ale greatly improved the drinking experience, too. Not only did the bitter flavor of these little flowers improve the astringent taste, but hops help a beer retain a head of foam. A thick layer of foam on top of a beer can greatly improve a beer's aroma. Plus, the climbing vine of the *Humulus lupulus* plant that the hops grow on flourishes in all kinds of climates, all over the world.

So hops made ale into beer. Beer that tasted better, smelled better, lasted longer and could be sold and shipped farther than just across the hamlet. Hildegard was really onto something.

And as she continued to write back home in Germany, her work was being read far and wide. The nine books of *Physica* educated readers all over the continent. Because of Hildegard's authority and influence, her knowledge of hops and its power to preserve beer spread across Europe. Hildegard's writings helped fuel alcohol's next great revolution.

In September 1179, Hildegard of Bingen passed away at her beloved convent. She was eighty-one years old, having reached twice the average life expectancy for a woman of her time. Perhaps she got a health boost from her daily rations of hoppy beer.

At the time of her death, Hildegard was a renowned abbess,

prophet, scientist, master composer, and prolific writer. And of course, a beer lover. For Hildegard and her other brewnuns, alcohol meant virtue, not vice. As part of their daily diet, beer sustained them and nourished them. Their ability to brew it for themselves contributed to their independence and self-reliance, which in turn fueled the unique freedoms they enjoyed.

Just as Hildegard and the brewnuns used the Church as an avenue toward autonomy, independence and power, the alewives were able to do the same thing with their own brewing. During a time when women could not even own land, many were able to eke out an existence and even thrive because of alcohol.

Whether it meant building a business, bolstering her power in the community or just feeding her children, brewing was the only trade a woman in medieval Europe could count on. It was the best way to earn a living with the tools in her own kitchen. Many alewives didn't have the luxury to muse about the morality of drinking: beer often kept them and their families alive, either financially or nutritionally. For the next thousand years (and still today), women all over the world found themselves in the same position. For poor women, alcohol wasn't sin, it was survival.

Unfortunately, the alewives were about to have some competitors who did not agree.

4

LI QINGZHAO AND THE DEVIL'S SCHOOLHOUSE

The High Middle Ages

Historians used to refer to the era after the fall of the western Roman Empire as the Dark Ages.

The derisive term originated with the Italian scholar Petrarch, who was of the opinion that after the light of Greco-Roman culture went out, Europe was dim. Modern scholars now consider Petrarch's term to be bullshit. Good riddance to Greco-Roman culture and its watery wine.

Although the West was a better place without the Roman Empire, things were about to get a whole lot darker there for alewives and drinking women. Things were darker for women in the East, too. In the new Song dynasty in China, women had fewer social freedoms and therefore fewer drinking freedoms to enjoy. Groups of loud and rowdy women drinking wine in a tavern were scarce during this dynasty.

But there was one woman in China keeping the light on for drinking women. She changed the game for women in literature, too. Looking for the patron saint of drunken poetry?

Sorry, Charles Bukowski. Li Qingzhao is the reigning monarch of booze and writing.

Born into a privileged family in 1084 in Jinan, in the Shandong province of China, Qingzhao was one of China's greatest poets. She is the only woman in Chinese history who achieved canonical status with poetry within her lifetime. During the Song dynasty, women's writing was marginalized (like it was in most other dynasties, the Tang being one of the exceptions). To make Qingzhao all the more extraordinary, she was known for writing things that women were not expected to write. One of her favorite subjects? Drinking wine.

It was not uncommon for women in the Song dynasty to be literate or even be writers, but there was a deep cultural ambivalence about them being educated[38] and permitted to write. The women who did write faced nearly insurmountable prejudice when it came to getting their work produced or circulated.[39] Women were considered part of the home, part of inner, private life. Like in ancient Greece, men were considered part of the outer, public life of the country. Having a woman write was one thing, but printing it and spreading it around? This was a big transgression of the cultural norms.

Qingzhao was lucky enough to be born to an upper-class family full of scholars and officials, so she had access to literacy from the get-go. Her father was a writer and an important government figure, and her mother was a poet. Qingzhao started writing at a young age and became acclaimed for her poetry as a teenager. When she was just barely eighteen, Qingzhao married fellow poet Zhao Mingcheng, and the two were wildly happy together.

---

38 Upper-class women, anyway. Lower-class women did not have much access to education.

39 Book printing became widespread in China during the Song dynasty. It did not become common in Europe until around the fourteenth century.

She wrote *ci*-poetry, a form of classical Chinese poetry with origins in the popular songs of the day. It is limited to a fixed number of characters that must conform to a strict meter and rhyme scheme. She was a ci-poetry virtuoso. It wasn't how Qingzhao wrote that garnered attention from peers and critics, however, but rather what she wrote about.

Li Qingzhao.

The Jin-Song Wars were a series of conflicts that started in 1125 between the northern Jin dynasty and the southern Song dynasty. In 1128, caught in the war raging across the Chinese countryside, Qingzhao and Mingcheng's house was burned down, and the couple fled to Nanjing. Within a year, Mingcheng passed away from dysentery while traveling for official business. Qingzhao never fully recovered from the emotional blow. War and

Zhao Mingcheng's death forever influenced her favored subjects for poetry. After the death of her husband, Qingzhao began to write about things that were unexpected, even frowned upon, for women to write about.

In her anger, she challenged government policies and criticized officials and took bold, antiwar stances in her work. In her grief, Qingzhao wrote about desire, sadness and loneliness. She also wrote about drinking. In the eyes of critics, these were subjects only men were supposed to write about. Only *boys* were allowed to be sad, drunk and horny. Women were just supposed to be quiet. Producing work about sexuality and alcohol was unprecedented for a female poet.[40]

A collection of her poems translated in 1979 by Ling Chung and Kenneth Rexroth featured many of Qingzhao's groundbreaking poems, such as "Plum Blossoms,"

> *...Even Heaven shares our joy,*
> *Making the bright moon splendid on your curving flesh.*
> *Let us celebrate with thick green wine in gold cups.*
> *I will not refuse to get drunk*
> *For this flower cannot be compared to other flowers."*

and "Autumn Love,"

> *...I drink two cups, then three bowls*
> *of clear wine until I can't*
> *stand up against a gust of wind.*
> *Wild geese fly overhead.*
> *They wrench my heart."*

During the Song dynasty in China, these were outrageous

---

40 Our wine-loving Yang Guifei from the last chapter was featured in one of Qingzhao's poems. Qingzhao describes Yang Guifei's "face flushed with wine." Apparently, the emperor had a storied obsession with her wine-flushed cheeks.

subjects for a woman to write about. Li Qingzhao—with her glass of wine—turned the world of Chinese poetry upside down.

As word slowly got around Europe that adding hops to ale made it last longer, people started to realize that there was a lot of money to be made off booze. There was already a profit to be made in the brewing industry, at least on the government side of things. Taxes and fees from the regulation of ale generated a sizable hill of coins. But now that beer could travel and be exported, government officials and businessmen all over Europe and England put the brewing industry in their sights. It was time for beer to get commercialized.

The advent of hops in the brewing industry should have been an incredible boon for alewives. Being able to make beer that was tastier, cheaper and more easily transported and preserved should have made them prosper. Hops were the best thing *before* sliced bread. But when this new and improved brew caught on, as historian Joan Thrisk says, "If a venture prospers, women fade from the scene." One of the biggest effects this had on the brewing industry was not just how beer was made, but *who* made it. The alewives' livelihood was in trouble.

And so were their souls.

The Christian Church—another growing industry—in twelfth century towns, villages and cities noticed that its main competitor for attendance on Sunday was the alehouse. The combined might of both brewing commercialization and the Church would spell certain doom for the alewives.

By 1300, brewing had begun a transformation from a small, localized industry into a commercial titan. Bigger business called for more regulation and specialization. Brewsters, attracted to the industry precisely for its lack thereof, started to get pushed out by wealthier businessmen.

Ale prices were set by the aletasters once a year, so depending on the rising and falling prices of grain, an alewife could make decent or even good money by brewing. Just as I have to pay an exorbitant price for a beer in Los Angeles compared to the two-dollar specials in the small Massachusetts town where I went to college, the brewsters selling ale in big towns made a lot more money than their sisters out in the rural countryside. If they got lucky, they sold their product to castles or aristocratic households, maybe even at a market if their town was large enough to have one.

Brewing was technically an unskilled craft because it required no education or apprenticeship to start, but there actually were quite a few skills involved. Besides making the beer, women had to negotiate with the local aletasters, grain suppliers, malt sellers, water bearers, servants and, of course, their customers. To succeed, they needed to be skilled businesswomen, craftswomen and saleswomen all at once.

Single and widowed brewsters sometimes faced challenges because they didn't have the help that many married women did, although they endured fewer taxes and fees. But they were also subject to less control, and many of them fared pretty well financially because of brewing. For the married women, their husbands were—in theory—in control of the brewing. Husbands could tell wives when and how to brew and whom to sell it to. They could take the profits if they wished. In practice, however, this was the one industry where women were in charge. On rare occasions, they banded together. In 1317, the brewsters of Exeter in England were so incensed by the prices that the local aletaster set that they got together and refused to brew or sell ale until the prices were adjusted.

The power that the brewsters possessed made local authorities anxious, even hostile. Women who refused to submit to male control over their beer were marked as disobedient, noncompliant troublemakers.

Noncompliant women armed with knowledge and bargaining power who challenged the economic dominance of men? A recipe for trouble.

Although sometimes women were hired as aletasters, it was usually a man overseeing an all-female industry. Women knew more about the trade because they were the ones actually making the beer and should have been eligible for the position. But what were seen as legal customs (traditions of sexism) trumped practical experience. Because this was an area where women were more knowledgeable, many men were paranoid about brewsters being deceitful and untrustworthy.

Besides the actual brewing, brewsters also ran into problems when they sold beer. Even without the presence of a sex worker plying her trade, an air (or shadow, depending on your moral views) of sexuality and sexual license had permeated the public sale of alcohol for over a thousand years. Booze has always lubricated romantic and sexual social rituals. The alehouse was a choice location for courting...or for cheating on your spouse. Certain social rules were relaxed, and customers felt a little freer, often a little too free. The women selling the booze had to be on their guard. Alewives and women serving drinks had to be on the lookout for grabby, rowdy men. Any concern about drunkenness or the sexual license at the alehouse was projected onto the alewives, not their customers. It was the alewife who bore the responsibility of supervising them. When men got drunk and flirty, or drunk and violent, it was her fault. If a tipsy man got handsy and the alewife turned him down, the trouble resulting from the rejected, angry man was blamed on her.

Every female bartender or server knows this difficult line to walk. She's got to be pleasant and attractive, but not *too* pleasant and attractive. If someone crosses a line, not only is it her fault, but she's got to deal with the ensuing conflict. Eight hundred years ago, it was part of an alewife's job to both control men's drinking and deal with their behavior. Drunken creeps predate ice cubes, indoor plumbing and even little bowls of salty snacks as an alehouse fixture.

There was also a male fear that troublemaking alewives would spread their ways to other women, like noncompliance was some sort of disease you could catch at the alehouse. Men were afraid that unruly alewives would encourage other women to disobey their husbands. In many ballads of the time, alewives not only disobey their husbands but they disobey all men. One ballad, "The Kind Beleeving Hostess," lamented:

> To speak, poor man, he dares not
> My hostess for him cares not
> She'll drink and quaff
> And merrily laugh
> And she his anger fears not.

Anxieties about the nature of ale-selling were projected onto the alewives, not the men who patronized them. Sexuality, misconduct and deceit were associated with the presence of women in the trade.

This was how the Church would turn the alewife into a witch.

The alewives weren't the only women making beer during this period. Contrary to popular belief, pilgrims and colonizers did not bring alcohol to North America.[41] Several groups of Native American peoples had their own types of alcohol and healthy relationships with them centuries before white settlers arrived to screw everything up. As usual, women in these tribes were the ones to do the brewing.

Tribes in the southwest region of North America used alco-

---

41   The idea that Native Americans are genetically predisposed to alcoholism is a myth used to justify genocidal crimes. Any kind of drinking must be understood in a cultural context before it can be considered a problem. The tribes that did make alcohol were doing fine before Europeans arrived.

hol for social and spiritual purposes. Women in the Othama and
Tohono O'odham groups who lived in the Sonoran Desert made
a wine from the saguaro cactus called *haren a pitahaya*. During
the late summer, the women in the tribe would get together
and gather the red fruit of the cactus with a long pole. It grew
at the very top—fifteen to thirty feet up! The first batches of
fruit were made into jams and jellies, but the last of the saguaro
harvest was reserved for wine making.

The haren a pitahaya was used in rain ceremonies held on
New Year's Day, which took place in late summer for the tribes.
All the adults in these tribes drank, regardless of gender, believing that as they were saturated with wine, the earth would be
saturated with rain. Many Tohono O'odham villages still practice these ceremonies.

The women of the Chiricahuas tribes made a couple different types of alcohol. One was *tula-pah*, a potent corn beer that
was particularly difficult to make. The women needed to ger-
minate the corn and then dry it before they mixed it with herbs
and barks. The whole concoction was boiled for hours, drained,
then boiled again. The final result was fermented for twelve to
twenty-four hours. Like English ale at the time, tula-pah needed
to be consumed quickly to prevent spoiling.

There was also *tiswin*, another type of corn beer. The Tohono
O'odham women made tiswin from the sap of saguaro cacti.
Just like tula-pah, it had a very short shelf life no matter what
it was made from.

Brewing usually turned into a large social gathering. Women
of the tribe made huge quantities of tiswin or tula-pah, and
everyone drank. Once it was ready to be consumed, the alcohol was served by the woman or women who made it. She'd use
a single-cup dipper that was passed around a circle of people.
This honored woman drank the choicest part of the brewing,
the sweet squeezings.

At these brewing parties, everyday social restrictions were relaxed, which created a socially neutral ground for women. After

they drank, women would assume traditionally male roles in singing or drumming circles. Teenage girls were sometimes allowed to partake, depending on how strict their parents were. For these women, alcohol became a key that granted entry to typically all-male spaces.

Although things were looking grim for drinking women all over Europe and Asia, some were still carrying the torch. On horseback, no less.

Drinking was very important to the Mongol tribes of eastern Asia in the twelfth century. It was central to both their diet and their culture. For a nomadic tribe, being able to have both a meal and alcohol on the go was key. Having them both together? Ideal.

Their principal boozy beverage was *kumiss*, a highly nourishing drink made from fermented mare's milk. The women of the tribes made it: they milked the mares, churned the milk until it bubbled, extracted the butter, and the remaining liquid was left to ferment. The resulting kumiss was a cloudy and slightly sour drink, high enough in calories to fuel a full day of riding on horseback. A massive amount of kumiss was drunk by the tribes on a daily basis, so the women were always busy.

For the people of the Mongol tribes, drunkenness was not an embarrassing state of affairs. It was honorable, even for the women. Mongolian women drank just as much as the men did. At feasts and celebrations, drinking was the primary activity. The seating arrangements were segregated by gender, and often there were drinking contests where men and women competed against each other. Swap out the kumiss for wine and you've probably been to a wedding like that.

Inebriation is shaped mostly by the way we are taught to express it. If drinking is a male-dominated activity, then expressing drunkenness is a male activity, too. In China, Li Qingzhao intrigued, shocked and even disgusted readers and critics by expressing her love of drinking.

After the death of her husband, Qingzhao settled down in Hangzhou, the new capital of the Song dynasty's government. She continued producing poetry and essays, and it's clear in her work that she found solace in both writing and wine.

By the East Hedges I cradle the wine goblet.
After sunset, a wind of dark scent filling my sleeves.
Don't say this does not waste away my bones.
The curtain rolled up in the west wind,
I know, my love, I have wilted
better than a daisy.[42]

Many literary critics of the time resented Qingzhao. These men believed she had a lack of shame and that women shouldn't write about things like desire and alcohol. She was regarded as some sort of unnatural creature, a boogeywoman with a quill and a goblet. Qingzhao's gender caused her poetry to be more harshly criticized.

"Such lines as these, how could a woman ever manage to come up with them?" said Zhu Xi, a male writer of the time. Even praise from the literary critics boiled down to a version of *pretty good…for a girl*. But Qingzhao didn't stop writing.

At age forty-nine, she had a short and ill-fated second marriage to a cruel man named Zhang Ruzhou, and the two divorced within months. This was the excuse that literary circles needed. Many used it as proof that Qingzhao was an immoral woman, and they mocked her life choices in reviews of her work. These men made fun of everything they could: the various tragedies of her life, her drinking, her divorce. As much as they disapproved of her, however, they could not argue with her talent. Qingzhao was unquestionably skilled with poetry. In a climate

---

42   From "Drunk Flower," translated by Kevin Tsai.

where all the literary conventions had been established by men, Li Qingzhao found her voice. And they couldn't deny her.

Before Qingzhao, there was a well-established tradition of poetry that had no strong sense of the personal identity of the subject. Most poems left the gender of the subject indeterminate. Qingzhao, however, wrote poems that were overtly feminine. Her work features female subjects that are independent, unconventional and unpredictable. Often, they are drinking. These women have a self-sufficiency to them, sometimes outspoken and sometimes refusing to speak. Expressing their loneliness, bitterness or anger, they each have a depth that is unique.

After the divorce, Qingzhao wrote her way out of the critical response. She kept producing poetry and clawed her way back to some semblance of respectability. Qingzhao had readers of all genders who loved her and her work. Still, elite culture at the time had a difficult time accommodating her. Most people didn't know what to make of her. Qingzhao's work was both traditionally unwomanly and yet absolutely feminine at the same time. She broke into a male-dominated industry and a male-dominated drinking culture, and she did it being unapologetically female. It put her legacy in jeopardy.

Alewives had a very particular look.

These women often wore tall, sometimes pointed hats in order to distinguish themselves and stand out in a crowded marketplace.[43] The ale stakes that advertised their product were essentially brooms—long sticks with a bundle of twigs tied to the end. They brewed their ale in large cauldrons. You might even see a cat or two hunting around the grain for mice.

Sound familiar?

It's no coincidence that the witch costumes available at Spirit Halloween stores look similar to a medieval alewife. Any neg-

---

43   These hats could be two feet tall. It's believed to have been a simple marketing scheme for brewsters. Easy for people to find!

ative depictions of male ale sellers in the thirteenth and fourteenth centuries focused on bad business practices. But for the
alewives, it was a different sort of attack. Those looking to dis-
parage an alewife went after her appearance, her sexuality and
especially her faith.

Alewife and her promotional hat.

Since the Church in western Europe was in competition
with alehouses for Sunday attendance, the alewives became its
enemy. Sermons of the time described alehouses as "deadly ri-
vals." At the time, it was said that "the tavern was the devil's
schoolhouse." Which meant that the alewives were the devil's
schoolteachers.

Women running alehouses were depicted as temptresses who
lured godly men to sin. Representations in writing and art of the

period show unpleasant images of willful, lusty and disobedient alewives drinking or selling ale. The Church fostered a fear
in men that the brewsters, with their little scrap of economic
authority and independence, had unnatural power over them.
Religious imagery often featured alewives cavorting in hell—
sometimes topless. Alewives were shown burning in hell more
than any other type of tradesperson.

PICTORIAL PRESS LTD./ALAMY STOCK PHOTO

A woodcut of a suspiciously alewife-like witch flying around with the devil.

A popular medieval poem, "The Tunning of Elynour Rum-
myng" by John Skelton, depicts a brewster named Elynour as an
ugly woman and a bad craftsperson. The poem suggests where an
alewife's power could lead...to a world where women are in control. The horror! The poem also contains allusions to witchcraft.
Elynour is described as witchlike: "she and the devil be sib."

All of these fictional narratives about alewives and drinking
women were slanderous and, in fact, downright dangerous. They

encouraged male suspicions about alewives and the community power that these women had.

By the mid-fourteenth century, brewing was being taken over by male businessmen looking to industrialize and commercialize beer. New regulations made it so that without capital and a husband, women couldn't get a foothold in brewing. Without legal independence (women couldn't sign contracts on their own), potential female brewers were unable to gain access to the industry. Single women and widows were the first to be pushed out. This, combined with the Church-encouraged prejudice, tolled the death knell for the alewife.

In Japan around the same time, similar problems afflicted the saké-making women. A combination of Buddhist and folk beliefs that women had a polluting nature gradually pushed them out of the industry. One myth posited that the spirit of the saké itself was female and having a woman around in the brewery would make the saké jealous and angry. Eventually, the saké brewery became an all-male space. These sexist beliefs would keep women out of the saké industry for hundreds and hundreds of years.

Li Qingzhao never stopped writing. It is believed that she passed away in 1155, at around seventy years old. Less than a hundred of her poems survive, and about half of them are focused on the joys and sorrows of drinking. Historians believe that both Qingzhao's gender and the subject of her work affected how much of it was saved. Her deft ability in self-expression made a mark on a male-dominated art form. There have been so many iconic male artists who reveled in their drunken feelings throughout history from F. Scott Fitzgerald to Charles Bukowski.

Before them, there was Li Qingzhao.

She was everything that a drinking woman symbolized at the end of the Middle Ages. Qingzhao was bold, independent, noncompliant, formidable, feared, criticized, excluded but, ultimately, undeniable. She used her writing to show that women's inner lives matter, that they're beautiful and powerful and crucial. By crafting poems that showcased women experiencing feelings and exhibiting behaviors that were supposed to be in the domain of men, she blazed a trail through the world of Chinese poetry. Helped, of course, by a glass or two of wine.

Our next drinking heroine transgressed gender norms even further by taking men's drinks…and their trousers, too.

5

THE DEVIANT MIRTH
OF MARY FRITH

The Renaissance

Mary Frith was vilified for, accused of, arrested for and some-times convicted of swearing, dressing in men's clothing, sex work, thieving, masterlessness,[44] "deviant mirth," performing on a stage forbidden to women, receiving stolen goods and, of course, drinking. Mary Frith was a whole lot of fun.

Also known as Moll Cutpurse,[45] Mary was born in England around 1584. Verified biographical information about her is tough to find. Not only was she a larger-than-life figure who was the subject of many legends and tall tales, she was a criminal. In fact, she was known as the first professional female criminal, and she was damn proud of it.

Even if it's not feasible to confirm this superlative, Mary is no-table in that she *chose* to be a criminal. At the time, the growing metropolis of London was a magnet for young, single women

---

44 A term for being unmarried.

45 Moll was a general nickname in the sixteenth century for a woman of bad reputation. Cutpurse was a term for a thief.

looking for work. The only trades that were viable options for them were usually jobs that involved cleaning and cooking. Women had been pushed out of the one industry they previously controlled—brewing—and the guilds for other trades refused to apprentice them.

Alewives were an endangered species by the year 1500. In London, which was one of the most populated cities in the world at the time, only one percent of the members of the brewer's guild were women, compared to thirty percent just fifty years earlier. This trade guild was the only one open to women, but they were still barred from holding any position in the guild office. Married English women could continue to brew after their husbands died but had to give it up if they wanted to remarry.

In 1512, a large brewery was built in the south of England specifically for making beer for the English naval fleet. The military was about the best customer you could sell booze to— they bought a lot of it. The huge scale of production needed to brew for armies and navies excluded women from this part of the industry. Women didn't have the legal ability to acquire the capital needed to start up a big brewery.

They did start working as employees *in* the breweries that were cropping up. In countries like Belgium, Luxembourg and the Netherlands in the sixteenth century, most brewery workers were female. Like the rest of western Europe, these areas had a history of female brewing. Women worked in these breweries as both laborers and administrative staff. Dutch breweries usually had a female clerk responsible for keeping track of outgoing beer and all brewery records. In the brewery itself worked the wringsters, women who were responsible for the mash. With long rakes and big, oarlike wooden paddles, they moved the malt around in the brewing vessels. The mixture was thick and tough to move: it had a consistency like bread dough. This was physically difficult work, and these women were strong as hell! In Scandinavia, mashing was work reserved for female brewery workers, as well. There, they were called brouwsters.

London, however, did not have widely available jobs for

women in breweries, and Mary was not particularly interested in cleaning or cooking for anyone. Aside from a service or housewife trade, illegal activities were the only avenue a woman with no financial backing had to earn a living. In fact, most of the activities Mary Frith enjoyed—dressing in breeches, smoking, drinking too much, going to the alehouse and conducting business—were considered criminal for a woman.

Maybe she thought *in for a penny, in for a pound.*

Mary started out as a pickpocket and a purse-snatcher but eventually moved up the criminal ladder. She became a receiver and dealer of stolen goods, and she was so successful that she soon amassed a fortune.

Mary Frith loved taverns and preferred to conduct all her business there. It was a common occurrence to see her in a tavern, in trousers, puffing on a pipe and sipping beer. Men didn't know what to get angriest about: her pants, her pipe or her tankard. People saw Mary participating in what were considered male activities and wearing breeches as more than just a transgression of the patriarchal order, they saw it as an assumption of power.

Taverns were growing in number all over England, especially in London. With alewives and alehouses a thing of the past, male-owned drinking establishments rapidly rose in popularity. Taverns were buildings planned and dedicated to be public, instead of a kitchen with some stools set out and an ale stake above the door. They were an almost entirely male space, but there were some women running them. By the early 1600s, about five to ten percent of English taverns were run by women, usually widows of brewers.

Women still drank in public, but in fewer numbers than in the days of the village alewives. All over England and Europe, female drinking culture moved into the private space of the home, and the kitchen became the place for women to drink. This shift had such an immense effect that centuries and centuries later, the kitchen continues to be the center of women's drinking culture in many parts of the world.

Alcohol was still ubiquitous in the lives of everyone of every class. It was an important part of everyone's nutrition, medical treatments and social life. Women also drank to relieve menstrual pains and labor pains. Someone going into labor was a cue for the local women to get together and prepare the "mother's caudle," a warm wine or beer with sugar and spices mixed in. Although its purpose was to strengthen a birthing woman and keep her spirits up, the other women present at the birth drank it, as well.

Once the baby was born, there was quite a lot of drinking at the birth celebration. New mothers were encouraged to drink, since physicians at the time believed alcohol helped their bodies recover from birth. (Which we now know is not true. No shots in the delivery room.)

Upcoming marriages were another reason to be boozy. The English tradition of bride-ale was essentially a fundraiser for newlyweds. A bride-to-be brewed a bunch of ale and threw a big party in the hopes that lots of friends, family and neighbors would attend and give her enough money to fund the wedding and help establish her future household. Sound like a bridal shower? This is where we get the word *bridal*. It comes from *bride-ale*. A bride-ale shower.

Women also drank just because they wanted to, for their own jollification. Female neighbors gathered in each other's kitchens and drank beer together to socialize. These women fostered friendships, shared community knowledge and gossiped together over a drink. It was like an episode of *The Real Housewives*, only with fewer high heels and more wimples. Drinking and preparing different types of alcohol in the home was an important part of women's culture.

Along with home brewing beer, being able to select and preserve wine was essential for a housewife. How to stretch wine, how to save wine that was about to go bad, how to make bad wine taste better and how to take undrinkable wine and cook with it were all skills a woman needed. As books became widespread throughout the world, collections of recipes and kitchen knowledge were printed for women. *The English Hus-wife* by

Gervase Markham (subtitled *Containing the Inward and Outward Vertues Which Ought to Be in a Compleate Woman*) was printed in 1615 and was full of recipes and remedies for mothers and wives. Beer and cider recipes were included, since a "compleate woman" needed to be able to make booze.

Groups of women still went out to the tavern for drinks occasionally. Rarely alone, of course. Getting a drink in public solo wasn't worth the risk to a woman's reputation. If a woman wanted to go to a tavern without her group of female friends, she usually sought an approved male escort, such as a husband or a brother or some other male family member. It wasn't unusual for women to join their husbands for a night at the tavern of drinking and gambling.

Besides the risk to her reputation, being a woman alone at a tavern posed a risk to her person. English taverns were a male-dominated space, and a sexually aggressive drinking culture developed there. Often, it was dangerous for female patrons. Sexual assault was common. Then, like it is today, for women it was just safer for them to be around other women.[46]

The tavern outings for groups of women were opportunistic, usually taking place after a day's shopping or selling at the local market, or perhaps when their husbands were away. This was more common in larger cities and metropolitan areas. There were many types of games for them to play, including dice, cards, "tables" (an ancestor of backgammon) and "shove goat."[47]

Even when drinking in a group, there was a double standard for women. In addition to their fears about female sexual promiscuity, men were now afraid of the sexual gossip being bandied about in groups of drinking women. Many ballads of the day illustrate male anxiety about female drinking behavior, depicting female tavern socializing as problematic.

---

46   Not so funny that women always go to the bathroom in groups, now is it?

47   It was related to modern shuffleboard and did not involve shoving actual goats.

An English writer, Ester Sowernam, recognized this double standard when she wrote in 1617:

> What a hateful thing is to see a woman overcome with drinke, when in men it is noted for a sign of good fellowship. And whosoever doth observe it, for one woman which doth make a custom of drunkennesse, you shall finde an hundred men! It is abhorred in women, and therefore they avoyd it, it is laughed at and made but as a jest among men, and therefore so many doe practise it.

There was the rare ballad that celebrated the fellowship of drinking women. In *Fowre Wittie Gossips Disposed to Be Merry*, the song encourages "Let every woman have her cup." In *The Seamens Wives Frolick over a Bowl of Punch,*

> We love our liquor to drink it all up.
> None of us but love a full glass or a cup...
> To e'ry good bowl they told it its doom
> Merrily danc'd it about the room.

The English royalty of the sixteenth century also enjoyed drinking. Henry VIII and his English court had a very boozy reputation, and their French guests were shocked to see how much royal English women drank. Decked out in sumptuous gowns, female members of the court chugged wine from flasks while they loudly talked and cheered on whatever entertainments the assembled were watching.

Mary Frith loved to have a group of women along on her trips to the tavern. After they were fortified with some beer, the crew accompanied Mary on some of her illicit adventures. The all-female gang was associated with such truly nefarious acts, such as dressing in menswear and participating in "levity." Mary did enlist their help with actual crimes, as well, such as thievery and purse-snatching. A group of drunk women dressed in men's clothing was shocking and scandalous to the fifteenth century English public. Some accused them of being supernatural, even shape-shifting.

Mary became so notorious that in 1611, two men, Thomas Middleton and Thomas Dekker wrote the play *The Roaring Girl*,[48] *or Moll Cutpurse*, a comedy based on her exploits. She attended a performance of it, and when the show was over, Mary hopped onstage, grabbed a lute and started playing dirty songs for the audience. The success of the play solidified her place in the pop culture of the time. Hundreds of years before the women of *Jersey Shore* were doing shots and becoming a pop culture phenomenon, Mary Frith was making waves in London.

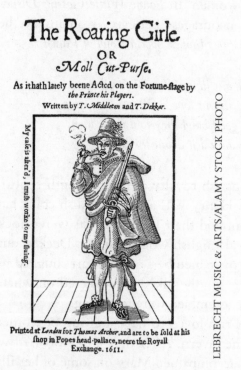

Poster for the play based on Mary Frith's escapades.

---

48   This is a play on the term *roaring boy* which referred to a young man who committed crimes, drunkenly caroused and brawled.

Just like many famous reality television personalities have discovered, Mary's celebrity didn't protect her from the authorities. The next year, she was arrested for wearing men's clothing. London law enforcement chose the least effective punishment possible for Mary. She was forced to stand in a public square and confess her crimes to a crowd, a silly punishment for someone who loved to perform. Mary made a dramatic show of regret and guilt, promising to be more modest, and apologized for her poor conduct...until someone in the audience realized that Mary was hammered and noted that she was always a maudlin, teary drunk.

Despite being arrested multiple times, Mary was fairly successful at avoiding prosecution. Whenever she was jailed, she used her vast fortune to bribe her way to freedom. But it wasn't her criminal activity that caused her notoriety. Mary wasn't a murderer or a kidnapper. She didn't pull off grand heists. She mostly picked pockets and sold stolen items. It was her behavior that made her a legend.

We've seen how closely connected the freedom to drink is to the power one holds in society. Mary Frith was a persistent reminder to a repressive society that all the women who were able might want to put on a pair of breeches and head down to the tavern for some beer and trouble, too.

Although the alewives of England and Europe had mostly disappeared by the 1500s, women were still brewing in other parts of the world. The brewsters of Scotland took a little longer to get pushed out of the beer industry.

In the sixteenth century, they still dominated the world of beer. In the town of Aberdeen in 1509, every single brewer was a woman. As in England, beer was a very important part of the Scottish diet. And like their English and European counterparts, the women of Scotland were attracted to brewing for its accessibility and versatility. One Scottish woman named Ellen

Bessat who lived in the early sixteenth century was a brewster, a cake baker, a seller of second-hand shoes and a receiver of stolen goods. Who says women can't have it all?

Scottish laws prohibited women from buying anything with their husbands' money except goods for the household, and if brewsters were caught breaking this law, their brewing equipment could be seized and smashed. They might even be forbidden to brew for a year and a day. So, the brewsters became adept at subterfuge. Many of them sold beer secretly to neighbors and friends without getting it officially approved, taxed or quality-checked. Women were heavily involved in the underground booze trade in Scotland.

The brewsters used a strong network of female knowledge to their advantage. Women knew the needs of their neighbors and local families. Friendship between brewsters allowed them to share this information and improve their ability to sell their product.

This may have contributed to why Scottish officials became increasingly uncomfortable with them.

In 1530, the Edinburgh Council remarked unhappily that it seemed as if any woman, even if she was unmarried, could set up shop as a brewster. (Yeah, dudes, that was the point.) The council tried to outlaw this practice. This all-male body wanted brewing to only be done by wives. They didn't want independent women making a living by selling beer. If women brewed, the council preferred them to do it as part of a household and in service to a patriarchal structure. By 1546, the council ruled to restrict brewing. All single women who lived alone seemed suspicious to the council and were ordered to leave town. Now, only wives and widows could make beer. If you were a single woman who was able to stay, it was possible for you to apply for a license to brew or sell beer in the local market, but most women couldn't afford it. By 1655, the percentage of female brewsters had gone from one hundred to twenty. These rules and regulations muscled them out of the industry.

But over in Africa, women were still brewing up a storm.

Alcohol has a long history in Africa that predates any European colonialism, and there is a deep-rooted tradition in many African societies of women brewing beer. In the eastern and southern parts of the continent, cloudy grain beers were an essential part of the culture and diet. Made from sorghum, the beer was thick, sour and, most importantly, a good source of nutrients and B vitamins. Just like women up in England, women in east and south Africa drank beer to supplement their meals.

Beer wasn't just for breakfast, though. Down on the southwestern edge of Africa, women brewed sweetened sorghum beer for important social occasions like celebrations, weddings, funerals, meetings and religious rituals. The *umqombothi* was typically brewed by matriarchs of big families, who had their own secret ingredients and traditions. Most umqombothi recipes were closely guarded family secrets and varied from region to region. It was usually made in a huge drum, in which maize malt and old beer were mixed with a porridge made from sorghum. This mixture was boiled, cooled and left for a few days. Sometimes, yeast came naturally from the open air. Sometimes, the brewer added yeast from previous batches after the mixture cooled. Either way, the end product was a thick, brown beer.

While it was Zulu tradition in southern Africa for the women to drink the beer first and test the quality, it was typically a male-only privilege to drink to the point of being drunk. Umqombothi is traditionally low ABV, so you'd have to drink a lot to get drunk, anyway. It was drunk from a communal *calabash* or bottle gourd. In the Zulu religion, the goddess Mbaba Mwana Waresa ruled over fertility, harvests and beer. Like

Ninkasi, she was believed to have taught humans how to make beer. Because of this, she was one of the most revered deities in the Zulu pantheon.

Zulu brewing women.

In what is now Namibia in the southwest, there was (and still is) a rich brewing culture. The women here made several different kinds of beer, ranging from lighter to darker brews, and developed a complex malting process. It probably helped that these women brewed beer daily and had ample opportunities to experiment. Beer was so important to every household's diet that a steady supply was needed.

Along with beer, a drink called *omaongo* was also crafted by women. It was made from fully ripened marula fruits, a yellow stone fruit with a tart taste. When the fruits dropped to the ground, the women and girls of the village got together to gather them, then they pressed the juice from the fruit and left it to ferment. The omaongo was made for the men of the village, but after it was finished, the women poured water over the leftover kernels and fruit pulp and left the resulting mixture to ferment for a few days. This was made into a weaker ABV drink for the women called *oshinway*. Pop a little paper umbrella in there and it's Namibia's version of a traditional girly drink.

In other parts of the continent, drinks made from palm and bananas were very popular. *Mbege* was a banana beer made in Tanzania by the women of the Chagga people. The Chagga lived on the slopes of Mount Kilimanjaro. The women started the brewing process by making a porridge from peeled bananas that had been boiled for hours. The porridge was left to ferment for a few days, then it was strained and *mso*—an infusion of malted millet—was added. The final creation was a thick, opaque beer which was yellowish-brown. Mbege was about the strength of the average beer today and had a mix of sweetness from the bananas and sourness from the millet.

The Yoruba-speaking women of Nigeria made alcoholic drinks from the oil palm tree, rafia palms and sorghum. Alcohol was called *u-un mumu* or *that which is drunk*. Once the men tapped the palm trees, the brewing of palm wine was a woman's job. The yield from the first few days of fermenting was sweet, with a low ABV. This wine was for the women. As the wine matured and became heavier in taste and higher in alcohol content, it became the drink for men. Women also made sorghum beer to supplement the wine.

Just like in Europe and England, brewing all over Africa was a female-dominated economy operating within a patriarchal order. In the sixteenth and seventeenth centuries, their dominion was largely uncontested. However, as white colonizers encroached, a threat began to loom.

Mead. Beer. Wine. Saké.

Up until this point in history, there were only fermented drinks. There was not a single martini or margarita to be found in all of the Middle Ages. However, at the same time as women were being pushed out of brewing across Europe and Asia, a new booze category entered the scene. Toward the end of the fifteenth century, people around the world were beginning to learn about distillation and how it could be used to make alcohol. Distilled alcohol became the biggest game changer in the world of drinking since those first early humans figured out how to make beer and mead.

Of course, a woman was behind this revolution. Let's rewind.

Somewhere between 100 and 200 CE (no one knows for sure), a woman named Maria was one of the greatest alchemists in the world. She called herself Maria the Jewess, and she is believed to have published important works of alchemy, including one called *Maria Practica*.[49] Maria was probably Syrian and lived in Alexandria. Very little biographical information about her is known.[50]

Alchemy was less of a science and more of a very loosely organized group of ideas that questioned the nature of the universe. It was based on observations of natural elements. Alchemists experimented with base metals, and you might be familiar with their quest to turn lead into gold. One of their great goals was to find the elixir of life, a potion that would grant the drinker immortality or eternal youth.

The original *Maria Practica* manuscript did not survive history, but the chemical knowledge and laboratory-equipment mechanics it described have shown up in other works. One of the pieces of equipment Maria invented was the *tribokos*, a three-armed distillation chamber. The tribokos consisted of an earthenware vessel for holding liquid, an alembic (a spigotlike still head for condensing vapor) connected to three copper delivery spouts, and glass flasks to receive the liquid. The vessel was heated from beneath, causing the vapor to rise up to the alembic and, once it

---

49   Making her history's first female Jewish author.

50   In the third century, the Roman emperor Diocletian started a systemic persecution of the alchemists in Alexandria and had their manuscripts destroyed.

cooled in there, to drip down to the delivery flasks. Today, we know this as an *alembic still*. Or just a *still*, for short.

Maria was looking for the elixir of life when she created the tribokos.[51] She never found the secret, but her invention did lead to the discovery of another magical elixir: liquor.

Maria's invention wasn't associated with alcohol until an eighth century scientist in Iraq named Jabir Ibn Hayyan (known as the father of chemistry) decided to see what would happen if he put wine in an alembic still. What followed was one of the most important moments in booze history.

Alcohol has a lower boiling point than water, 173 degrees Fahrenheit versus 212. So when you boil something like wine or beer, the alcohol vaporizes and rises first. Using an alembic still, it's possible to collect that vapor. Once it's cooled, that vapor turns back into a liquid. Ta-da! You've got distilled alcohol. Known at first as aqua vitae (the water of life), distilled alcohol—spirits—became the foundation for every kind of liquor you can enjoy today. Whiskey, tequila, vodka, gin, rum, even the cherry liqueur inside those little chocolates.

Jabir studied the resulting liquid from his experiment scientifically, but he didn't drink the stuff. Let's fast-forward.

It wasn't until the 1400s that distillation spread, when scientists across Asia and Europe began to experiment with the technology, taste the results and write about their findings. The first place distilled spirits became popular was Germany, and most of them were distilled from wine. Originally, the liquor was sold to the public for medical use. Apothecaries called it brandy, from the German *gebrant wein* or *burned wine*. People bought small amounts of brandy as a health tonic. They were essentially buying shots of brandy to cure all manner of maladies, from dental pain to bladder disease.

---

51   It's believed that Maria worked with another female alchemist, a woman who called herself Cleopatra, after our beloved wine-drinking Egyptian queen.

A hundred years later, at the start of the 1500s, distilled spirits finally entered mainstream drinking culture. What scientists called aqua vitae became French *eau de vie*, Scandinavian *aquavit*, Russian *vodka* and Gaelic *usquebaugh*, shortened to *usky* or *whiskie*. Its medicinal value was in its rejuvenating and pain-relieving effects, but soon people began to want those effects even when they weren't sick or injured. For a general tonic that folks drank daily for their well-being, there became a mighty thin line between medicinal consumption and recreational tippling.

Up until this point in history, people only drank fermented beverages. Beers were about 5% ABV, and wine and saké hovered around 15%. Distilled spirits could be anywhere between 30 and 65%.[52] No one really knew how to drink distilled spirits yet. Imagine having a glass of vodka after only drinking beer your entire life. No one had thought to restrict it. Elizabeth I even declared that her subjects should have all the aqua vitae they wanted.

As soon as distilling caught on, women got in on it. If she had the equipment, a woman could easily distill alcohol in her kitchen. Soon, upper-class women from England to Hungary who could afford a still were distilling spirits at home. Half of the thirty distillers in Munich in 1564 were women. In England, the percentage was even higher. There, most spirits were being produced by women. Just like ale, it started as a domestic product, the result of small, home-run operations. By now, brewsters had mostly disappeared, but female distillers took their place.

The countries where distillation really took off were in climates that were too cold to support the growth of grape vines.

---

52 The United Kingdom didn't adopt the system of ABV percentages until 1980. When distilled spirits were first popularized in the 1500s, they were tested and taxed with a simple "proof" test. If gunpowder that was soaked in the liquid could still be lit, it was considered "proof" that, yes, the liquid was distilled spirits. Any alcohol that passed the test was above proof, and alcohol that didn't was under proof. There was a higher tax on "proof spirits." The problem with this basic test is that proof could mean anywhere from 40 to 90% ABV.

Grain-based spirits became popular as an alternative to expensive, imported wine. In the sixteenth century, places like Ireland, Germany, Scotland, Russia and Scandinavia had a distillation boom.

In Russia, vodka became all the rage. It was easy to make, affordable and helped ease the bite of the cold Russian winters. By the early 1500s, vodka was a menu option alongside beer in local taverns. Russians drank cyclically, with long periods of sobriety and hard work followed by drunken holidays and celebrations. Here, the women drank with the men. Seventeenth century German scholar Adam Olearius described Russian women who drank elbow-to-elbow with their husbands until the men passed out. The women then sat on top of the sleeping men and continued to drink and toast each other.

During village festivals, young, unmarried girls were allowed to drink vodka or beer. They participated in circling dances, where the girls dressed in their finest clothes, sang folk songs and performed a dance in the middle of a banquet. Sometimes they'd sing about mythology and legendary beasts, but sometimes they'd sing about the glory of vodka.

Vodki delicious, I drank, I drank
Not in a cup or a glass, but a bucketful I drank
I cling to the posts of the door
Oh, doorpost, hold me up,
The drunken woman, the tipsy rogue.[53]

Women drinking was so normalized in Russia that a key part of the dance had the girls pretending to stumble around, imitating a drunken woman.

The good news for women was that distillation offered a way to fill the economic void that brewing left behind. Spirits now

---

53 From "Rural Life in Russia," an essay written by Lady Verney, featured in 1906's Russia As Seen and Described by Famous Writers.

had a high market demand and could easily be made in a kitchen with a minimum amount of training and equipment.

The bad news for women was that distilling became another way to mark a woman as a witch.

Between the mid-sixteenth and early seventeenth centuries, prosecution for witchcraft was at its peak in Europe. It was a dangerous time for a woman to make concoctions in her kitchen and have an extensive knowledge of healing with local herbs. Female distillers were looked upon with suspicion, just like the brewsters had been.

Witches symbolized an inversion of Christian values. A witch was the antithesis of a woman who quietly obeyed her husband, feared and worshipped God, produced children and stayed inside to tend the home. Some of the main things witches were accused of included (but were not limited to) drying up breast milk in those who were nursing, causing women to become barren, making men impotent, and killing children. These accusations came from a desire to protect the patriarchal order. Anything that threatened it—lesbianism, dressing in men's clothes, interfering with cycles of reproduction and nourishment of children—was punishable by death. Anything that allowed a woman to operate outside it, such as—oh, I don't know—achieving financial independence by selling spirits she made in her home, was suspect.

A drunken woman was also the antithesis of a good, compliant, God-fearing woman. Some women were accused of being witches for reportedly singing dirty drinking songs. Many artistic representations of witches' sabbaths from the sixteenth and seventeenth centuries show women who are clearly drinking and partying. The male fear of witches' sabbaths can be traced all the way back to the male fear of female Bacchus worshippers. Seeing a group of uncontrollable, uninhibited, powerful women drinking together would probably make a medieval witch-hunter wet his breeches.

Drunkenness in men was thought to enhance both their honor and their natural characteristics, while in women it destroyed their honor and inverted the gender hierarchy.

Women's bodies were thought to be cooler and moister than men's, so it was believed that they were naturally more sensitive to liquor's fiery quality. A drink turned up the heat on their naturally cool temperaments, purged their female characteristics and thereby inverted the natural order. Alcohol enhanced men's naturally hot natures, improving them and making them more virile. Basically, scientists from this period used bullshit biological ideas to support the oppression of women. Don't drink liquor, ladies—that's man-juice! There were even myths of drunken transmutation, of women drinking too much and then sprouting penises from their stomachs.[54]

It was believed that drinking weakened a woman's ability to resist the devil, when really, it was that drinking strengthened a woman's desire to resist the patriarchy.

Add trouser-wearing and committing crimes to public drunkenness and it's easy to understand why Mary Frith caused such a stir in London. In order to get the authorities off her back, she took some drastic action. She got married.

A couple of years after her arrest for wearing men's clothing, Mary married a man named Lewknor Markham. Not much is known about Lewknor, although it is possible that he was the son of Gervase Markham, the man who wrote *The English Huswife* and thought a "compleate woman" needed to know how to brew beer. It was common belief that their marriage was a sham in order to give Mary more business power and keep authorities from harassing her. The two didn't even live together.[55]

---

54 While they are hilariously ridiculous, myths like these were also dangerous and reflect a long legacy of misogyny against trans women.

55 At this point, you're probably wondering, and yes, signs point to Mary Frith being somewhere on the LGBTQIA+ spectrum. But since we don't have her own word on the subject, we can't know for sure. Because so much of her life has been sensationalized (we can be fairly certain she wasn't a shape-shifter), it's tough to say. Three years after her death, a supposed autobiography was anonymously released, but it wasn't written by her. Maybe she just liked drinking and wearing pants. I know I do.

This arrangement gave Mary more freedom to keep wheeling and dealing down at the tavern and continue her brisk stolen-goods business. Try as they might, the London authorities could never stop her. By the time she died in 1659, Mary had amassed a vast fortune that she left to relatives.

Mary was buried in the graveyard of St. Bride's Church on Fleet Street in London, a church dedicated to Saint Brigid, the Irish holy woman who conjured all that red beer. Mary would have approved.

Until her death, Mary Frith was a thorn in the patriarchy's side. Carousing around London in her breeches after a few pints of beer, puffing on her pipe and causing trouble, she was an obtrusive, insistent reminder that drinking wasn't just for men. When she went down to the tavern and had a pint, it was interpreted as an act of rebellion. She broke the rules *in public*, where everyone could see her. In an era when women were pressured to do their drinking in private, she refused.

Stay inside, don't drink, keep quiet, be obedient. Mary Frith wasn't the first woman to say *No, thanks* to all of that, and she wasn't the last. Soon, with the rapid spread of industrialization, many more women around the world would follow in her path. One woman in particular used the economic and political power behind distillation technology to help solidify her empire.

And Mary?

She was buried in her breeches.

6

THE VODKA EMPIRE OF CATHERINE THE GREAT

The Eighteenth Century

As the eighteenth century dawned, alcohol wasn't the only thing getting revolutionized.

Industrialization was spreading like wildfire in the 1700s, and European countries were gobbling up the globe with colonization. These two forces began to change drinking culture for women in every corner of the world. They also set the stage for one of the world's greatest rulers to craft her empire. She used the political power of distilled spirits to help her do it.

Russian consumption of alcohol has always been legendary. Since vodka entered the scene in the 1500s, travelers have remarked on the country's truly astonishing ability to put it away. Many were surprised to see Russian women drink just as earnestly as the men. Upper-class women were drinking wine, and lower-class women were all about beer and vodka.

Eventually, the government realized how much money there was to be made off alcohol. In the 1540s, Russian ruler Ivan the Terrible established state-owned and -regulated taverns called *kabaks*, and within a century, the government had a partial monopoly on booze. In 1648, peasant revolts broke out across the country over their right to make and sell alcohol, but they were unsuccessful. The following year, the Law Code of 1649 extended government control to all the Russian provinces and established a complete monopoly of the sale, distribution and even production of alcohol, be it vodka or beer. By the eighteenth century, the government was making a huge profit off of the country's prodigious drinking habits.

This was the Russia that Catherine the Great was set to rule.

Born in Stettin, Germany, on May 2, 1729, as Princess Sophie, she was the daughter of a German prince, and her mother's family ruled the Duchy of Holstein. They did not possess a vast amount of wealth or land, but Catherine's family was well connected to the royal families of Europe. Even when she was young, she showed political skill and an early affinity for power. She wrote later in life that she had "the idea of a crown running through my head like a tune."

Catherine also showed an early affinity for beer. On a trip to Moscow when she was a teenager, Catherine wrote to her father that she got sick on the journey, but it was of her own doing. She was ill because "I drank all the beer I could find."

Trips to Moscow were a necessity for young Catherine because she was engaged to her second cousin, Russia's Grand Duke Peter III, whom she detested as soon as they met. But he was her golden ticket to the Russian throne. In 1744, when she was fifteen, they were married. "To tell the truth, the Crown of Russia attracted me more than his person," Catherine penned in her diary later in life. If we're being generous, we could call Peter *wacky*. It's more accurate to say that he was immature, abrasive, tyrannical with his staff and taken to decadent (and annoying) flights of fancy.

Catherine kept her eyes on the prize. She did her best to tolerate her irritating new husband and set about assimilating herself into Russia. She changed her name, converted to the Russian Orthodox Church and quickly learned Russian language and culture. Most importantly, she taught herself how to survive in Russian politics. She won the affection of both the public and strong political allies. Before long, a coup was in the works, and Catherine used vodka to help make it happen.

The earliest reference to alcohol in Vietnamese history is found around 1400, when women made alcohol by fermenting rice. By the seventeenth century, however, women in Vietnam had fallen in love with distilling.

Small-scale kitchen distilling was the norm across the countryside in the 1600s and 1700s. Distilling fit easily into the household of the regular Vietnamese family because it was a convenient and efficient way to use up extra rice. *Rượu* was (and is) a generic term for any liquor distilled from rice. It was made by many Vietnamese women to drink themselves, to give to extended family or to sell to neighbors at a nearby market. With distillation, they were turning surplus grains into a product that could be bartered or sold. One woman's trash is another woman's booze. As an added bonus, the mash left over from the process was a great source of pig food.

In eighteenth century Vietnam, distillation was closely associated with the kitchen. The word *nau* means both *to make alcohol* and *to cook*. The tools for distilling were easy to come by and included things that were already found by the hearth, such as pots for heating the fermented mash. Overall, distilling rượu was a physically undemanding task that a woman could do while tending to a household. This allowed women to play a central role in its small-scale production and sale, especially in the colder months. The lower temperatures made for more efficient fermentation, and who doesn't want a drink of hard liquor when it's chilly outside?

If she was in a pinch, a woman could drink or sell the rượu right away. The liquid would burn all the way down, but it was drinkable. Most of the time, rượu was poured into glazed earthenware containers and was aged for at least a month underground, or somewhere else suitably cool, dark and humid. This process made the final product much smoother. There can be huge taste variations between different types of rượu, depending on the container it is fermented in, the time it fermented and the type of rice and yeast used. *Rượu đế* was the most common during this time period, which has a slightly bitter but smooth taste that is similar to Japanese saké.

If she wasn't in a pinch and wanted a higher-quality booze, a woman distilled the rượu a second time. (Spirits today are usually distilled at least two or three times, but we'll get to that later.) This produced an even smoother, almost perfectly clear rượu. She might infuse it with botanicals like jasmine, chamomile, rose petals, lotus flowers or apricot. Of course, if she went through all the trouble to distill it twice and infuse it with something aromatic and delicious, a woman charged a lot more money for it.

Rượu was usually sold and stored in hollowed-out gourds called *bau* or *be rou* or glazed earthenware called *sanh* that were sealed with corks made of compressed and dried banana leaves. Bau and sanh were common sights at local markets, since rượu was both a dietary staple and a key part of rituals, ceremonies, weddings and New Year's celebrations. It was also an important component of medicine. Like a glass of red wine today, it was thought that a small amount of rượu was good for you.

Moderation, however, was crucial. For women, especially. Widely held religious beliefs made gender the main factor in someone's alcohol consumption. Confucian and Buddhist feminine ideals stressed modesty and propriety.

Out in the Vietnamese countryside, ideals and reality didn't always align. In rural areas, alcohol was consumed by everyone, regardless of gender. Public drinking was the purview of men, so Vietnamese women drank mostly in the home. Their drinking culture was a private one that, like many women all over the world, revolved around the kitchen. At least that way they were closer to where all the booze was kept.

Thousands of miles away, Europeans had invaded both North and South America, pushing out or appropriating native alcohol practices. In the wake of a violent seizure of land, during the seventeenth century English settlements grew over the eastern coast of North America like a plague. And where there were settlements, there were taverns.

The early American tavern was quite similar to its English counterpart. Whether they catered to an upper- or lower-class clientele, taverns in early America were an all-white, all-male space. Women from any class rarely entered a tavern to drink. Stepping into a tavern was a major risk to a woman's reputation.

Most white women in early colonial America were married women, brought over with their husbands or brought over to become someone's husband. Legally, they were dependent on their spouses and could not be held responsible for their debts. Husbands not only didn't want their wives seen in the local tavern, they also didn't want them running up a tab they had to pay for.

Women were so rare in taverns in early America that laws governing alcohol and drinking behavior hardly mention them. As in England, if you were a woman in a tavern, it was assumed that you were a server, a sex worker or the wife of the owner. Most women preferred to avoid taverns altogether.

Native American women and Black women were not allowed in at all. In 1687, New England laws made it illegal to sell alcohol to Native Americans. (Although there is evidence that illegal trade still took place. Native American women sometimes bought rum or brandy from white sellers and resold it.)

Early American taverns were known as *ordinaries*, and the only ones where you might glimpse anyone who wasn't white and male were the so-called disorderly ones. These were the colonial version of a sketchy dive bar, places that didn't give a shit about fostering a *proper* tavern environment. Ordinaries that catered to a low-class clientele often tolerated a mix of genders and races. There were laws in place stipulating that servants and enslaved people could not be entertained without express permission from the people who enslaved them. Because these rebellious ordinaries served women, enslaved people and Native Americans, they were constantly under suspicion of harboring folks who were plotting against the government. Local constables were regularly summoned to these establishments for a variety of offenses. Sometimes it was noise complaints, sometimes it was staying open too late, but mostly it was being "in defiance of good order." Karens have been active in America for centuries.[56]

Women rarely appeared in court on alcohol-related offenses. If they did, it was most likely for selling liquor without a license. Just like elsewhere in the world, selling homemade alcohol was the chosen occupation for poor women. The most economically vulnerable white women—singles, widows, sailor's wives—brewed or distilled and hung a makeshift sign on their door, not unlike the alewives.

It was difficult for a woman to get a tavern license in colonial America because it was believed that women were too weak—physically and mentally—to enforce rules and handle violent drunks. Taverners were supposed to be people who could

---

56 Many elite clubs in the early years of America were formed so upper-class white men could drink without women, Black people or poor people around. If a club said its members were *mixed*, it meant that it tolerated white men of different Christian denominations. So diverse!

be trusted to maintain order. Some colonies like Massachusetts limited the number of taverns in smaller towns to one and kept those licenses reserved for prominent local white men.

Despite an overwhelming bias against them, there were a substantial number of female taverners in colonial America. For many towns and cities, it was an economic decision, since most of the women applying for these licenses were single or widowed, and the town would rather have them selling booze than depending on neighbors for support.[57] Some cities, like Boston, only licensed women to run inferior taverns that sold cheap beer, but no food, no lodging and no liquor. If a woman wanted to sell liquor, she could do so as a street vendor.

It was rare for a woman to operate a higher-class tavern, and the few who did really put officials in a bind. New England Puritans expected women to serve men, which was all well and good for a woman running a tavern. But they also expected women to obey men. What happened when someone got drunk and rowdy? Female taverners were responsible for the conduct of their customers. Officials feared that this situation—a woman having any sort of authority over men—would throw a monkey wrench into the gears of the Puritan order. What's next, women having rights?

To keep this in check, some women were granted their tavern licenses on the condition that they be subject to a male supervisor chosen by the all-male town council. Overall, however, it was easier for male officials (and less nerve-racking) to have

---

57   One colonial widow, Alice Guest, used her circumstances to create one of the period's most unique taverns. Widowed in 1685, Alice was in dire financial straits and living in a cave on the bank of the Delaware River in Philadelphia. She applied for a license to turn her cave into a tavern. It sounds like a rough situation, but her cave tavern (cavern?) was ideally situated to service the huge number of sailors and immigrants that arrived in the city by ship. It became so successful that Alice was eventually able to build a wharf for it and buy herself another house. However, she never moved the business to a more proper location, and it is speculated that the tavern's unique interior lent it a certain value and increased customer attraction. Alice Guest might have been the world's first themed-bar owner.

women sell booze as street vendors. It undermined the threat of women having too much power over men. Female tavern owners were even discouraged from participating in the men's conversations, and street sales prevented this, as well.

Sometimes, operating a tavern put a woman at risk for losing more than her reputation. Like female distillers in Europe, New England alcohol-makers and sellers were in danger of being persecuted as witches. In 1692, the first woman to die as a result of the Salem witch hysteria was a tapster (a female taverner). Her name was Sarah Osborne, and she owned and operated the Ship, which was considered the best tavern in town. After an argument with her in-laws over who would be receiving the profits from the tavern, Osborne conveniently became one of the first to be accused of witchcraft. Her position at the Ship made her a powerful and prominent woman in town, but it also made her susceptible to suspicion and, ultimately, to fatal mass hysteria and misogyny. She died in jail.

As you can imagine, women were largely not a part of the public drinking culture of colonial America. Like elsewhere in history, this reflected their relative lack of societal power. Taverns were crucial to popular culture, professional partnerships, the creation of neighborly bonds, the maintenance of community, and the dissemination of news and local knowledge. A lot of important stuff happened at the tavern, a place where women were unwelcome. They drank as they lived—in private.

But believe me, American colonial women drank. Everyone in early America drank. There wasn't much to drink that wasn't alcoholic. People were still (rightly) nervous about water, so if a woman was thirsty, there was usually a choice between beer, cider, rum or brandy. For children, there was small ale, which was just a weaker beer. A kids' beer, if you will. The average white farmhouse in New England drank over a hundred gallons of alcohol a year, between beer, cider and distilled spirits.

The colonists needed those gallons of booze, since they depended on alcohol for the calories. A common breakfast for a housewife was toast broken into small pieces and doused with beer. Plus, besides the nutritional benefits of alcohol, getting buzzed was one of the very few pleasures available to people in the early modern world.

Because most women weren't literate, there are scarce written records describing the female drinking customs of colonial Americans. What we do know is that they involved a lot of communal indoor drinking. From everyday gatherings like sewing circles to big events like births, funerals and weddings, women gathered inside and drank together. They spent the day quilting, eating, drinking and talking.

It's commonplace today to make fun of women-centric book clubs, where there's more wine drinking than book discussion, but for hundreds of years, the only place women could gather, drink, relax and socialize was in a neighbor's kitchen, surrounded by other wives and mothers. There is a long-standing tradition of driving women to some sort of behavior, then mocking them for it. (Sort of like making beauty a woman's most powerful and important currency, then laughing about how long it takes her to get ready.) In colonial America, men drank everywhere. At home, in court, even in church. Men almost always controlled the taverns. The only place a woman controlled was her kitchen. So while women were banned from public drinking, they still had a drinking culture. It was a private one, but it was robust.

When they weren't getting together to drink alcohol, women also gathered to make it. A wife was considered to be lazy and useless if she didn't make alcohol for her family. As English colonist John Hammond said in the mid-1600s, "They will be adjudged by their drinks, what kind of housewives they are."

Colonial women were in charge of brewing beer, pressing

cider, making mead and distilling liquor. As the technology spread, women all over the world distilled spirits in their kitchens. In early America, women used fruits and berries from their gardens for their spirits. They didn't bother with wine. There were many early failed attempts at wine before people realized that New England's climate was not hospitable to grapes.

It was, however, very hospitable to apples. The earliest record of apple cultivation in New England is from 1623, after which a booming apple growing tradition began in the region. In 1635, America's first named variety of apple, the Roxbury Russet, was cultivated in Massachusetts. It was known for its superior suitability for cider.[58]

With all these apples around, colonial women made quite a lot of cider. Most of it was pressed by hand, since cider presses were large and expensive, and few women owned them. They pressed and beat the ever-loving hell out of the apples (which was hopefully cathartic) in a wooden trough. The juice was collected underneath the trough, and the remaining pulp transferred to woven bags. Women pressed the bags into tubs to collect the remaining juice, and those tubs sat covered in cloths or boards for at least twenty-four hours. After several more rounds of pulp removal (a time-consuming process), the juice was poured into casks. Finally, the juice was left to ferment.

The process was repeated for different kinds of fruit. Women made ciders from not just apples but peaches and persimmons, along with beers from corn, molasses, spruce and birch. The recipes were saved in cookbooks that women made for their daughters and daughters-in-law. The cookbooks included recipes for cordials or liqueurs, which were preparations of distilled spirits with fruit, herbs or spices added. Cordials, in the age before refrigerators, helped preserve fruits out of season. Women also used them as tonics for various health problems.

---

58   The variety is not widely grown any longer. We salute you, Roxbury Russet.

These cookbooks were treasured heirlooms that passed through the female side of the family for generations and were incredibly valuable.

Despite the fact that all this booze was made by women, it was considered to be the property of the man of the household. The origin of a batch of cider or beer was often obscured because the wife who made it was the legal dependent of her husband. Thomas Jefferson had a well-regarded brewery on his estate at Monticello, but it was his wife Martha who was in charge of it. She was a beer enthusiast. Before it was even up and running, Martha was involved in the planning and architecture of the building. Eventually, her daughter (also named Martha) took over and became an accomplished brewster.

Martha (the younger) was very keen on her beer being made with fine ingredients,[59] and it was served to staff and guests alike to great appreciation. In her first year, she (along with the many enslaved people at Monticello) made over a hundred and seventy gallons of beer—over eighteen hundred glasses. Martha's beer was so lauded that her father invited his friend James Madison to attend a brewing session.

It might have tasted great, but colonial beer certainly wasn't pretty. Dark and cloudy, it was a good thing that glassware was still not widespread yet. Most beer was sipped from pewter mugs or wooden tankards. There also were heavy black leather jugs known as blackjacks that were waxed, bound and trimmed with silver and used mainly for beer. Most brews were around 6% ABV, a similar strength to beer today. (A Budweiser is 5% ABV.)

Brewing at large facilities was impossible without the work of enslaved people. Enslaved Black persons in early America had their own drinking culture, but because they weren't allowed the ability to record their own histories, trustworthy information is

---

59 Like our girl Hildegard, Martha was very fond of hops and loved a bitter, hoppy beer.

scarce. Most histories written by white authors of the time were racist, derogatory and of very little use. We do know that alcohol was frequently provided to enslaved people for holidays and celebrations, where fiddling, dancing and drinking took place. Births, weddings and funerals were all usually accompanied by alcohol of some kind.

Planters also supplied alcohol like rum and whiskey to the people they enslaved as a reward for tough labor, like bringing in the seasonal harvest. (Many enslavers resented the cost of this practice.) There is some historical record of enslaved women making alcohol when they could. Since making alcohol was a tradition for women in most parts of Africa, many women carried that knowledge with them when they were captured and shipped to America. There is even evidence of young Black women creating cocktails out of their whiskey allowances, crafted with water, sugar and herbs.

Many peoples who were colonized and enslaved by Europeans have a complicated relationship with alcohol. While it was certainly used as a tool of control by enslavers and colonizers, alcohol was also used for temporary rebellion by those enslaved. Author and scholar Laura Serrant has written about the complex history of alcohol and Black women in the Caribbean, saying in her 2015 paper "The Silences in Our Dance," "Alcohol as positive escapism not only allows for the possibility of 'self preservation effects' on the individual, but also the opportunity for groups to develop ways of being which act outside what is usually expected of them.... For slaves, this allowed for 'rebellion,' challenging the social order, enabling them to say, feel, dance or display behaviors that would not be acceptable to their masters and to defy the efforts to silence them and render their culture invisible."

For many enslaved women in the 1700s, celebrations and social drinking helped foster community and preserve a crucial

and imperiled link to a culture that white slave owners ruthlessly attempted to strip them of.

Despite the fact that Catherine's husband was unpopular with
the people of Russia, the Imperial Guard and, well, just about
everyone but his mistress, Peter became emperor in 1761. But
being his queen was just a stepping stone for Catherine.

The unhappy couple never warmed to each other. It reportedly took nine years for them to consummate their marriage.
Catherine and Peter both took lovers, but Peter flaunted his.
He publicly bragged about his sexual conquests and took to dis-
tancing himself from Catherine. This caused some big problems for him. First, because Catherine, using a mix of political
savvy and well-placed charm, *was* popular. Second, Catherine's
lover was one of the leaders of the Imperial Guard, an influential man among a group of men who already hated Peter. Soon,
Catherine and her lover devised a plot to secure her the throne.

On the night of the planned coup, Catherine promised the
group of assembled soldiers a large distribution of vodka if they
overthrew her husband.[60] The men immediately proclaimed al-
legiance to her. She marched at the head of her new loyal army
and led them to Peter's location.

Hours later, Peter was arrested, and Catherine was then
crowned the empress of Russia, the last one the country would
see. That night, she was able to use her political prowess to secure her empire without a single drop of blood spilled.

But quite a bit of booze was. As soon as she was crowned, Catherine made a declaration to open all the drinking establishments
to her troops. She made the world's most beloved announcement:
Drinks are on me![61] Soldiers and their wives hauled out every-

---

60 This is also how you convince groups of college students to do things.

61 Three years later, royal compensation was still being processed for the
    Petersburg wine and beer merchants.

thing available. Wine, champagne, vodka, beer, mead. Alcohol was poured into tubs, kegs, whatever happened to be around. Catherine the Great was born.[62]

PICTORIAL PRESS LTD./ALAMY STOCK PHOTO

Catherine the Great looking particularly pleased with herself.

Catherine secured her position with a commitment to Russian Orthodoxy and traditional Russian ways, but she also guided the resurgence of the country's military dominance and an awakening of Russian culture. The new ruler garnered fame early in her reign for writing "Instruction," a manifesto which described her ideal government for Russia. Catherine was deeply influ-

---

62 A few days later, Peter was found dead. While there was a lot of confusion and conspiracy theorizing around his death, the official ruling was that he died of a stroke and hemorrhoidal colic. There was no evidence but lots of suspicion that it was Catherine's (or her conspirators') doing.

enced by the Enlightenment and emphasized the importance of morality for government officials, taxes, criminal justice and the economy. She recognized vodka as the spirit of Russia and fostered ties to other European monarchs by sending bottles as a gift. An avid reader and writer, she also sent bottles to luminaries and authors like Goethe.

The new empress was smart about the way she used alcohol, and she wanted everyone else to be, too. She drew up new parameters of moderation for Russia's nobility. Catherine wouldn't abide a drunken court dragging her down.

While she stressed the importance of moderation, Catherine also recognized how integral alcohol was to the daily lives of her subjects. Soon, she would make major legal changes to overhaul how alcohol fit into the economy of her country.

By the 1700s, distilled spirits had taken the globe by storm. In the Netherlands, during the Dutch golden age of naval power and prosperity, the national spirit was genever. Genever is a clear, distilled spirit made from malted grain and flavored with various botanicals, the most important of which is juniper. The taste of juniper berries masked the harshness of the distilled spirit. When Queen Elizabeth I sent English troops to support the Dutch in their war for independence from Spain, the soldiers brought back a taste for this strong, floral liquor.

The English market for genever grew rapidly. Soon, "strong water houses" were popping up all over the country, especially in London. Folks started calling it *gin* for short. In the early eighteenth century, the English government needed new revenue, and landowners needed a market for surplus grain. Gin was cheap, easy and quick to make.[63] Thanks to a period of relative prosperity (and mobility), more and more people had disposable

---

63 It was also pretty gross. Early English gin was so strong that it would have made your hair turn white. Drinking it was like taking a shot of nail polish remover. It wasn't until the mid-1700s that people refined the distillation process and made it with higher-quality ingredients.

income to spend on new drinks like coffee, rum, tea, chocolate and this new distilled spirit called gin.

In 1702, Queen Anne helped popularize gin further. She was an enthusiastic supporter of the spirit and encouraged its consumption. The queen even increased its production when she canceled a charter issued to the Worshipful Company of Distillers which gave it the sole right to distill in and around London and Westminster. In the wake of the cancelation, hundreds of small distilleries popped up in those regions.

The spread of industrialization and the spread of gin went hand in hand. Gin was a modern drink, an urban drink. It was the drink of the thousands of young women flocking to cities— London in particular—in search of factory and administrative jobs. It was the beverage of the first modern woman.

The problem for these women was that London did not live up to the hype. There were very few jobs open to women, and they didn't pay very well. Those who did find employment found themselves in an unfamiliar situation. They were away from their families, with free time and money to spend. So where did they go to amuse themselves after work?

They went to the gin shop.

The tavern was a male space where men went to drink. The gin shops, however, were new and not yet imbued with masculine tradition. Women were still overall not accepted in the public drinking culture at the tavern, but it was okay for them to go into the gin shops. Especially since it was largely women that ran them.

Just like the alewives from centuries before, women who ran gin shops (or dramshops because they served *drams* or small amounts of gin) could set up with minimal equipment and education, and no capital. It was one of the few occupations a lower-class woman could try her hand at, and soon, it was dominated by women. Technically, a license was required, but a license cost money.

So most women who distilled and sold gin did so illegally.

Selling unlicensed gin carried a great risk for them because they were much more likely to be charged, convicted and sent to prison for this crime than men. To avoid detection, many women sold gin out of hastily constructed shacks[64] so they could pack up and skedaddle at a moment's notice to escape the authorities. Some went one step further and sold gin on the go out of baskets, boats, even wheelbarrows. These mobile gin-slinging women did really well at large public events like hangings, and the local taverns resented them for poaching their clientele.

Because of the thousands of women who both sold and drank it, gin was called *the ladies' delight*. The spirit immediately took on a feminine identity, called Madam Geneva or Mother Gin.

The gin these women sold was not the delicious kind you might mix with tonic today. Usually, it wasn't even technically gin, since it was rarely made with juniper. In fact, it was rarely made with anything good. This gin was typically distilled from malt and mixed with things like oil of turpentine, salt, pepper and perhaps ginger or almond oil as a substitute for more expensive ingredients like coriander. The final product was around 57% ABV. Modern Everclear, by comparison, starts at 60%. If flushable toilets had been widespread in the eighteenth century, you could have used this gin to clean them.

By and large, these female illegal gin sellers were dirt-poor. Hawking gin in a shack or on the street was the only thing keeping them from destitution. They had the most to gain and the most to lose. But some women did have proper stalls, shops and cellars. There was even a small, elite group who were publicans or licensed distillers. In the mid-1700s, the London Company of Distillers was made up of almost two hundred and thirty distillers, and four were women.

The revolutionary thing about gin shops is that they specifi-

---

64 Serving your gin in a shack meant you could provide seating and protection from the elements, which encouraged customers to stay for a spell and spend more money on your gin.

cally catered to female drinkers. Their customers were usually maids having a tipple after work, servants grabbing a drink on a break and housewives stopping in while they shopped for groceries. Many of them sold other household goods like candles to better serve and attract their clientele.

Gin shops were frequently packed with customers. There were often male customers (some who came just to meet women), and women sometimes drank with them. Women also sipped gin with other women. Dramshops were the first place in London's history where it was okay for a woman to drink in public without a risk to her reputation. It was a female-centric *public* space, an entirely new idea for the city.

CHRONICLE/ALAMY STOCK PHOTO

A London dramshop.

The gin shop was actually the precursor to the bar as we know it today. Women changed the shape of the drinking establishment. Literally. Working women didn't have time to sit at a table and drink their gin. So licensed gin shops often had a long counter to order from. A busy factory worker could walk up, quickly down a glass and head back to the factory. This bar, the long counter for serving drinks, was a fixture of the female-centric dramshop.

Now, they certainly weren't as nice as taverns were. Most gin shops (especially the unlicensed ones) were small and cramped. Many were purposely hidden, often in a spare room or a squalid basement. To be fair, however, most of London was cramped and squalid at this time. Some of the gin shops were secret, known only to locals and had the same pop-up atmosphere as the original alehouses.

The problems started because people didn't really know how to drink spirits yet. London was like a city full of college kids, learning how to drink liquor for the first time. Consumers thought you could drink the same amount of gin as any other type of alcohol. If you drank a pint of ale, why not drink a pint of gin? The flood of cheap gin on the market caused the Gin Craze, which swept London and peaked from 1720 to 1751. There was mass drunkenness in the streets of the city and countless cases of alcohol poisoning and alcohol-related deaths.

The Gin Craze prompted a panic about who was drinking the gin. The upper classes were appalled by the widespread drunkenness in the lower classes, but especially by the lower-class women. Single, young working girls turned notions of femininity upside down by drinking for fun instead of getting married and having children. They scared the living hell out of London society.

The upper classes didn't want to see poor wives or mothers drink, either. Married women, who were more rooted in their neighborhoods and subject to more scrutiny, often kept bottles of gin at home. Soon, gin was being called Mother's Ruin. The destitute, drunken mother or wet nurse became the poster person for a new temperance movement (social campaign against the consumption of alcohol).[65] Reformers took up the cause to stop women from drinking.

---

65 This was when the temperance movement began in England, but another one started around the same time in North America. Native American activists began a campaign to restrict alcohol in their communities in order to protect themselves from the destructive influence of the white settlers.

Naturally, the new temperance movement wasn't for the women's benefit. The anti-gin movement was more about control and eugenics than women's health care.

England was in the process of becoming a great world power. The British Empire was fueled by the tremendous numbers of lower-class children who grew up to be sailors, soldiers and laborers. Government leaders wanted the English working class to buckle down and start producing more people to toil for low wages, to fight in England's wars or to help it colonize the globe. A bigger working-class population was better for England's economy, or so reformers wanted everyone to think. By not having children, independent, gin-drinking single women were screwing with England's labor supply.[66]

Newspapers ran sensational stories of drunken women murdering their children for gin money and gin-addicted wives bringing about the ruin of their families. There were many depictions of ugly, old hags who drank gin alone in their hovels. The stigma against elderly, single women (who were completely useless to the might of the British Empire) was enormous. Urban legends of spontaneous human combustion flourished during this time. Most of the supposed victims reported were old women who lived alone. Supposedly, they were found charred to a crisp, often with an empty bottle of gin conveniently near the remains. Now, ladies, you don't want to end up like that, do you? It was just better for everyone if women stayed sober, shut up, got married and started making more workers.

In 1736, the government passed the first Gin Act. Designed to tamp down consumption, it slapped a retail tax on gin and established laws for gin-selling licenses. Reformers fixated on gin as the main cause of crime and immorality (not, you know, poverty), and the gin shop became their number one target.

This campaign was about punishing the poor and poor women

---

66 Perhaps the only good thing that came out of this was doctors petitioning for sobriety in pregnant women.

specifically. Dramshops were a place for the poor to congregate, one of the only public places where poor people—and especially poor women—were welcome. If poor women were in a gin shop, they weren't at work or at home making or caring for children.

Women made up twenty percent of the licensed gin retailers but seventy percent of those charged under the Gin Act. Sometimes, locals got together and attempted to rescue these women when they were put under arrest. Loyal customers, neighbors and friends tried to protect them from patrolling inspectors.

Within four months of the first Gin Act, riots broke out. Women played an important role in these riots, and they were usually the ones inciting them. They often joined the physical fray by yelling and throwing dirt and stones.

Over the next fifteen years, a total of eight different acts and repeals were passed by the English government trying to tax and control the people who sold and drank gin. None of them quite worked until the final Gin Act of 1751. This one raised taxes and prices of gin further, prohibited distillers from selling gin to unlicensed shops, and banned gin in prisons, poorhouses and workhouses. Finally, gin consumption dipped. Folks also generally had less disposable income by this time, and most had figured out that drinking a pint of gin wasn't the best idea. The Gin Craze followed the same arc as most crazes. The novelty (and low price) encouraged the masses to try it when it first became popular, and after about a generation the shine wore off.

The Gin Act of 1751 successfully pushed English women out of the trade. Up north in Scotland, however, women were still running unlicensed liquor shops. They weren't selling gin, though. These were the first whisky women.[67]

Whisky (and whiskey) is a spirit distilled from a mash of fermented grains. Today, it's usually aged to mellow it out, but early

---

67 Yes, whisky with no e. If it's from Scotland, Japan or Canada, it's *whisky*. If it's from Ireland or the United States, it's *whiskey*.

Scottish whisky was potent, unaged stuff that quickly became a popular drink throughout the country. So popular that in 1725, the English government, which became officially united with Scotland in 1707, passed the Malt Tax Bill for Scotland, which raised the cost of distilling and selling whisky. Most distillers were either forced to shut down or go underground. This was just fine for women.[68] They were used to selling booze illegally.

The first person in Scotland to ever be arrested for illegal distilling was a woman named Bessie Campbell, in 1506. During that time, Scottish authorities arrested and murdered women suspected of practicing witchcraft (which of course actually meant practicing folk medicine and distilling at home), so Scottish women became skilled at avoiding the authorities and secretly making illegal whisky.

In 1699, a law in Edinburgh was passed that forbade women from being employed in taverns, as they were "a great Snare to the Youth and Occasion for Lewdness and Debauchery." This contributed to the rise of unlicensed drinking establishments known as shebeens. Shebeens were usually run and managed by women, and whisky was their specialty. The women of the shebeens sometimes even made it themselves. To avoid paying exorbitant malt taxes, many distilled whisky covertly at home. Most illegal whisky makers worked at night, when the smoke from the fires beneath the stills was hidden. This is why illegal whisky became known as *moonshine*.

Lots of women drank whisky in shebeens, in both urban and rural areas. They drank it at home, too, whether at the end of the workday or the start of it. It was a common morning ritual in the Western Isles for the mistress of the house to give her servant women a glass of whisky to begin the day. Women working

---

68   Although it did cause a lot of unrest, just like the Gin Act of 1736 did in England. Riots broke out in Glasgow. Women also played a prominent role in these riots, marching in the street and beating drums as a signal for the mob to assemble.

in the fields drank whisky to stay warm. In the eighteenth century, grocers began selling it, and wives often grabbed a bottle to bring home. This practice started a significant economic pattern that continues today. The grocer was the domain of housewives and mothers, which meant that the person responsible for choosing and buying liquor for the home was a woman. (Liquor companies still haven't quite acknowledged this fact hundreds of years later, but we'll get to that later.)

Across the globe, Indigenous South American women were making their own moonshine. These *clandestinistas* weren't just trying to dodge taxes, though. They were actively resisting their Spanish colonizers.

In the sixteenth century, the Incans were a people with a vast empire in the Andean region of South America, which extended from modern-day northern Ecuador down the Pacific Coast to the Maule River in the middle of Chile. Their empire was the largest in pre-Columbian America and their capital was in Cuzco, which is today south-central Peru. Incan women, unsurprisingly, were the ones responsible for making alcohol.

They fermented a beer out of corn called *chicha*, which was made in a similar way to early Japanese saké. The women of the village put rolled balls of corn flour in their mouths, chewed until their saliva broke down the starches into sugars and then spit all of it into a bowl. The mixture was then boiled and diluted. This liquid was put into a container and left to ferment for two to three days. Voilà, corn beer! All you need is a bowl and your own face. Chicha would usually reach an ABV of about 5%, the same as your average beer today.

Women also played an essential part in distributing chicha. The corn beer was used in important social and political rituals, like marriages, funerals and war ceremonies. So whoever made and sold the chicha had some power in the community. Elite women (who could be widows or even single) often owned rural alcohol-producing farms or establishments that sold it. This was a way for them to have some autonomy. Their involvement in the production and distribution of alcohol reflects how relatively egalitarian Incan society was, at least in regards to gender.

Women chewing corn in preparation for chicha brewing.

ALAMY STOCK PHOTO

The Spanish came along and ruined everything in the late 1500s when they conquered the Incans. By the seventeenth century, many different Indigenous peoples in South America were oppressed under Spanish rule. One of the strategies the colonizers used to control native populations in regions that are now Guatemala, Peru, Bolivia and Mexico was to regulate alcohol.

Fermented beverages had been important in religious and political rituals in South America for thousands of years prior. Along with chicha, a sacred drink called *pulque* was made from the sap of the agave plant. Pulque is a thick, sour fermented alcohol that looks a bit like skim milk. For the Aztec people, whose empire spread throughout central Mexico and parts of South

America, pulque was closely linked to women. Mayahuel was a goddess in Aztec mythology, the first woman to figure out how to get sap from the agave (or maguey) plant. Unless it was being used for religious purposes, the only people who could drink it daily were elderly or pregnant women. Pulque was made and consumed by women, but not sold. To the Aztec people, it was a sacred drink, not a commercial one.

After Spanish colonization, however, pulque lost its sacred status, and it became a common beverage. By the 1600s, even the Spanish were drinking it.

In small Mexican villages, peasant women dominated the pulque economy. They were exclusively in charge of pulque selling, with shops called *pulquerias*. If the village was too small to have its own pulqueria, women sold it from the doorways of their homes. Making and selling pulque allowed these women a bit of economic security, and sometimes they even climbed the social ladder. Everybody wants to be friends with the lady who sells good booze. If a woman moved from the countryside to set up shop in the city, the money and security from pulque helped her adapt to a new, urban home and learn to navigate life under Spanish rule.

Women also frequented pulquerias as customers. In fact, everybody did. Large crowds were to be expected at the pulqueria (which was essentially the neighborhood bar), especially during religious festivals. Pulquerias grew to be so popular that they started making the Spanish nervous. Colonizers saw them as centers of transgression, rebellion and disorder.

As Catholics, the Spanish saw moderation and restraint as important virtues. They associated drinking with religious traditions, not parties. But for Indigenous Mexican people, moderation was a sliding scale according to the occasion. For them, drinking rituals were part of their government, and pulque was an important piece of their cultural identity. The Spanish realized that controlling pulque was a way to control native people and that taxing it was a good way to make money. They worked overtime to do so during the early colonial period, passing laws that restricted both the sale and consumption of alcohol.

The first restrictions stipulated that only elderly native women could run pulquerias, but they must have a license and limit the number of customers they served. The Spanish even tried to pass ordinances that segregated pulquerias by gender, but around 1752 they gave up. It was too difficult to keep husbands, wives and families from drinking together.

These laws caused many illegal pulquerias to pop up all over Mexico. In Mexico City, Spanish women opened up unlicensed taverns, where they sold untaxed pulque made by native women outside the city. Native women also operated small, illegal pulquerias. These clandestinistas made and sold their pulque in secret.

Down in Peru, native women continued as brewers and vendors of chicha under Spanish rule in *rancherias*, or native neighborhoods. They were called *chicheras*. By then, chicha was no longer made by chewing corn. Chicheras now malted their corn before mixing it with water for fermentation. Along with chicha, they also made *guarapo*, another fermented beverage made from the sap of maize stalks. It was sort of a sweetened version of chicha.

Enslaved African women who were brought to Peru carried their native brewing knowledge with them. Free African women sometimes became brewers themselves, and Afro-Peruvian female brewers drew on both African and Peruvian techniques to make beer.

Besides making the stuff, women drinking alcohol vexed the Spanish. Women drinking and dancing at Peruvian taverns shocked their Catholic colonizers. They were seen as an affront to the rules of Spanish colonial society. The Spanish attempted a decree forbidding women from going to taverns alone, but it failed just as gender segregation in pulquerias failed in Mexico. Native women did not accept Spanish colonization passively.

An independent woman making or drinking alcohol (or both) went against the patriarchal structure that the Spanish government worked so hard to protect. Just like women in London, if women in Lima were out making their own money by selling alcohol, or hanging out with their friends at the tavern after work, they weren't home, making children and obeying their husband.

Many native Peruvian men refused to marry these non-compliant women. While Incan culture had permitted more freedoms for women than the Spanish did, it was still a patriarchy. By drinking on their own or with each other, these women managed to separate themselves from oppressive, misogynistic structures present in both native and colonial cultures.

Unfortunately, women in other colonized countries did not fare as well.

Over in the Caribbean, a new distilled spirit was taking the islands by storm. Rum is a spirit distilled from molasses (a by-product of sugar) or sugarcane juice. In the 1600s, it was discovered by enslaved Caribbean sugar-plantation workers. They figured out that if you distilled fermenting molasses, the end product was a delicious spirit. Rum quickly spread in popularity, was taken over by enslavers and took its terrible place in the triangular enslaved-people trade between North America, Africa and Europe.

In Jamaica in the seventeenth century, most of the female taverners selling rum and rum punch were white women.[69] Known as rum-punch-women, they bought rum in large quantities (we're talking between sixty and five hundred gallons at a time) and resold it. These women were plentiful in the notorious Jamaican city of Port Royal, an infamous pirate haven. Since it had a lot of pirates, Port Royal also had a lot of ale and punch houses. Though there were many women who worked in them, they were generally considered improper women, on

---

69 Rum punch was a mix of rum, water, sugar, some sort of citrus like lemon
    or lime, and spices, like cloves, cinnamon or nutmeg.

the fringes of society. Some of them did distill their own rum (or *kill-devil* as it was also called), and they sometimes passed on their recipes and businesses to their daughters.

There is no known history of female pirates getting together to drink in Port Royal, but a girl can dream.

In France, a new type of watering hole changed public drinking for women.

Just like their English versions, French taverns were men's spaces. A woman entering one was seen as an intruder. But in the suburbs of large cities like Paris, a more female-friendly alternative appeared.

Guinguettes were drinking establishments that were larger and more focused on food, dancing and entertainment than just booze. They were named after *guinguet*, a sour white wine that was made locally. And just like London's gin shops, guinguettes were a new type of public drinking establishment outside of the masculine tradition of the tavern. Since female drinkers were not intruders here and instead were welcomed as customers, guinguettes became associated with women.

Guinguettes' location outside of the city made them more of a weekend destination, a place to drink that was slightly more glamorous (and outside of the city's tax zone). Women spent the day walking through the suburbs, shopping and stopping at various guinguettes for some wine. Many were open-air establishments and featured beautiful gardens and greens. They were an escape from everyday city life.

Soon, however, there would be no escaping the revolution that was developing in France. The French people found a lot of inspiration in the American Revolution and thought that if Americans could rout the British, maybe the French populace could overthrow their monarchy. Royal families all over Europe and Asia started to get nervous, maybe even a little jumpy if they heard someone mention the word *guillotine*.

★ ★ ★

Over in Russia, Catherine kept a close eye on the French Revolution. It made her paranoid of threats to her power. She certainly wasn't interested in having her head chopped off. The empress knew that she needed to secure her position and bolster her rule. Before she did that, Catherine inspired a beer revolution.

In 1766, she agreed to sign a commercial treaty with England, despite being wary of its growing martial power. During the negotiations, Catherine found that London stout suited her taste for strong, dark beer. In order to secure herself a steady supply, Catherine contracted an English brewery, Anchor Brewery in Southwark, to brew the stout and ship it to Russia for her and her court. The stout needed to survive the long journey and still be delicious and drinkable when it arrived. For this to happen, the brewmasters at Anchor realized that they needed to change up its recipe. They brewed a rich, dark stout especially for Catherine at a higher ABV, which gave it a longer shelf life (supposedly for up to seven years). She fell head over heels for the stuff.

The new beer was a strong export stout. It was 12% ABV, which is about as high as the average wine. Catherine bought tons of it for herself and her Russian royalty to drink. With the empress's enthusiastic stamp of approval, the style became known as an *imperial Russian stout*. You can still buy this kind of beer.[70] Even today, an imperial type of beer is one with a higher-than-average ABV.

This development revolutionized the beer industry. Imperial Russian stouts and porters (another dark style of beer) were able to be shipped all over the world. Yet another incredible beer innovation that you can thank women for.

Back in Russia, the high prices of state-controlled vodka and the government monopoly on access to distilling led to widespread unrest throughout the country. Catherine realized that

---

70 It is delicious and definitely worth a try.

the government restrictions on spirits needed to be reorganized before she was really in trouble.

What she ultimately decided to do was dole out distillation rights to Russian nobles, which granted them the ability to distill vodka on their own estates. It was a system that lowered vodka prices for the peasantry and earned a lot of tax revenue for her. Although this was a big improvement on the previous system, the peasantry was still not allowed to make their own vodka, and illegal distilling was common.

The healthy new revenue stream helped fuel Catherine's massive expansion of Russia. Her reign is considered the golden age of the country. She worked on a huge amount of internal development and annexed Poland, Prussia and Austria. (Clearly it was not the golden age for any of these countries.) She even founded schools for upper-class girls.

Even though she became more conservative as she aged, Catherine was a devoted patron of the arts and lifted a ban on the private ownership of the printing press. This caused a blossoming of the Russian publishing industry and a flourishing of intellectual life. Catherine was always irritated by men who underestimated her. She hated people that "could not imagine that a consistent pattern of action could be the product of a feminine intellect."

Under her hand, Russia became one of the great powers of Europe. Catherine was responsible for stimulating the country and ushering in a period of modernization. All fueled by a pint of her signature stout. Catherine the Great died in 1796 after reigning as empress for thirty-four years.

Alcohol legislation has always been about so much more than just moderating drinking and preventing drunkenness. It's about controlling people: who is allowed to drink and where. It's about stifling threats to authority and forcing certain types of people, poor people especially, and poor or native women *especially*, into certain types of approved behavior. It's about who can partake in this industry and make money off it. Just as it was in the ancient world, controlling who has access to alcohol is about who has access to political and economic power. Catherine was fortunate enough to be the one making the rules, and she became the first politically powerful woman to harness the economic power of booze.

Whether it was gin-drinking women in London, or chicha-drinking women in Lima, or pulque-drinking women in Mexico City, patriarchal structures all over the globe—under the guise of public health and propriety—used laws controlling alcohol to suppress them. But they were never completely successful. Women always found a way to secretly brew, distill, sell or drink in pulquerias, shebeens, hidden dramshops or their own kitchens. In the coming century, they continued to lead this booming underground alcohol market in communities all around the world.

Catherine the Great used alcohol to secure her empire. The next woman you'll meet had an empire that was *made* of it.

7

THE WIDOW CLICQUOT AND THE DELICIOUSLY FEMININE

The Nineteenth Century

Vodka. Whiskey. Gin. Rum.

A whole tasting flight of new distilled spirits was now available to toast the coming of the modern age. It was time to start refining these drinks: the way they tasted, how they were made and how they were served. After all these years, fermented drinks needed an update, too. During the nineteenth century, one that experienced a big innovation was champagne.

The name that most people associate with great champagne is Dom Pérignon. But that guy *hated* bubbles in his wine. The seventeenth century French monk was famous for his skills with blending wine, not making it sparkle.[71] The name you should think of when someone mentions champagne is Barbe-Nicole Clicquot, the grand dame of sparkling wines.

Barbe-Nicole was born December 16, 1777, in Reims, France—

---

71 In fact, he was actually tasked with figuring out how to remove the offending bubbles from the wine the monks were making. The claim that he invented champagne was a very misleading marketing campaign started by the company (which only named it after him) long after he died.

what is now the heart of champagne country.[72] She grew up during the French Revolution, the blonde, gray-eyed eldest daughter of a wealthy textile businessman. Wine ran in Barbe-Nicole's blood. Her great-grandfather Nicolas founded the world's first champagne house in 1729.

By age twenty, she was married off to François Clicquot, the son of another wealthy textile businessman. François's father also dabbled in the wine trade, and the new couple wanted to make that small offshoot of his company blossom. Within their first year of marriage, Barbe-Nicole and François hatched a plan to transform the Clicquot family business into a champagne house.

They started out simply as wine brokers. Barbe-Nicole and François didn't make wine of their own but rather acted as distributors for local vineyards. This was before sparkling wine was even called champagne. Even in the Champagne area of France, it wasn't named champagne until the 1860s.

The couple owned several vineyards, and together they assessed the potential of their various properties. During this time, wine drinkers had to depend on the reputation of a winegrowing region. Wine bottles did not come with labels, and there were no publications that reviewed or recommended wine. In fact, wines usually weren't sold in bottles. Wine came in casks, unless it was really fancy stuff. By the 1600s, Champagne was known as a region with fine wines, and many of the vineyards that Barbe-Nicole and François owned were in prime locations there.

Now, we're not talking about the type of champagne you pop on New Year's Eve. Wines in the early 1800s would be considered dessert wines if they were sold in stores today. They were cloyingly sweet. A typical bottle of modern champagne contains around twenty grams of sugar. Early nineteenth century wine

---

72   This is the Champagne region of France. In order to be called champagne, sparkling wine made here must be crafted under legally defined rules called appellation. I'll go deeper into this later.

was at least *ten times* as sweet and often served cold and slushy. It was more like a Slurpee from 7-Eleven. *Le Slurpee.*

It wasn't golden in color, either. This wine had a brownish pink hue, the result of the large amount of sweet syrup and brandy that was added. Finally, it wasn't even as bubbly as sparkling wines today. Early nineteenth century glass wasn't able to withstand the pressure. The bottles exploded at about half the force that wine bottles endure today.

Making sparkling wine is quite a difficult process, even if you do have a bottle that can take it.[73] It demands the alchemical expertise of a master blender. See, wine transforms into sparkling wine through a second fermentation. Because of the cold winters in the Champagne region, a second fermentation often happened when the temperature dropped before the yeast in the wine finished gobbling up all the sugar. When things warmed back up in the spring, the yeast continued their feast. They exuded more carbon dioxide, but the wine had already been placed in sealed casks, trapping the bubbles within.[74] Eventually, winemakers figured out that they could make wine sparkle on purpose. If they added yeast, dissolved sugar and brandy to the wine before it was bottled (and stored in bottles, instead of casks)—*voila!*

Before Barbe-Nicole became interested in champagne, there was a woman who popularized it.

Claude Moët was a French champagne maker who, around 1750, traveled to Versailles to drum up some royal taste for his wine. When he got there, Moët spoke to a group of young

---

73 Much to the chagrin of the French, sparkling wine was actually invented in England.

74 Remember how Dom Pérignon hated bubbles in his wine? In the 1660s, he and his other monk pals at the abbey at Hautvillers were asked to find out why the local wines had bubbles in them. No one had figured out the issue of a second fermentation yet, and the bubbles drove local winemakers crazy. They called it the devil's wine. Dom Pérignon never ended up figuring it out. See above footnote.

women who were eager taste-testers. They found it "deliciously feminine" and wanted to drink more of it. One of these women was Madame de Pompadour, King Louis XV's official mistress.

She became one of Moët's most loyal customers and insisted that his champagne was served at royal functions. Madame de Pompadour was one of the earliest and most influential figures to recognize that the sparkling wine of Champagne was very, very special. She claimed it was "the only wine that leaves a woman beautiful after drinking it." Getting an endorsement from Madame de Pompadour in the eighteenth century was like getting an endorsement from Chrissy Teigen today.

History doesn't say whether or not champagne made Barbe-Nicole Clicquot more beautiful, but she was certainly enamored with making it. And she wasn't the only one.

When Barbe-Nicole was getting into the business, Moët was already a very successful wine company. They were also distributors of wine, and nearly half of the winemakers they got their product from were women. All of them were widows.[75] Women were a key part of family-run businesses in France in the generation before Barbe-Nicole. By the time she wanted to become a winemaker, the practice was looked down upon, and there was a growing prejudice against businesswomen. In 1804, the Napoleonic Code went into effect, and part of its legal framework steered women toward becoming mothers and wives and not much else. But this didn't deter her. Barbe-Nicole loved wine making.

While they were developing their wine company, Barbe-Nicole had to stay in the background while François made all the financial decisions. After the couple finally began to bottle their own wines, she got to be involved at the vineyards. Barbe-Nicole traveled to inspect the progress of the grapes and rose before the sun to watch the early morning harvests, which lasted around twelve days. Baskets full of grapes were brought in from the vineyards and gently poured into the presses. She loved to

---

75 Sadly, most of their biographical information is lost.

study the process and happily watched the grapes as they were pressed, mesmerized by the sounds of groaning rope and wood.[76]

Things were about to change for Barbe-Nicole, however.

In 1805, the year after the Napoleonic Code made it more difficult for women to be in business, François passed away from typhoid fever. At twenty-seven, Barbe-Nicole found herself widowed. Instead of losing her beloved burgeoning wine business, she convinced her father-in-law to let her keep it. More than that, he also agreed to invest in her, to the tune of nearly half a million in today's dollars. The deal was conditional, though. Barbe-Nicole must apprentice for four years with a partner of her father-in-law's choosing. His pick, Alexander Jérôme Fourneaux, was both a wealthy merchant and an experienced winemaker. He agreed to partner with her and show her the ropes.

Newly widowed, Barbe-Nicole found that she could now manage her own life. In a strange way, a widow had more legal freedom in nineteenth century France than a married or single woman. She had the social privileges of a married woman but the financial freedoms normally afforded to a man. Barbe-Nicole was about to take advantage of them both.

To find one of the world's most unusual beers, look no further than the Amazon rainforest. The Makushi were (and are) a Carib-speaking people who lived there, in the North Rupununi region of what is now southwestern Guyana. Using local rainforest plants, Makushi women made a wide array of fermented alcohol.

Fly was made from purple potatoes and sugar, and there were wines made from fruits like pineapple, mango and cashew apples. But the mainstay was a type of beer called *parakari* made from fermented cassava bread. It was an extremely social drink,

---

76   There are usually multiple pressings of grapes. The first one or two are
     the finest, but the quality of the juice decreases from there. Table wines
     are typically made of third, fourth or fifth pressings.

a vital part of both everyday and ritual life. Cassava beer was the glue that kept Makushi society together. (And still does.)

Cassava is a bitter, woody sort of root that was fundamental to the Makushi in the nineteenth century because their traditional way of life and much of their diet relied on it. The Makushi measure of success was a thriving cassava farm. The parakari that the women made from cassava was therefore held in very high esteem and integral to their cultural identity. It's also a special beverage, completely unique in Indigenous Amazonia (and perhaps the entire world). Instead of using saliva from chewing, like many other Indigenous beers did, parakari is fermented with fungus.

First, women harvested cassava roots and ground them into flour. Gardeners cultivated hundreds of different varieties of the roots, some of which were considered superior for making beer. The flour was then baked into bread and burned ever so slightly. Next comes the important (and tricky) part. The women made a temporary structure out of banana leaves to act as a fungal incubator and placed the bread, broken up into pieces and soaked in water, inside of it. *Parakari mama* powder was then sprinkled on top, and this fine green powder acted as an inoculum for fungal growth. It was made from dry cassava leaves that had been placed on the fungus of the last batch. Think of it as the Makushi version of that sourdough starter you've been keeping in the back of your fridge for months.

The structure was closed up and left for three days, with more banana leaves added every day. When there was a good amount of growth, the women took the wet, moldy bread, placed it in buckets and put it in a cool, dark place. If it was left for a few days, the liquid in the buckets became a sweet beer with a low ABV. If left for a week or longer, it became a beer that was strong and bitter. After being strained and watered down, the final product was smooth, thick and, depending on how long it was left in the bucket to ferment, either cream-colored or a light brown.

In addition to the fungus, the Makushi women also got a little supernatural help.

Until the 1960s, it was common for Makushi women to get tattooed with symbols that were thought to endow them with special skills. Along with symbols to help with cooking, many women got fermentation symbols. These brewing charms were believed to imbue the woman with a superior ability to make alcohol and were usually tattooed around the mouth, chin, forearms and hands. The symbols and patterns depicted different insects. Very particular arthropods, in fact.

If a woman wanted to enhance her ability to brew sweet beers or make sweet wines, she got tattoos of an arthropod known for making sweet substances, such as a bee. In the Makushi language, the verb *yekî* means *to sting*, but it also means *to get drunk*. If a woman wanted to make drinks with an extra kick, she got tattoos of creatures who wield painful stings. A scorpion tattooed on her hand meant a Makushi woman's beer came out strong and bitter. A bee tattooed on her forearm meant her mango wine would be sweet and delicious.

The Makushi women no longer get fermentation charm tattoos today, but they have a newer practice that might be even more impressive. Instead, they catch the real insects and sting their own hands with them. Are there any home brewers you know willing to stick their hand into a swarm of fire ants to make sure their beer is strong enough? I doubt it.

Up in nineteenth century America, no one was getting brewing tattoos, but a marvelous innovation in drinking culture was developing. Please give a big round of applause for...

Cocktails!

Cocktails have a special place in the history of the United States. The craft of mixing cocktails was the first American art form and the first piece of American culture to capture the world's interest and palate.

With distilled spirits available, it was inevitable that people eventually started to mix them with other spirits and see how they tasted. The exact origin of the cocktail (and even why it is called that in the first place) has proved elusive for historians. What we do know is that by the mid-1800s in America, they were widespread. Traditionally, a cocktail is made with spirits, sugar, water and bitters.[77] The types of spirits, sugar and bitters vary widely. Soon, fruit juices, cordials and liqueurs joined the list of possible cocktail ingredients.

Jerry Thomas, a legendary mixologist (yes, that term has actually been around for that long) active in the mid-1800s in California and New York, is known as the father of bartending. In 1862, he wrote the *Bar-Tender's Guide*, the first drink recipe book published in the United States.

Wait. What about all those cookbooks filled with drink and cordial recipes the colonial women had been passing on to each other for hundreds of years?

Dr. Nicola Nice, who created the acclaimed gin liqueur Pomp and Whimsy in 2017, thinks Jerry Thomas needs to share the spotlight. During a 2020 interview with the Speakeasy podcast, she said,

> You read about obviously everything from Jerry Thomas onward and it's kind of been this sort of legacy of bartending that's been passed down through male generations and yet you have to ask yourself the question, well, where did they get their recipes? And who might have influenced him and what might he have been drinking at home.... I think we can all say that his legacy has been incredibly influential, but at the time, who would have had the most influence? ... Jerry Thomas sold eight thousand copies of his book in the first edition. Isabella Beeton [who

---

77   Bitters are an alcoholic concoction of various herbs and botanicals. They started out as medicinal but eventually got added to drinks. As you might expect, the flavor is usually bitter.

was English but whose books were sold internationally],
who was probably the most successful, prolific household
management writer, she sold over two million copies in
the same time period. The only book that outsold Isabella
Beeton was the Bible. This is a Kardashian level of influence. When you think about who is reading this and who
is being inspired by it and who is using the recipes and rep-
licating them...we need to give women more credit for the
impact they've had.

Mrs. Beeton's Book of Household Management was published in
1861, the year before Jerry Thomas's book came out. Along with
tips on taking care of your home, Beeton's book contained recipes for beers, ales, cordials and all sorts of cocktails and punches.
There was even a recipe for a cocktail called The Brain Duster,
a name which would be at home on any modern cocktail menu.
In 1866, Malinda Russell self-published *A Domestic Cookbook:
Containing a Careful Selection of Useful Receipts [Recipes] for the
Kitchen*, the first (known) cookbook published by a Black person
in America. It also had recipes for drinks and cordials.

Because women's work in the home is and has always been
undervalued, their contribution to the history of cocktails has
been all but erased, despite laying the foundations for the craft.
It's nice that Jerry Thomas made cocktails, but could he do it
while watching children, cleaning the house and making dinner?

In the nineteenth century, women's drinking culture in America continued to be mostly private. There were big changes in
the country's alcohol habits, but they still excluded women. Poor
women, especially. After the revolution, upper-class Americans
looked for a way to keep the riffraff out. They didn't want any
poor people, women or people of color around while they were
drinking (or doing anything, really). Then, along came the hotel.

The first hotels were built in America in the late 1700s, and
they really caught on in the 1800s. Hotels were a dramatic depar-

ture from even the fanciest taverns. They were huge structures that cost a lot to build, and they offered private, high-quality sleeping quarters. Most hotels had a bar, which was a space, usually with a long counter and tables and chairs, that was dedicated to serving liquor and other alcoholic drinks (and sometimes, but not necessarily, food). Many hotel bars had policies, like dress codes, that helped segregate drinking spaces by class.

Before the American Revolution, taverns were supposed to charge fixed rates for their goods and services. Afterward, however, this practice declined, which meant that taverns and hotels could now price the working class right out of their bars. Many hotels jumped on this ability to keep poor people out, and they became the place where proper people went to drink properly. Upper-crust public drinking culture became more about class segregation than gender segregation. This led to elite, white women being allowed to participate in celebrations, parties and events at hotels. Men drank at these occasions, and eventually women were allowed at the bar, as well.

For the rest of the women of America, public drinking was only a possibility at the other new development in hospitality: the saloon. American drinking culture in the eighteenth century became split between the hotel and the saloon. Saloons were the place for the middle and lower classes to drink. A saloon was essentially a less fancy bar that sometimes served food and sometimes featured entertainment. It was a mostly male space that sort of followed the rules of a medieval alehouse: women usually drank in a saloon only if they were accompanied by a man or a group of other women.

Dance halls had a bit more gender balance in their customers. Overall, these were brightly lit, festive spaces in the back or on the second floor of a saloon. The main attraction for a dance hall was, as you can imagine, dancing. Everyone who just wanted to sit around and have a beer hung out in the saloon down below. Most of the people who went to dance halls were working-class couples. It was a popular place for those who were courting to dance to live music and drink.

It was common for a man taking a woman to a dance hall to buy her drinks, as well as for single men there to buy a woman a drink in exchange for a dance. This was called treating. While this practice helped many women (who had limited freedoms and occupational choices) afford to go out for the night, it also created an ambiguous air of expectation. Treating caused many men to think that if he bought a woman a drink, she was obligated to, well, take your pick: date the guy, sleep with him, etc.

The legacy of social pressure and expectation caused by treating is still felt by women in bars today. Getting a free drink is always nice, of course. But to take the pressure off and clear the air of any expectations, it might be a better idea, as Liz Lemon says, to buy a woman some mozzarella sticks instead.

Alcohol was still an important part of the diet of most Americans, especially those belonging to the lower classes. Many women brewed and distilled illegally at home to avoid high license fees, and there was a lively alcohol trade that took place entirely in kitchens. Some women hid bottles all over their homes to avoid detection from local authorities, in places such as oversize pipes under sinks and behind secret panels in walls. Tenement women were experts at this.

Women who didn't brew or distill needed to buy their alcohol. When they grabbed a bucket of beer to bring home for their families from the local saloon, it was called *rushing the growler*.[78] Some saloons installed a side door where female customers could enter and buy beer or whiskey during the day. This side door was called a *ladies door* or a *family entrance*.

However, there were some women who walked in the front. As America spread west, so did its drinking culture. It was a

---

78 If you've ever been to a brewery and had your waitress offer you a growler— a large, glass bottle filled with around a gallon of beer—you can thank these nineteenth century moms!

mostly male population heading to the Wild West in the early 1800s, but it wasn't uncommon to find women who flouted social norms on both sides of the bar. There are records of at least two dozen female bartenders serving up drinks in the West. In Wichita, Kansas, one Rowdy Kate ran a saloon with her husband, appropriately named Rowdy Joe. Kate was infamous for outdrinking (and outshooting) her customers.[79] She earned her nickname because of the violent way she dealt with disorderly patrons, especially when Joe was gone.

Along with women mixing and serving drinks, there were some known as bloomer girls,[80] who wore bloomers, drank, smoked, gambled and generally did things women weren't supposed to do. In the dusty atmosphere of the Western saloon, bloomer girls drank cordials and brandy as they listened to live music, such as accordion players. Bitters and whiskey mixed with honey were more popular in the South.

WORLD HISTORY ARCHIVE/ALAMY STOCK PHOTO

Bloomer girls.

79 She reportedly shot and killed at least five men, including two ex-husbands.

80 Bloomers were basically a skirt with a divider between the legs, sort of a dress-shaped pair of wide-legged pants. There was a huge craze for them in the mid-1800s after they were popularized by writer Amelia Bloom in her temperance journal. Amelia would probably have been pretty unhappy to see women wearing them to go out drinking.

Some of the Wild West's most notorious personalities were drinking women. Gunslinger and horsewoman Martha Jane Canary, also known as Calamity Jane, was part of Buffalo Bill's Wild West show and a legendary drinker. She wore men's clothes, chewed tobacco, cursed up a storm and liked to march into a saloon and shout, "I'm Calamity Jane, and the drinks are on me!"

One American folk song went,

My Lulu, she's a dandy
She stands and drinks like a man
She calls for gin and brandy
And she doesn't give a damn
And she doesn't give a damn

The gold rush in 1849 was the catalyst for a massive influx of people of all races and genders to the American West. Women made up an increasing percentage of the population, and soon there were many saloons that admitted them. In the legendary gold rush city of Deadwood, South Dakota, so many women wanted to drink that some saloons created a separate drinking area for them in the back, accessed through a side entrance.

Not all places were so accommodating, though. Some towns and cities passed laws forbidding women from entering the front door.[81] Many men feared women taking over. Gynophobic saloon owners put up *Men Only* signs in their front windows, like children putting up a *No Girls Allowed* sign on their treehouse. Even up in Alaska, where many lower-class American women traveled to frontier boomtowns, a saloon could lose its license by employing women or allowing them to drink there.

In the 1800s, England's female drinking culture had retreated into the home once again. Victorian sensibilities demanded mod-

---

81 Some progressive and crafty saloons got around this law by installing a second door right next to the main door.

esty and propriety out of women, who were supposed to dedicate themselves to the domestic sphere. They were expected to
live an inner life and leave anything public to the men of the
country. Behavior that deviated from this ideal was condemned.

The changes that the previous century saw to the role of
women in English society—more independence, more women
in the workplace—challenged the notion of male superiority.
Male reform leaders pushed back and targeted working-class
women, especially the ones who liked to drink. By the time
the Victorian era began in 1837, women enjoying almost anything at all was associated with sinfulness. They were seen as the
weaker sex who were more prey to temptation, so it was better
for everyone involved if they just stayed at home. Maybe even
closed inside a stockings drawer or hatbox. Just in case.

Public drunkenness was now a crime for which people could
be prosecuted, and women were condemned for it more than
men were. Women drinking in public absolutely scandalized the
Victorians. An elite socialite named Lady Jessica Tatton Sykes
often caused a stir with her appetite for spending, drinking and
seducing men. Refusing to be shamed, she turned it around on
her critics, saying, "After all, I have only a man's vices."

In both England and America, women were expected to be
the angels of the home. Not only were they to practice strict
moderation for themselves but they were also responsible for the
moderation of everyone in the house. Victorian ideals created
an impossible situation for women: have none of the power, yet
all of the responsibility.

None of this stopped women from drinking.

Victorian women's drinking was sly. Society demanded that
they serve as paragons of morality, so women had to get sneaky.
Upper-class wives held so-called tea parties, where the partic-
ipants delicately sipped sherry or gin from beautiful tea cups.
Gin cordials (liqueurs made with gin, sweeteners and flavorings) were wildly popular among women, either purchased or

homemade. Working-class women often bought their gin from the local grocer, tucking a bottle amid their other items.

The craze might have been over, but the English still loved their gin.

Alcohol was still a part of women's lives in many other ways. Bathing in it was thought to promote health until the mid-nineteenth century (although this is not where the phrase *bathtub gin* comes from). Upper-class women who were sick took warm rum baths to restore their strength. Wine, boiled with herbs like thyme and sage, was applied to the face to promote even, fair complexions. Mead mixed with rose petals was rubbed on the body for beautiful skin. White wine with flower blossoms, dabbed onto the affected area, was thought to reduce freckles and spots. Women cooked white wine with rhubarb and shampooed their hair with it to lighten their locks. They also dyed their hair redder with red wine and radishes. Women who could afford it even bathed their infants in spirits rather than water, a practice which mercifully no longer exists.

The nineteenth century saw the rise of public houses, a.k.a. the *pub*. The pub was a huge improvement on the cramped, squalid alehouse. Instead of a smoky hearth, there was a stove to keep everyone warm. In front was an actual business facade with a sign. The pub was purpose-built for the selling and drinking of alcohol. Thanks to the gin shop innovation of the previous century, many pubs featured a bar to order from. Drinking vessels became standardized, and alcohol was now served in pewter mugs or glasses. Wine, beer and several types of spirits were on the menu. An English pub in the 1800s looked much like pubs do today. Probably with more top hats, though.

Many women worked in pubs alongside their husbands, even though they were discouraged from being customers. If the husband was in charge financially, the wife was the one who managed everything else. The pub woman served drinks, dealt with customers, kept tabs, made small talk—all duties bartenders still do today.

Along with a bar, another common sight in the pub was the *snug*. Snugs were small, private rooms where women could drink away from the prying eyes of passersby. They were more ornately decorated than the rest of the pub and usually had no windows. Pubs were typically split into two areas, the *taproom*, where the working-class men went to drink, and the *parlor*, where the upper-class men hung out. The Victorians were all about segregation. Snugs were the place for women to drink.[82] The benefit of the gender segregation was thought to go both ways. Women were shielded from men's drinking behaviors, like cursing, and men were spared the scandalizing sight of a woman having a drink. The horror!

Women who drank in snugs were not rebellious ladies looking to stir up trouble by drinking in public. They were middle- and upper-class women who wanted the same thing that women today usually want when they go to a bar. They wanted to relax, have a drink or two and maybe socialize with some friends.

Over in France, some entire establishments catered specifically to drinking women.

In the seventeenth century, cafés began popping up. Today we associate cafés with coffee and writers pretending to work on their novels, but these were more like restaurants. They usually had full menus and full bars. In the nineteenth century, there were several Parisian cafés that were owned by women and had a mostly female clientele of authors and artists. Specifically lesbian authors and lesbian artists. The English gin shops were female-centric, but please thank the French lesbian community for history's first public drinking spaces that catered specifically to women.

---

82 Snugs were used by anyone who wanted a private drink. They were also the preferred spot for clergymen, politicians, and married men and their mistresses.

These cafés weren't secret places, but they were discreet. There was no law against female homosexuality, so French authorities were much more concerned with male homosexuality and mostly left known lesbian meeting places alone. Before these cafés opened, private salons did exist where women could meet, drink and socialize. But places like Le Hanneton, La Souris and Le Rat-Mort were landmark watering holes. These establishments were revolutionary in that they were owned and operated by—and catered specifically to—women. They were special places where social boundaries were blurred and women of all class backgrounds could have a glass of wine, smoke and relax in public.

Some of those glasses were filled with Barbe-Nicole Clicquot's champagne.

Once it was agreed that Barbe-Nicole was to apprentice under Alexander Jérôme Fourneaux, the two of them invested money—a ton of money—in the Clicquot wine business. Veuve[83] Clicquot Fourneaux & Co. was born.

At the start, Veuve Clicquot made about seventy-five percent of their own wine, getting the rest from other local winemakers. The business was successful from the start, and the brand name rapidly earned a reputation for excellence. Their wine was fantastic.

Things went well for the partnership for years, but in 1809, disaster struck. The Napoleonic Wars caused economic unrest throughout Europe. Ports were closing all over the place, and the export market was strangled. By 1810, Veuve Clicquot Fourneaux & Co. was done for. With their agreed-upon four-year apprenticeship over and the business in shambles, Alexander chose not to continue working with Barbe-Nicole.

---

83 French for *widow*.

She wouldn't quit, though. This short, stubborn woman wanted to keep making champagne.

Barbe-Nicole convinced her father-in-law to reinvest in her wine, to the tune of 30,000 francs (almost 220,000 US dollars today). Thus began Veuve Clicquot Ponsardin (which was her maiden name) & Co.

She was determined to make this new iteration of Veuve Clicquot work. Blockades, closed ports and unstable currency made shipping internationally difficult, so Barbe-Nicole focused on the domestic market and sold wine in her own country with grapes mostly raised on her own land. She sold her jewelry to bolster her finances. Her workday started at seven o'clock in the morning and didn't stop until ten o'clock at night. Most of her time was spent in her home office in Reims, where she maintained her account books and feverishly dashed off pages and pages of correspondence. She constantly communicated—with suppliers, salesmen and clients.

All her work paid off. After the first year of transition, she was making profits. They weren't huge, but they were still profits. At the time, she was one of only a few independent women in France who owned a business with that sort of capital.

Things continued this way for a few years, until 1814, when the war that was tearing up Europe arrived on her doorstep.

Russia marched into France, and Reims found itself occupied by Russian troops. Instead of looting and burning like Barbe-Nicole feared they would, the Russian troops bought—not stole—lots of bottles of champagne from the widow during their occupation. They absolutely loved the stuff.

The next year, in the spring of 1815, the Napoleonic Wars ended, and half a million foreign soldiers in the Champagne region popped bottles of the local sparkling wine to celebrate. This forged champagne's cultural identity as a drink of celebration. In Reims, it was bottles of Veuve Clicquot that Russian officers toasted with. Demand for Barbe-Nicole's champagne skyrocketed, and her production increased tenfold.

When they went home, the Russians brought their love of champagne with them. For decades, it had been a drink for the rich. Now, in one fell swoop, a tremendous number of working-class men developed a taste for this special wine. Champagne was now an international phenomenon.

Barbe-Nicole had one huge problem with capitalizing on the Russian demand: there was a ban on international trade because of the war. She realized that this was actually a once-in-a-lifetime opportunity. Before peace was secured and exports were legal again, the widow took a colossal risk and sent a secret, illicit shipment of champagne to Russia.

The champagne arrived in good condition, and she was way, way ahead of any of her competitors (her biggest being Moët) who were still waiting for the trade ban to be lifted. Not only was it the only champagne available, it was *excellent*. The bottles were Barbe-Nicole's 1811 vintage, a year with a perfect harvest that had made an exquisite and powerful wine. Soon, there was an absolute mania for Veuve Clicquot. It sold for ridiculous prices. The entire shipment of over ten thousand bottles sold, and she made a phenomenal profit.

Buyers raved about the quality of Veuve Clicquot. The king of Prussia toasted with it on his birthday that year. Czar Alexander announced that he would drink no other wine.

But Barbe-Nicole's true genius was that she already had another, larger shipment on the way, before the success of the first had even been confirmed. This second shipment of Veuve Clicquot also arrived successfully, still far ahead of the competition.

Dressed in the black widow's clothes that she would wear for the rest of her life, Barbe-Nicole became one of the most famous women in Europe. She was a celebrity. A bottle of

Veuve Clicquot was one of the most highly valued products in the world.

This widow was just getting started.

While the French were making champagne and the English were making gin, the Irish were still making whiskey.

Barley flourished in the dampness of Ireland, so it became the main crop that was distilled into spirits. Unaged, distilled whiskey was called *poitin*—Irish moonshine. If barley wasn't available, women made it from almost anything, from oats to potatoes. Poitin was clear and tasted harsh, no matter what it was distilled from. Irish women made it at home, and they brought their spirits along when they went to community events. Sometimes it was mixed with goat's milk, mint or honey.

In 1661, the Irish government imposed the very first whiskey tax. At four pence a gallon, the tax forced mothers and wives to start hiding their stills in the hills. By the 1700s, English taxes put small distilleries out of business across the country. In the Ireland of the 1800s, most of the bootleggers were poor women who made spirits to support their families.

By then, England had swallowed Ireland. The Act of Union in 1800 created the United Kingdom, and soon Ireland faced even more aggressive taxes and English informants on the hunt for illegal whiskey distillers.

For many Irish women, making whiskey was their only source of income. Ruthless English informants focused on them, seizing their property or their livestock if they suspected the women of distilling. Old age didn't exempt them, either. When neighbors fought back against the informants and tried to protect the distillers, England bolstered their forces. Informants' numbers were increased, and they were given muskets and other weapons to help suppress the Irish.

These Irish women would not be suppressed, however. They kept distilling. A popular 1830s folk ballad went,

When I was at home
I was merry and frisky
My dad kept a pig
And my mother sold whiskey

Ireland's most legendary poitin distiller was a woman named Kate Kearney. She lived in the Gap of Dunloe, and the English never caught her. This was during the famine, in the mid-1800s. Kate gave her poitin out to anyone who was hungry and needed sustenance, a tall order during a time when a million Irish people died of starvation. She distilled a mix of grains and herbs, sometimes mixing her final product with goat's milk to make it more nourishing. Kate Kearney and her secret whiskey remain in the folklore of Ireland to this day.

One of the world's most famous Irish whiskey brands is Bushmills. In January 1865, the owner died and left the distillery to his wife, Ellen Jane Corrigan. It was already a successful whiskey company when Ellen Jane took over, but she made it soar. Listing herself as E. J. Corrigan to hide her gender, she handled the company's business affairs and bought much of her barley from local widows and employed many women. Under her hand, Bushmills grew in size and won awards. Perhaps most importantly, she introduced electricity to the distillery. Ellen Jane initiated the steps needed to make the company into the international brand it is today.[84] During a critical stage of the distillery's development, Bushmills relied on women.

---

84   The current master blender there is a woman named Helen Mulholland. Studies show that Bushmills is one of the alcohol brands most enjoyed by women.

Scottish women were no strangers to the world of boot-legging, but they were skilled in distilling legal whisky, too. By the 1800s, more than thirty women managed scotch distilleries.[85] One distillery was run by a woman named Helen Cumming and her husband in the mid-1800s. Helen sold her scotch at a shilling a bottle through her kitchen window. In 1872, her daughter-in-law Elizabeth took over and expanded the enterprise, building a bigger, more modern distillery. In 1893, she sold it to John Walker & Sons, which is now the Johnnie Walker brand (currently the world's best-selling blended scotch).

Irish and Scottish women were so good at distilling that they were as in demand as American mail-order brides. Men in America paid for women to move from Ireland or Scotland, marry them and make whiskey.[86] One whiskey wife, please!

Instead of barley, women in America made whiskey with rye, wheat or corn. George Washington is called America's first distiller, but there were scores of women making whiskey before him.

To make whiskey, a woman filled a big tub with malted grain meal and water. She stirred the mixture, maybe sprinkling more meal into the mash before she left it to sit for a few hours. Then, more water, malt and grains were added and stirred. Soon, the mash could be distilled in a big pot still, similar to the ones in use in Ireland and Scotland. Pot stills were and still are pretty simple, just a large version of Maria the Jewess's ancient design. A new type—the column still—was patented in 1830, but home distillers in America usually stuck with the simpler pot still.

---

85 Besides the *e*, the difference between Scotch whisky (or just scotch for short) and Irish whiskey is mainly the taste. Scotch tends to be distilled from malted barley and has a heavier, deeper flavor. Irish whiskey tends to be made with unmalted barley and given an extra round of distillation. It has a lighter, smoother flavor. Not all scotches have a smoky, peaty flavor. It depends on where in Scotland the scotch is made.

86 They were advised to bring a bottle of whiskey along on the sea voyage to America to help with seasickness.

It's a good thing that so many women knew how to distill, because in the early 1800s, there was a whiskey boom in America. In an effort to bolster American products, Congress taxed rum (a spirit made outside the country) but not American-made whiskey. The spirit soared in popularity. Some legal distillers were women, but they're difficult to track through history. Like Ellen Jane at Bushmills, they usually used initials instead of their full names to avoid prejudice. We do know that there were at least fifty women who ran distilleries in America during this time.

There were also many illegal distillers, women who began a long tradition of female American whiskey bootlegging. These women were tough and often armed, ready to defend themselves against the law. Some were known for violence. In the late 1800s, Mollie Miller, of Polk County, Tennessee, was the head of a notorious whiskey making outfit. She killed at least three taxmen and five informants. Also of Tennessee, Betsy Mullens managed a large bootlegging operation. When the authorities came to arrest her, Betsy—who weighed around six hundred pounds—dared authorities to carry her out of her house if they wanted to take her to jail. She was never arrested.

In the south, many women hid their operations in the hills or mountains. In the north, the woods were the best place to hide your still if you didn't have an attic or spare bedroom. Out west, women filled covered wagons with barrels of whiskey and packed satchels with bottles for transporting to customers.

Over in Russia, women were doing the same thing with vodka. In the late nineteenth century, rural Russian women dominated the underground world of bootlegging. Catherine the Great opened up the vodka industry during the previous century, but the Russian peasantry was still not legally allowed to distill. Even so, women made vodka at home and offered it at local fairs and bazaars. Armed with several glasses and a bottle, they walked around and sold drinks on the spot to traders.

These wives and mothers operated completely independently from their husbands. Money that married women earned from selling vodka was their own. Many women used the profits to support their families, sometimes even donating it to their church. Not all bootleggers were tough, gun-toting gang leaders. Some of them were the kindly, shawl-wrapped grandmothers who shared your pew on Sunday.

These women became the key to Russia's vodka culture when, in 1894, the government passed another state vodka monopoly law. Many taverns closed, which forced most drinking to take place at home, where women were ready to accommodate. In rural areas, where many men left families and wives behind to find urban jobs, women took up both the heavy manual labor of the farm and the desire for some vodka at the tavern at the end of the day. They even got together to drink after a big sheep shearing or on holidays. Unmarried rural women had their own alcohol-infused celebrations. On the seventh Sunday after Easter (known as Whitsunday), they gathered in the woods to drink, sing and decorate birch trees.

If a Russian woman joined the workforce and spent more time outside the home, she was still responsible for the drinking that went on inside it. Women whose husbands drank too much were blamed for not being good wives. They were advised to be sweeter and more charming. If a husband spent too much time out drinking, it was assumed that his wife didn't keep an attractive enough home.

This idea, that women had all the responsibility for drinking but no power to enforce it, was the soil in which the seeds of the women's temperance movement were planted. And it wasn't just in Russia and Victorian England.

In the nineteenth century, temperance movements sprang up in countries all over the globe: Japan, America, Finland, Mexico, Sweden, Norway. They set the stage to change women's role in politics forever.

★ ★ ★

Barbe-Nicole Clicquot was now the first woman in modern history in control of an international commercial empire.[87] All the bottles of Veuve Clicquot champagne were sent out with her brand burned into the cork, an anchor that still graces the bottles.[88]

THE PICTURE ART COLLECTION/ALAMY STOCK PHOTO

The Widow Clicquot.

She was in the right place at the right time. Capitalism was taking over economies across the world, and the craft of champagne was shifting from an industry of rural artisans to big business.

In the vineyards, *vignerons* were the skilled workers guiding

---

87   Women like her are still a rarity. Only one woman has been at the helm of Veuve Clicquot since Barbe-Nicole, and her name is Mireille Guiliano. She left the company in 2014.

88   Bottles sold today also feature her signature on the label.

the grapes to maturity. Men were considered to be the most skilled and paid the most. There were also *vigneronnes*, skilled women who worked the trade. Their elevated status was recognized by the option to hyphenate their married names with their maiden ones. Vigneronnes' skill with grape cultivation made it so they could be seen as more of a person and less like their husband's property. They still earned much less than the vignerons (about 600 francs a year, compared with the men's 1000) but enjoyed some independence and social power.

Down in her cellars, Barbe-Nicole had a problem. She couldn't hurry wine. In 1815, demand for "a bottle of Widow" was so great that the company was having trouble filling orders. To make matters worse, the grape harvest that year was abysmal. By the next year, she completely ran out. Veuve Clicquot was out of finished champagne.

She couldn't speed up the fermentation, but Barbe-Nicole realized that she could speed up the means of production. The most time-consuming part of the process was disgorging the wines—clearing the champagne of the yeasty debris trapped in the bottle after the second fermentation. It was a huge pain in the ass. All the traditional ways of doing it had big drawbacks. If she poured wine from one bottle to another, it destroyed the effervescence and usually wasted wine in the process. Tilting and shaking the bottle took forever. Filtering it ruined the quality. She was determined to find a new way to do it, one that would get her champagne fast.

All her cellar workers laughed when she announced her mission.

After some experimenting, Barbe-Nicole realized that if she stored a bottle of champagne on its neck, all the debris would settle on the cork, making removal quick and easy. If she stored all the bottles that way, it could revolutionize her champagne production. Again, all her workers chuckled and told her it would never work. So she had her own kitchen table moved down into the wine cellars and drilled full of slanted holes. Barbe-Nicole and her cellar master Antoine Müller tinkered with storing the champagne in the holes, neck down. After a month and a half of experimenting, Barbe-Nicole discovered that she was right. With one quick flick of the cork, all the debris shot right out of the champagne with minimal effort and no adverse effects on the wine. It was her turn to laugh.

Barbe-Nicole and Antoine immediately set about using this method, *remuage sur pupitre*,[89] for all their champagne. Soon, they were able to quickly disgorge large quantities of beautifully clear and brilliantly sparkling wine.

Within a few years, Veuve Clicquot was exporting nearly 200,000 bottles of champagne annually, compared to just 20,000 in 1812. Barbe-Nicole drove her competitors mad. No one could keep up with her. The folks over at Moët were absolutely frantic to figure out how she was producing clear wine so quickly. But her cellar workers were so loyal to Barbe-Nicole that the secret of remuage sur pupitre stayed safe at Veuve Clicquot for almost ten years.

While Barbe-Nicole Clicquot was developing her empire in Champagne, Tatsu'uma Kiyo was building one out of saké in Japan—the largest saké empire in the entire country.

By the 1700s, saké-making techniques were refined, and advanced technologies were in use. Gone were the days of rice chewing and spitting. Women were still largely barred from the saké brewery for various misogynistic superstitions, however. There were exceptions, like the large Sakura Masamune brewery, managed by the widow of its former owner. On the whole, however, there were no women allowed to run things.

---

89 *Remuage* translates to *riddling*, and the A-framed wooden racks that stored the upside-down bottles were called *pupitres* or *riddling racks*.

Until, that is, Tatsu'uma Kiyo figured she could create an empire behind the scenes.

Kiyo was born in Nishinomiya on July 16, 1809, as an only child. She was sharp and full of energy and ambition. The daughter of a brewing dynasty, Kiyo had saké in her genes. Her family's brewery, the Tatsu'uma House, had been founded in 1662 and was one of the largest and earliest saké breweries in Japan. They both brewed saké and crafted their own barrels in Nishinomiya. The nineteenth century was a good time to be making saké. It was one of Japan's major industries, and there was a lot of money to be made.

As a child, Kiyo spent a lot of time in her family's brewery, learning how to do everything from wash barrels to supervise the male workers. By the time she was old enough to marry, she was a saké expert.

In 1830, at the age of twenty-one, she was married off to the son of another brewing house. (The wedding celebration must have been a jovial affair.) The couple had at least six children before Kiyo was widowed in 1855. At forty-six, she found herself with a massive business to run in an industry that didn't want women around. So she found a loophole.

Kiyo hired a *bantō*, a male clerk that she trusted completely and trained to essentially be her deputy. He handled all the open negotiations and face-to-face meetings, while she stayed behind the scenes, pulling all the strings. With this facade in place, Kiyo began to build herself an empire.

She was an innovator. Kiyo was one of the earliest brewers to ship saké to bustling, faraway Edo, which earned her a ton of profits. To facilitate transport, she bought her own ships. When faster, more reliable steamships were invented, she bought those. Eventually, Kiyo started her own shipping company, along with marine and fire insurance companies to protect her cargo. She even established an exchange and financial facility to protect her brewery against the fluctuations of rice prices.

Kiyo was a managerial and entrepreneurial genius. Like Barbe-Nicole Clicquot, she recognized the power in a famous label. In the 1830s, she began to buy saké in bulk from other breweries when she had a particularly bad rice harvest. Kiyo experimented with ways to blend those other sakés with her own brew and sell it under the Tatsu'uma House brand. She pioneered strategies that are still critical to the survival of saké breweries today.

Outside of the brewery, as her children grew up, she married them off to the children of other brew houses. This bolstered her business relationships, making Kiyo sort of like the queen of the saké version of *Game of Thrones*.

She was meticulously involved with the everyday running of the brewery, as well. Kiyo sometimes washed the barrels herself to ensure the level of cleanliness that she expected. In the late 1800s, Tatsu'uma House was producing twenty-two thousand *koku* every year. (One koku is equivalent to about forty-eight gallons.) Kiyo was making three times as much saké as her nearest competitor. For fifty years, hers was by far the largest and most prosperous saké brewery in Japan.[90] With her trusted bantō handling the face of things, Kiyo wielded an incredible amount of power in the industry.

In 1900, at age ninety-one, Kiyo passed away. Despite the influence she had during her lifetime, she is relatively unknown today. Historians believe it is the result of an old tradition in Japan where women who become successful in business are actually an embarrassment to their families because of the humiliation they caused their competitors. At the time of her death, Kiyo's business was still three times as large and successful as any other saké brewery in the country. Her grave in the Tatsu'uma

---

90   The company, which is now called Hakushika, is still one of Japan's leading brands.

family plot is unremarkable, small and practically hidden off in a corner. She has been largely forgotten by saké history.

Barbe-Nicole Clicquot was fortunate enough to not suffer such a fate.[91]

By 1841, she finally retired at age sixty-four. (The same year her biggest competitor, Jean-Rémy Moët, died.) She stayed involved on an executive level in the champagne house, essentially becoming a one-woman board of directors. By then, she was an international icon, albeit a faceless one. Barbe-Nicole never traveled to any of the markets her champagne was sold in.

Veuve Clicquot was the brand responsible for internationalizing the champagne market. Today, the Widow Clicquot would have been a billionaire. The method she and Antoine developed completely revolutionized sparkling wine. Remuage sur pupitre is still used in many champagne houses to this day.

Whether it was shaping the new art of cocktails or establishing secret distilleries to subvert oppressive regimes, women in the nineteenth century were a powerful, unseen influence in the world of alcohol.

Work in the kitchen and in the home has been systemically devalued and outright dismissed for thousands of years. It's impossible to confine alcohol or cocktail history to the bar because so many types of people were not allowed to work or drink there until very recently in modern history. Alcohol was a deeply important part of the private home lives of peoples all over the world in the nineteenth century, not just the goings-on in the public taverns, hotels, saloons or pubs. Many of women's recipes and innovations are what various alcohol industries and companies are built on. Barbe-Nicole was one of the few female innovators who got the acclaim and success she deserved.

---

91 If you want to learn more, you can read Tilar J. Mazzeo's excellent biography, *The Widow Clicquot*. Tatsu'uma Kiyo, at this time, has no biography written about her.

So many names and stories have been lost to time. Having a legacy is a privilege afforded only to a few. Often, it's about class. Like we see with Barbe-Nicole and Kiyo, sometimes it's just about when and where you were born. As the next century dawned, however, women's powerful influence would no longer remain hidden.

In July 1866, Barbe-Nicole Clicquot passed away at the age of eighty-nine,[92] still dressed in her widow's black.

She owned a beautiful estate in the country outside Oger, about thirty miles south of Reims. It overlooked acres of idyllic vineyards where she could watch chardonnay grapes growing in the warm summer sun. There, she loved to entertain. Until well into her old age, Barbe-Nicole hosted grand parties full of artists, writers, politicians and sometimes international royalty.

She just had one rule: the only beverage served was her champagne.

---

92   At a time when most French women didn't live to see the age of fifty.

8

ADA COLEMAN'S AMERICAN BAR

The Twentieth Century

By 1900, the world of drinking looked essentially like it does today, and not just because modern mixologists love sporting suspenders and old-timey mustaches. In nearly all industrialized societies, there were bars, bartenders, cocktails and most of the types of alcohol you'd expect behind a bar today. (Or versions of them, anyway. No birthday-cake-flavored vodka yet.) Drinks were served in glasses, and ice was finally incorporated into the craft. The first decade of the twentieth century is considered to be the golden age of the cocktail, when most of the classic cocktails people still drink today were invented.

It was also the heyday of the world's first female celebrity bartender.

Ada Coleman was born in England, sometime around 1875. Her father worked as a steward at a golf club owned by Rupert D'Oyly, a successful hotelier and producer of musical theater. When her father passed away, D'Oyly offered Ada a job at the golf club. She was about twenty-four years old.

Right away, it was clear that Ada was a natural in the service industry. She was charming, incredibly friendly and, most importantly, this young, light-haired woman was sharp as hell. Soon, D'Oyly transferred her to one of his more prestigious establishments: the impressive Claridge Hotel in London. The gorgeous luxury hotel had been recently rebuilt with modern facilities like elevators and en suite bathrooms. Today, it's still known for hosting royalty and their guests. In 1899, Ada worked in its flower shop.

The wine merchant at Claridge's, a man named Fischer, took Ada under his wing not long after she started work. He taught her how to mix a cocktail and handle a shaker. The first drink she ever made was a manhattan, and Ada took to bartending immediately. She absolutely loved making cocktails and asked to try her hand behind the bar.

Behind the bar was where Ada Coleman was meant to be.

Flower shop forgotten, Ada excelled at her new job. It was undeniable: she was a cocktail prodigy. Her phenomenal drinks were matched only by her gregarious personality. D'Oyly noticed her new skills and transferred her to one of his other high-profile locations.

The Savoy Hotel in London, D'Oyly's most famous and successful property, had just beautifully renovated its bar, which was called the American Bar.[93] It soon became the throne of the new queen of cocktails.

In southern Africa, the consumption and brewing of beer had been a fundamental part of the culture of rural populations for centuries. And it was female brewers controlled the industry.

In the 1860s, Dutch colonizers established a settlement in Umtata, down near the Cape of Africa (what is now the Eastern Cape province of South Africa). The settlement was located on

---

93 This hotel bar was one of the first places in Europe to serve American-style cocktails. Remember when I said that cocktails were the first American art form and first cultural product to catch on all over the world? The Savoy called its bar the American Bar to make sure folks knew it was serving those cool new American drinks.

the banks of the Umtata River. The colonizers annexed the surrounding region in 1884, and Umtata became the seat of a white government ruling over a population of mostly Black African people. All those native African women making beer became an increasingly large concern for that government.

Umtata developed into a way station for scores of Black male migrant workers. These men were ideal customers for brewers—they were thirsty and had money to spend. Migrant workers became a great source of income for women looking to sell their beer. Rural female brewers started traveling to Umtata for this express purpose, and soon beer was a booming industry there.

If Umtata was too far away, there were many other towns in southern Africa that had a bustling beer industry for women to join. Durban, a coastal city a few hours to the north, was another hub for beer sellers. In 1902, the city saw hundreds of women arriving every day. These brewers traveled by train and carried huge tins and gourds full of beer. It was mostly women, but even girls as young as twelve came to sell beer. They also sold things like chickens, eggs and herbs, but beer was the main attraction.

Before the boom of migrant labor in cities, rural southern African women were usually homemakers and agricultural workers. They spent their days raising children, cooking, tending crops, gathering wood and, of course, brewing sorghum beer. Brewing was still women's work in southern Africa in the nineteenth century. Beer had both nutritional and social importance and played a huge part in rural hospitality.

The brewers soaked the grains before they ground them, cooked them and mixed them with sprouted sorghum to make a mash. This mash was then fermented into a thick, low ABV beer called *utywala*. Women usually brewed at home, but they gathered to brew together when a lot of the beverage was needed for a large event. Sometimes, just the act of brewing was enough for a big social occasion. Beer parties are the best parties.

With the spread of urbanization in the 1800s, beer became

a lucrative product in southern Africa. Women started to brew for commercial purposes, instead of just making beer for their families. Besides brewing, there were not many other paths available for a woman to earn a living. But just as it was for the ale-wives and chicha brewers, being a brewer wasn't only a way to get money. It also offered independence. Some women brewed on the side to make extra cash, but others turned it into their full-time job. Most of the women who traveled to cities like Umtata and Durban to get into the beer trade were single and had few other options to support themselves.

It was the independence of the brewers that worried white government officials.

In fact, the brewers were a double threat. The sale and consumption of alcohol by native Black populations had long been the subject of fierce debate by white colonizers. If these women were supporting themselves by brewing, they were not working for wages at white farms and businesses. White governments and business owners were concerned about the availability of a Black labor force. By being their own breadwinners, the women were also challenging the white, patriarchal order of colonized society. Plus, Black populations drinking a native brew were rejecting the white expectations of propriety and sobriety.

These expectations were for native populations, of course. The rules were different for whites. A French count visiting India in the 1800s noted the excessive drinking of the British colonizers there, even the women. "You will be thunderstruck by the enormous quantity of beer and wine absorbed by these young English ladies!"

A white panic started to develop around African alcohol consumption and the prominence of women in the trade. As the ranks of female brewers and beer sellers swelled, authorities attempted to suppress them.

As we've seen, alcohol legislation is usually not just about drinking.[94] It's about *who* is drinking. These laws usually specifically target poor populations, poor women specifically, and poor nonwhite women most of all.

An act was passed in 1899 that prohibited the sale of liquor to Black Africans in South Africa. The government knew it would be nearly impossible to police the consumption of utywala, so the law did allow the sale of what was termed *native beer* by native women. But authorities were terrified of women establishing themselves and gaining power in the trade, so the sale was allowed as long as it wasn't a permanent business. That meant women couldn't open a storefront or a bar and were forced to sell beer in a transitory way. Or by going underground.

Like their Irish or Scottish equivalents, South African shebeens (the forerunner of speakeasies) flourished as the beer trade continued to grow with the spread of migrant labor. Most of them were controlled and run by women known as shebeen queens. Shebeen queens usually set up shop in a rented house. The rooms that weren't filled with seats for drinkers were filled with tins, drums and casks full of illegal beer. Sometimes, the house was totally dedicated to brewing, and customers went to a shed in the backyard to listen to or play music, drink and dance.

They talked, too. Shebeens became the sanctuary for rebellion. Whispers of uprising and overthrowing the white government took place there between sips of sorghum beer. Shebeen queens were the greatest enemy of the white population, noted one white government official.

Thousands more rural women took advantage of the legal right to temporarily visit towns and cities and sell beer. Many were wives or relatives of men who had traveled to the city for work, and they used beer selling as a way to visit their loved ones.

Women's control of the beer industry was so extensive that white officials started to test ways to interrupt it. In Durban,

---

94   There are notable exceptions to this, such as drunk-driving laws. We can all agree on that one.

some suggested laws that restricted women's use of the railway system to travel into the city. In 1908 in Umtata, a policy was enacted that required the use of permits for beer sellers. Only legal residents of the city could brew and only limited quantities at a time (just five gallons). This quashed the ability for rural women to travel to cities to sell beer and hindered economic opportunities for thousands of them.

In 1907 in Durban, a full quarter of the Black women in the city had traveled there to be beer sellers, brewers or both. The visibility of a large, transitory Black female population made white officials and residents anxious. They were convinced of the immorality of Black women, especially the unmarried ones. White ideas of native African respectability were woven together with a completely imaginary moral and racial hierarchy. If a woman was independent and supporting herself, she wasn't part of the ideal unit of the married couple. She was not as easily controlled and probably full of vice.

Racist ideals about morality aside, white officials were right to be nervous.

In the coming decade, Black women became not just an essential part of a native uprising, they *were* the uprising.

What was happening to native beer and its brewers in South Africa in the early twentieth century was also happening to pulque and the women who brewed it in Mexico.

In the early 1900s, in a nation reeling from colonialism, pulque (along with many Indigenous products and practices) was now considered to be inferior. What was once a beverage that was integral to the cultural identity of Mexico was made out to be dirty and low-class. This greatly impacted poor women's dominance of the trade. The handmade aspect of pulque, the fact that it could be brewed in a small kitchen without training or expensive equipment, was what made it possible for poor women to make a living from it. Now, pulque that was hand-made in a kitchen was considered unhygienic, a base beverage.

During the first decade of the twentieth century, Mexico was under the regime of Porfirio Díaz. Just like the Spanish, the Por-firian government saw pulque and pulquerias as the source of the undesirable and improper parts of society, like laziness and drunkenness. Laws and regulations were enacted to restrict pul-que production and pulqueria business. For women who made their living selling it on the street or in a tavern, this created an impossible situation. How could they maintain their social standing when they sold a drink that was thought of as an un-hygienic vice that was holding back society? Especially when it was one of the only ways they could make a living? Many of these women protested and wrote to the government to stand up for their rights to sell alcohol. Sadly, over time the Porfirian attitudes toward pulquerias diminished their popularity and therefore an entire trade that was accessible to women.

Alcohol has always been a class divider. These new social pressures certainly tamped down on women's drinking culture, but mostly for poor women. The biggest thing that prevented women from drinking was poverty. Due to their social status, elite Mexican women rarely were arrested for public drunken-ness. So although poor women could afford to drink less often, they were more likely to be arrested when they did and over-indulged. Poor women paid a far greater price for both drink-ing and making alcohol.

It has been pathologized for so long, people forget that for thousands of years alcohol hasn't just been for getting trashed. Alcohol use is portrayed as a bad thing, a sin, a vice. But alco-hol has been *used* as an integral part of diets and economies by native women across the globe. Making or drinking it was an important way to connect to traditions and cultural identities. For many women in places like Mexico and South Africa, it was a way to stay alive. Laws and regulations that restricted native alcohol culture for the sake of morality or propriety or public safety were usually just poorly disguised oppression—misogyny and racism wearing glasses and a silly mustache.

Ada Coleman was singular for her talents behind the bar, but she was also singular because she was back there at all.

At the time, women working in bars were called barmaids. It was bar*maid* because most bars and pubs in England and America specified that no woman over twenty-five needed to apply for the job. At twenty-six, women presumably withered to dust and blew away in the first strong breeze. At the advanced age of twenty-four, Ada was nearly too old.

Barmaids were usually women who just needed income, not women looking to hone a craft and start a career. Being a barmaid might have been a little more lucrative or at least a little more fun than the other job options available, but few women signed up because they were excited about the industry. Some thought that barmaids were bad for society and that working in a bar was detrimental to a woman's morals. In London, there were social campaigns created to convince women not to work in bars.

In America at the turn of the century, there were around fifty thousand male bartenders but only one hundred and forty-seven women. In Canada, that number was even lower.[95]

That's how many women were making drinks in *public*. But if you counted up the women mixing up drinks at home, the number would be sky-high. As cocktails spread in popularity, housewives needed to learn how to make them. Wives and

---

95 The notable exception to this is bottling. By the turn of the century, in the United States and Canada, the lion's share (or lioness's, in this case) of women's involvement in the booze industry was in packaging and labeling. These women washed, filled and corked bottles by hand. Because it was similar to kitchen work, it was largely considered the purview of women. Even after bottling machines took over, many distilleries and breweries had women packing the bottles for shipping.

mothers influenced the ingredients that were used in cocktails, along with the tools used to shake, store and serve them.

The Victorians loved accessories. There was nothing a rich, Victorian adult loved more than an object specifically crafted for a single task. Mixing drinks was no different. This meant that in the early twentieth century, there was a myriad of serving dishes, glasses, utensils and containers. Etiquette manuals for women in both England and America specified the types of alcohol and all the accessories that went with each one for every type of function imaginable. Afternoon teas, garden parties, balls, ladies' luncheons, formal dinners, you name it.

At a formal dinner, a guest might find five different glasses at each place setting. One each for water, champagne and different types of wine and sherry. There were crystal glasses for the very rich, plain glasses for the middle class. Catalogs aimed at female customers advertised all sorts of options, from whiskey and sherry tumblers to wine glasses.[96] Dedicated cabinets for liquor were also featured in these catalogs, along with elaborate sideboards for wine. The whiskey decanter, today the symbol for sophisticated masculine drinking, started out as a marker of feminized alcohol. Whiskey, in a beautiful cut-glass decanter that sat on an elegant sideboard, was everything that upper-class female drinking culture was at the turn of the century. Decorative, social, made specifically for home consumption.

In the early 1900s, besides professional bartenders, no one knew more about the intricacies of making and serving cocktails than the well-to-do white American or English housewife.

The first cocktail book written by a woman was released in 1904. *One Hundred and One Beverages* was penned by May E. Southworth, and it is true to its word: it contains a hundred and one different recipes for hot and cold cocktails. Southworth was

---

96 Most wine at this time was imported from France and about four times as expensive as whiskey. If you were ordering wine glasses, you were probably rich.

not a bartender, however. This cocktail book was part of a series she had written containing a hundred and one recipes for different types of things. *One Hundred and One Beverages* went right along with *One Hundred and One Salads*. It was expected that a woman would be able to make a cocktail, just as she could cook a roast or bake a pie.

These manuals also had strict advisories on drinking behavior for women. Popular American cookbook and etiquette author Eliza Leslie specified in one of her books that "on no consideration let any lady be persuaded to take two glasses of Champagne. It is more than the head of an American female can bear."

The exception to rules like these was when a man asked you to drink. At formal dinner parties, there was a practice called challenging. If a man lifted his glass to a woman, it was rude of her to refuse the challenge of taking a sip. This, along with the practice of treating in dance halls (from the last chapter), helped to create the female obligation to drink at the invitation of men, which still, in over a hundred years, hasn't fully disappeared.

American women of all classes drank all the time, not only at formal dinner parties. They drank because doctors told them to.

The most widespread cure-all in America at this time was alcohol. Patent medicines (heavily advertised, over-the-counter cures) at the time contained, on average, 22% alcohol. That's double the average alcohol percentage in wine. One of the most popular brands was Lydia Pinkham's Vegetable Compound, an herbal tonic for women said to alleviate everything from menstrual ailments to weakness and hysteria.[97] Whiskey companies targeted women, touting the medicinal qualities of their product. The most notorious of which was Duffy's Pure Malt Whiskey. The brand was immensely popular with women, partially due

---

97 Lydia Pinkham's parents owned a grocery store in Lynn, Massachusetts, and were staunch temperance supporters. They refused to sell alcohol but couldn't compete with other stores that did. So Lydia started selling her homemade remedy, which they were fine with, because it was—ahem—medicinal.

to the endorsements it advertised. Apparently, a one-hundred-and-sixteen-year-old woman from Buffalo, New York, named Mrs. Burton claimed that "Duffy's Malt has been my steady companion for twenty-five years. I am waiting on myself, and feel that so long as I can get some Duffy's Malt Whiskey, I will live twenty-five years longer."[98]

Overall, women in America were encouraged to drink often. At the behest of a male guest, to relieve all their so-called womanly issues and to stay healthy. Really, women could drink all the time, just as long as a man was telling them to do it. They were still expected to be the angels of the home, a living example of propriety and morality, responsible for the behavior of everyone in the house.

But all this private, unregulated medicinal drinking had dark consequences.

After distilled alcohol became commonplace all over the world, people began dying from what doctors called *intemperance*, an umbrella term for what we now know as alcohol poisoning, alcoholism and other alcohol-related medical issues. Soon, intemperance became nearly synonymous with immorality. If you were poor and died, it was frequently assumed that the cause was intemperance, instead of exposure, malnutrition or disease. Alcohol was the scapegoat of urban problems. Intemperance was used as a way to condemn poor, marginalized women who lived in morally suspect circumstances. It was a vicious cycle. Alcohol was a medical panacea, often the only available and accessible painkiller for those who could not afford to see a doctor. Even if a woman could afford to see a doctor, alcohol was probably what he would prescribe.

Because of the stigma surrounding intemperance, the middle- and upper-class women who were suffering from the effects of alcohol abuse often weren't diagnosed. To protect her social standing, a doctor would often record a vague diagnosis and ultimately

---

98   These claims, of course, were not verified. The company went bankrupt in 1911. But I do hope that a nearly immortal Mrs. Burton was still out in New York somewhere, swigging whiskey.

provide little to no help. Most doctors were reluctant to talk about the effects of alcohol abuse with a woman at all.

Since women were not supposed to be a part of the country's public drinking culture, medical warnings for alcohol focused on men. If any literature mentioned women, it was only on the dangers of alcohol to fetuses and to the family structure, not the health of the woman herself. Consumption of those boozy health tonics was not considered drinking. If alcohol was medicinal, after all, many women wouldn't even realize that drinking too much of it could cause them any health problems.

Even though the number of women who were struggling with alcohol abuse were fewer than the number of men, their notoriety was greater. It was a breach of the social order. They were the fallen angels of the home. In American society, a woman was only supposed to be associated with alcohol abuse in two ways. Either she was a victim of her husband's alcohol abuse or she was speaking out against it as part of the temperance movement.

Temperance had already been building as a political movement in the century prior. Since alcohol had become the scapegoat for all the rising problems of industrialization and capitalism, many thought, well, maybe everything will be better if we all get rid of alcohol. Maybe prohibition of alcohol—legally forbidding it—was the answer.

By the 1840s, the Prohibition movement, sometimes called the dry crusade, entered the American political stage. It started locally and then rose to a state level. In 1851, Maine became the first American state to ban alcohol for public consumption. By 1855, thirteen other states in the Midwest and Northeast followed. The laws differed, from prohibiting commercial manufacture to prohibiting the sale of alcohol to prohibiting the public consumption of it. By the early 1900s, Prohibitionists had their eyes on the Constitution, and alcohol had become a political powder keg.

Joining the temperance movement became attractive for many women in the country. It was them, after all, who were held responsible for the morality of the nation but given no power to do anything to uphold it. Many women supported Prohibition, but female temperance activists were dismissed by both male politicians and men-only temperance societies. In response to this rejection, female temperance societies were born. In 1852, organizations such as the Women's New York State Temperance Society formed and started to hold meetings.

Although the idea of a woman's political movement *sounds* pretty cool, most female temperance societies were very conservative and mostly white. The literature they wrote and distributed was in support of a patriarchal society. Their ideas enforced strict gender roles and emphasized women's domestic moral responsibility. To them, the main horror of female drinking was the negligence of a woman's household and familial duties.

It was a confusing message. These societies wanted to rally women to claim political power, but at the same time to limit it. The most well-known of the female temperance societies was the Women's Christian Temperance Union (which from here on out will be shortened to WCTU, because I don't want to type all that out). When they were founded in 1874, they didn't even endorse the new political idea of women's suffrage. It took them nearly ten years to get on board.[99]

There were some Black chapters of the WCTU, and many women joined, seeing the temperance movement as a way to get involved with a political system that excluded them. But in many states, the chapters and events were segregated. Ida B. Wells, legendary journalist and activist, clashed with WCTU president Francis Willard over racist remarks that she had made in a newspaper interview.

These two movements—temperance and women's suffrage—are often linked. Because temperance was one of the country's big issues around the same time that women were pushing for

---

99 The all-male Prohibitionist Society actually endorsed it before the WCTU did.

the right to vote, many believe that one was a consequence of the other. It caused a lot of brewers and alcohol companies to oppose suffrage. They assumed that all women in America were against alcohol and, if allowed to vote, would vote for Prohibition. But the actual history is much more complicated.

In Colorado, where women had been granted the right to vote in 1893, a 1909 law banned Denver women from drinking at night in restaurants and cafés. The Women's Public Service League, a women's group dedicated to working for public improvements, protested the law. They opposed any measures that restricted the actions of women but did not restrict those of men. The WPSL declared that access to public institutions should be available to everyone (as long as you were white).

People who were opposed to women's suffrage held this up as an example that giving women the right to vote would only promote their degeneracy. If you let them vote, they'll only fight for the right to drink! When Denver government officials responded to the WPSL's complaints, they claimed that they passed the law because of complaints about female drunkenness. Not wanting to seem pro-lady-drunkenness, the WPSL withdrew their complaints and stopped the protests. Another clash between women's rights and the idea of women's propriety.

There were women all over the country whose thoughts on both suffrage and temperance varied widely. Women might be in favor of both or neither. They might be for one but not the other. Despite what many temperance societies wanted America to believe—especially the WCTU—women were not a monolith.

Support for Prohibition continued to grow among people of all genders and America prepared for its biggest and most spectacularly failed experiment.

While both American and English societies were trying to keep women out of bars, Ada Coleman was still reigning over hers.

In 1903, Ada became the first female head bartender at the

American Bar in London's Savoy Hotel.[100] She immediately got on with the rarified clientele. Ada was charismatic and witty, and she made excellent drinks. Soon, she was the preferred bartender for celebrity customers like Charlie Chaplin and Marlene Dietrich, along with royalty like the Prince of Wales. They all called her Coley.

Cocktail historian Ted Haigh has noted that it was Ada and her drinks that made the American Bar famous. Many customers came because they wanted to meet Ada and get a taste of what she was shaking up.

Ada Coleman bartending at the Savoy in London.

And boy, was she shaking them up. Being the head bartender involved much more than chatting with celebrities. Ada had to shake or stir hundreds of drinks a night from recipes she'd memorized, along with overseeing the running of the American, the

---

100   She is still the only woman to ever hold this position.

drink menu and the other bartenders, and making sure all the customers were happy.

While she was technically skilled at the craft of making cocktails, Ada was brilliant at inventing them, as well.

Ada Coleman is most well-known in the cocktail industry today for being the creator of the Hanky Panky, a drink still featured on menus across the world. She invented this beverage for a comic actor of her time named Charles Hawtrey. He was a regular of hers, especially if he was working in London. Hawtrey had a habit of walking into the American and saying, "Coley, I am tired. Give me something with a bit of punch in it."

It was the punch part that got Ada thinking. She said in a 1925 interview for the newspaper *The People*, "It was for him that I spent hours experimenting until I had invented a new cocktail. The next time he came in, I told him I had a new drink for him. He sipped it and draining the glass, he said 'By Jove, this is the real hanky panky!'"[101]

What Ada made for Hawtrey was a stirred cocktail with gin, sweet vermouth and Fernet-Branca, which is a type of Italian amaro.[102] Truly, the kindest thing you can say about Fernet is that it has "a bit of punch to it." The name stuck, and so did the drink.

Ada Coleman wasn't the only one inventing new tastes in the world of booze. Over in France, another widow had inherited Barbe-Nicole Clicquot's champagne throne.

Today, champagne is categorized on a scale from dry to sweet. Brut champagnes are dry, while sec champagnes are sweeter. In the late 1800s, the sweeter the wine or the champagne, the more it was considered a girly drink. Trendy, rich women in England served champagne with afternoon tea—the sweeter, the better. Less sweet wines, those were for men. But it was a

---

101   In England during this time, *hanky panky* meant *magic* or *witchcraft*.

102   An amaro is a bitter herbal liqueur. *Amaro* is Italian for *bitter*.

woman, Madame Louise Pommery, who invented brut champagne in the first place.

Louise Pommery inherited the House of Pommery and Greno
when her husband died in 1860. The business mostly focused on
wool and textiles, but they also made champagne. The Greno
part of the company was her late husband's business partner,
and he encouraged Pommery to get involved. Upon witness-
ing her keen business sense, Greno ceded the entire operation
to her. Soon, she sold off everything associated with wool and
concentrated on making champagne.

Her first order of business was having a brand-new facility
built in Reims, the same city that Barbe-Nicole was born and
lived in. The new facility consisted of gorgeous buildings, carved
with massive bas-reliefs that celebrated champagne.

Other champagne houses had experimented with dry champagne, but no one had made a serious effort because of the risk
and the cost. Brut champagne is more expensive and trickier to
make. It requires higher-quality grapes that are more fully ripened
and at least three years of aging instead of the one year that sec
champagne requires. Plus, the market adored sweet champagne.
Why pay more to make a champagne there was no demand for?

But Pommery was adamant about making a different kind of
champagne. She wanted something new and singular.

Her experiments failed at first. The champagne tasted awful,
and the color was off-putting. Her financial manager thought
she was making a mistake and wasting her time. Pommery just
tried harder.

She contacted vineyards and promised them that she would
purchase their entire harvest, just as long as their workers would
pick the grapes exactly when she instructed them to. (Sudden
weather changes could be disastrous to grapes, so to avoid wasting a harvest, many growers would pick grapes before they were
fully ripe.) Pommery also promised to absorb any losses they

might face, just as long as she could have the grapes harvested exactly as she specified.

Finally, in 1874, she succeeded.

Considered one of the finest champagne vintages of the century, Madame Louise Pommery's brut was so good that there were poems written about it. It was a phenomenal hit among customers worldwide. The champagne commanded such a high price that her financial manager was forced to eat his words. To celebrate, she declared her birthday—March 18—an annual holiday at the House of Pommery.

Pommery's brut was the first truly dry champagne sold commercially. By the early 1900s, the House of Pommery was one of the biggest and most successful champagne houses in France. Her creation transformed the entire industry. Even Veuve Clicquot sells a brut champagne today.

Champagne was still a popular drink in the early 1900s, but there was a new spirit filling the glasses of French women.

Absinthe is a beverage with a lot of mythology surrounding it. Called the Green Fairy, absinthe is a distilled, anise-flavored spirit with a high ABV (vodka is about 40% AB; absinthe can be between 45 and 70%). It's naturally green-colored, which comes from the herbs and other botanicals used to make it.

During the start of the twentieth century, many believed that absinthe caused a particular type of madness, and it was said that its drinkers experienced hallucinations. None of that is true. Its wide popularity, especially in France, combined with its extremely high alcohol content gave rise to all sorts of ridiculous claims. By 1914, it was banned in France and many other countries. One of the beliefs that caused these bans was that absinthe was a particular vice of women.

Dr. J. A. Laborde was an "absinthism" expert. He supported the idea that addiction to absinthe was a separate issue from alcoholism, with its own symptoms. (Also not true.) In 1903, he wrote:

Woman has a particular taste for absinthe and if she intoxicates herself rarely with wine and alcohol, it has to be recognized that in Paris at least, she is frequently attracted by les aperitifs and, without risk of exaggeration, I would say that this intoxication has been for several years as common among women as among men.

Absinthe itself, like gin, was given a feminine identity. Scores of gorgeous art nouveau posters advertising absinthe featured women. Even today, the beverage is personified in art as a female fairy, decked out in green.

Poster advertising absinthe.

ALBATROSS/ALAMY STOCK PHOTO

Absinthe appealed to Parisian women not just because it was an elegant drink or because its preparation often involved beautiful, intricately crafted absinthe spoons,[103] but because when they were stuffed into a corset, it was (and is) difficult to drink too much fluid. Being able to have a small amount of a drink that was as powerful as a glass of wine was just more efficient. Many Parisian women drank their absinthe neat to cut down the liquid further. Centuries away from the Gin Craze, women had their spirits drinking all figured out.

Ada Coleman's involvement in the London cocktail community wasn't limited to the American Bar at the Savoy. One of the perks of being one of Ada's beloved regulars—besides the fantastic drinks—was the chance of getting invited back to her home after the bar closed. She was known for throwing huge, lavish parties where scores of happy guests danced, sang, laughed and listened to music long into the night.

One person who wasn't invited was the other bartender at the American, a woman named Ruth Burgess. Not much is known about Ruth except for the legend that, although they worked at the same bar for years and years, Ruth and Ada did not get along. Allegedly, the two women never even worked a shift together. The story goes that when Ruth got hired at the American, she asked Ada to share some of her famous cocktail recipes, and Ada refused. After that, the two women never spoke again. (Again, this story is not verified. It's just as likely that a newspaper, seizing on a rumor of animosity between two women in a male-dominated industry, fabricated the report.) Even if they didn't get along, it is still amazing that one of the most important early cocktail bars was headed up by two women.

In 1925, the Savoy shut the American Bar down for renovations and announced the retirement of both Ruth and Ada. Ada

---

103 The traditional French way of preparing absinthe involves taking said absinthe spoon and placing it on top of a small glass of absinthe. Then, you place a sugar cube on top of the spoon and drip ice water over the sugar cube until it melts entirely into the drink.

was around fifty years old, and after she left the American, she never returned to bartending.

Ada Coleman passed away in 1966 when she was ninety-one. Looking back on her career, she estimated that she had poured a million drinks in her over twenty years behind the bar.

Ada is an icon in the world of cocktails and known as one of the most influential bartenders of all time. As of 2015, her most famous creation, the Hanky Panky, is still one of the world's best-selling cocktails, according to Drinks International. It was featured in *The Savoy Cocktail Book*, a book of recipes compiled by her replacement at the Savoy, Harry Craddock, in 1930. Craddock worked under Ada for five years at the service bar before the American closed for renovations. Bold of him to include her recipes in the book, considering that in the foreword, Craddock declared that "Wine was created for the solace of man, as a slight compensation, we are told, for the creation of woman..." I wonder if he was brave enough to express sentiments like that when Ada was his boss.

Ada Coleman is proof that women have an equal ability to make magic with a cocktail shaker, if only someone would give them the chance to do so. She wasn't unusual in her ability to make an incredible drink. She was unusual in her ability to do it in public. In a time when society was doing its damnedest to keep women making cocktails at home for free, Ada was given a shot (no pun intended) at making them for a celebrity clientele at one of the most famous bars in the world. Her talent ensured that her mark on the history of cocktails will never fade.

Soon, in America at least, political changes would force *everyone* to make their cocktails in private. Immense shifts in the country's drinking culture were on the way, and for women, things would never be the same.

9

GERTRUDE LYTHGOE, QUEEN OF THE BOOTLEGGERS

The 1920s

Prohibition.

This is usually the point in alcohol history that people associate with women. To be sure, there were many fascinating women rallying and organizing and protesting on behalf of the temperance movement. Many people even blamed women for Prohibition.

But that's not the whole story.

There were just as many, if not more, women on the other side of the fence. Women drinking in speakeasies, smuggling whiskey, making moonshine and even fighting in Congress for Repeal.

Temperance wasn't just happening in America. All over the world, temperance organizations battled to ban alcohol while new, modern women bobbed their hair, lit cigarettes and poured themselves a drink.

In fact, one of the most successful bootleggers[104] of the period didn't operate out of America at all. The throne of her booze

---

104   Named for a practice used by smugglers in the 1800s who kept alcohol concealed in their boots.

empire was in the Bahamas. Gertrude Lythgoe, or Cleo as she was called, was known as the Queen of the Bootleggers, and she made international headlines as she ran her high-quality whiskies over the ocean into the United States.

She was born on March 1, 1888, in Bowling Green, Ohio, to white English and Scottish parents.[105] Cleo was a nickname she got because people said she looked like Queen Cleopatra, and it stuck (perhaps some foreshadowing for the boozy direction her life would take). Her mother died when Cleo was young, and with her father unable to care for her and her siblings, she was sent to live with an aunt. It was clear from an early age that she was extremely smart. Known for having a quick mind, she loved school and reading.

Cleo grew into a tall, slender young woman and started her career working as a stenographer in San Francisco. She later moved to New York City to work for the American post of a London-based liquor exporter. When Prohibition began in 1920, it drastically changed the course of her life.

Let's back up first, though, and see how it came to be that alcohol got banned in America.

Before the 1920s, the temperance movement had been active in America for decades, and lots of different societies and organizations were dedicated to the cause. These reformers staunchly believed that if alcohol was illegal, some if not most of the evils of society would disappear. Increasing numbers of women were involved, especially after the formation of the WCTU. Those who suffered at the hands of alcoholic husbands were particularly supportive, including notable temperance activist Carrie Nation, who was known for attacking saloons with an ax.[106] Many of them believed it would be easier to ban alcohol than it would be to ban violence against women.

---

105   This will be important later.

106   Here's Carrie!

However, many temperance supporters of all genders didn't fully understand what exactly it was that they were supporting.

Most average Americans who supported temperance believed that the movement would close saloons, not prevent them from having a drink at home. They didn't quite get that temperance meant all alcohol would be banned everywhere. In fact, most Americans didn't even think that moderate drinking was drinking per se. The terms *drinking* and *drinker* brought to mind a sloppy, impoverished drunk who hung around saloons all day. Many believed that enacting Prohibition would only affect the lower classes and the places where they drank. Products like wine, cordials and sherry (upper-class beverages) and medicinal tonics were usually excluded from lists of reportedly dangerous intoxicants.

In the early 1900s, activists were also fighting for women's suffrage. Opponents of both movements purposely entwined the two, hoping people would believe that if women were given the right to vote, they'd take away the country's booze. Women's rights activists (like Susan B. Anthony) were adamant about keeping the two issues separate, but many female-led temperance organizations like the WCTU were successful in convincing the country that they spoke for all women. This caused breweries and distilleries to regard women as their enemy. The State of Texas had to bring a suit against the Texas Brewer's Association in 1915 for antisuffrage election manipulation (spreading disinformation, intimidating voters, rigging votes in favor of candidates who didn't support suffrage), and a year later, the US Brewer's Association was indicted for similar charges.

Hate groups like the Ku Klux Klan were big temperance supporters that rallied hard for Prohibition. To them, saloons and other drinking establishments encouraged people to mingle and cross gender, class and race divides. It's a pretty good rule that anything the KKK endorses is a bad idea.

On December 18, 1917, the Senate proposed the Eighteenth Amendment, which established the prohibition of alcohol. There was a lot of support for the amendment all over the country, even in wet strongholds like New York. People supported it for social reasons, believing that the abolishment of saloons would solve poverty and crime. Religious groups backed the amendment. There were also groups with an economic angle, like tea companies and soda fountain manufacturers, whose eyes turned into dollar signs at the thought of a thirsty country cut off from beer. In January 1919, when a thirty-sixth state approved it, the amendment was ratified as part of the US Constitution. A year later, in January 1920, America became a dry country.

America's Great Experiment had begun.

The same year, the Nineteenth Amendment also became part of the constitution, giving white women the right to vote. (Black and Native American women were not guaranteed that right until 1965.)

For many middle- and upper-class women, their lives didn't change much. They didn't drink out in public often anyway, and they definitely did not go to saloons. Most of them had an extensive stock of liquor and wine at home. But what Prohibitionists failed to consider was the strong connection between upper-class entertainment and sociability (an area controlled by women) and alcohol.

It's a terrible idea to underestimate the power of rich ladies and their parties.

So. It was now illegal to sell, import, transport and make alcohol, whether it was fermented beverages like beer or distilled drinks like whiskey. It wasn't illegal to *consume* it, though. Prohibition completely transformed the country's drinking culture, just not in the way anybody predicted. Everything went underground. Soon after Prohibition went into effect at the start of 1920, a robust illicit drinking scene exploded in America.

Because, of course, people still wanted to drink.[107]

---

107   Even prominent members of the WCTU still drank. Some of them were spokeswomen for Lydia Pinkham's Vegetable Compound!

For centuries, since European settlers colonized the country, American women's drinking culture was centered around domestic, private places. Now, the only place anyone could drink was in private. Prohibition ended up being one of the best things for drinking women in America because it turned the gendered rules of alcohol upside down and brought everyone to where women drank. To paraphrase a quote from the film *Watchmen*, I'm not stuck in here with you. *You're stuck in here with me.*

With the closure of all the public drinking spaces in America—saloons, pubs, hotel bars—came the time of the *speakeasy*. A speakeasy is any secret and illegal establishment that sells booze. Speakeasies during Prohibition ran the gamut between seedy and shabby, and elegant and upscale. But most ordinary Americans could not afford to regularly step into even the dingiest of speakeasies. See, Prohibition made drinking a vice for the wealthy. More than anything, it underscored class division in America, since most prohibition laws are more about *who* is prohibited.

There was still plenty of good-quality booze to be found in America, if you knew who to talk to and had the money to pay for it. This illegal alcohol was egregiously marked up because of the titanic disparity between the demand for it and the supply, plus the risk in either secretly distilling it or transporting it to the United States undetected by authorities. Customers might find themselves paying twenty-five dollars at a speakeasy for a bottle of champagne, which equals about three hundred and eighty dollars in 2020.

Along with the exorbitant drink prices, speakeasies often featured first-class entertainment. Patrons got to watch singers and dancers—some of international fame—while they sipped their expensive scotch. There were usually also full menus, with dining options equivalent to the finest restaurants in whatever city the speakeasy was in. In fact, speakeasies really gave hotels and restaurants a run for their money, even putting some out of business. Most rich people in America wanted to drink during their nights out, and for that, they had to go to a speakeasy.

Within a few years of Prohibition, there were thousands of speakeasies. These were usually concentrated in big cities like Chicago and New York City. It was said that Forty-Fifth Street in Manhattan was the wettest street in America.

To get in, patrons had to first find the speakeasy, which might be in the basement of a gorgeous mansion, a nondescript office building, a retail store, a tenement building, a restaurant, a rooming house or a tearoom. Then, they might have to knock twice on a sliding panel, ring a bell in a particular sequence or whisper a password or phrase to a shadowy face behind an iron grille to be allowed inside.

Unlike in pubs or saloons before Prohibition, there were lots of women to be found in speakeasies. In fact, for the very first time in history, men *wanted* women around when they were drinking. The presence of women made it less suspect to the authorities. During a press conference in 1924, Bishop Thomas Nicholson, president of the temperance organization the Anti-Saloon League, expressed his disapproval at how "drinking among women is rapidly increasing." Lois Long, a star reporter for the *New Yorker* in the 1920s, surprised her male editor with how much she could drink as she made her nightly rounds of the speakeasies (or *speaks* as she called them).

Speakeasies were the first places in American history to actually cater specifically to their female customers. Some decorated the place in a way that was meant to appeal to women. Some even hired attractive male bartenders. This, in particular, was a symptom of an interesting new development in American female sexuality.

Up until this point in history, women didn't date. If you were an upper-class woman, you might be roped into an arranged marriage. Or you might, along with women of the middle and sometimes lower classes, be courted. But the speakeasy, with its privacy and its encouragement of women's participation, helped to develop a brand-new (and scandalous) openness about female desire and sexuality. Women found themselves with a little more power in the romantic market. Dating and drinking at a speakeasy were two of the most popular hobbies of a new kind of American woman: the flapper.

Flappers were young women known for wearing shorter skirts (we're talking knee length, here), bobbing their hair, smoking cigarettes, drinking and generally flouting social norms. Helen Lowry wrote for the *New York Times* in the 1920s, saying of the flapper that "she is the first woman in history that has not been checked at home when man went forth alone in search of his pleasures. And because of her we have with us the most merry, least jaded nightlife yet."

But what if a woman couldn't afford to go out?

Well, she did the same thing that women do today: drink at home.

Prohibition contributed to the development of another American pastime: the cocktail party. The safest and cheapest place to drink illegal alcohol was in your own home. The middle class of 1920s America loved a cocktail party. Stores began selling tools and accessories for home mixology, like shakers, serving trays and cocktail glasses. Since middle-class Americans didn't have the money for a bottle of champagne, they usually drank lower-quality bootleg liquor. These spirits really needed to be mixed into a cocktail to be palatable, a cocktail being the best way to mask the harsh flavor. Hostesses didn't want their guests to take eye-watering sips of straight bathtub gin.

Prohibition forced an explosion of cocktail recipes. Girly drinks during this time included cocktails like gin rickeys (gin, lime juice and soda water) or gin fizzes (a similar drink, but with lemon juice and sugar). Highballs, which are just liquor (usually whiskey) and soda water (or maybe tonic water or ginger ale) served in a tall glass over ice, were popular drinks for everyone, no matter the gender.

Many female celebrities of the day had their own favorite drinks. Silent-film star Louise Brooks[108] loved an orange blossom, which was a very popular orange juice and gin cocktail during Prohibition, a precursor to the modern screwdriver. Brooks loved hanging out at the summer home of media mogul William Randolph Hearst and drinking with Hearst's mistress, actress Marion Davies. Davies was also a lover of orange juice cocktails, but she preferred to drink mimosas. She was part of a women's drinking club with actresses Norma and Constance Talmadge and screenwriter Anita Loos.[109] Davies was such an avid booze enthusiast that she imported an entire bar to her Santa Monica beach house. It was built in Surrey, England, in 1590 and, over three hundred years later, reassembled in California so Marion Davies could mix orange juice and champagne on it.

Mary Pickford—film star, producer and one of the founders of the Academy of Motion Picture Arts and Sciences—had a drink named after her made with rum, pineapple juice and grenadine. The Singapore sling, a classic cocktail still popular today, was invented at the Long Bar in the Raffles Hotel[110] in Singapore by Chinese bartender Ngiam Tong Boon. Originally, it was made with gin, cherry brandy, Benedictine, lemon juice, bitters and soda water. Pink in hue, the Singapore sling was crafted to be a girly drink, a way to hide the fact that the rich, white tourist women visiting the bar were drinking alcohol.

Someone needed to make all this booze.

There were many, many female moonshiners before Prohi-

---

108 Louise Brooks was a massive fan of gin. When asked why she retired from Hollywood, she replied, "I like to drink and fuck too much."

109 She penned the film *The Fatal Glass of Beer*.

110 The award-winning head bartender of which, at the time I am writing this, is a woman named Priscilla Leong.

bition, but the 1920s were truly their heyday. From distillers to transporters, it was believed that female bootleggers outsold men five to one. Some of them were well into old age, such as Margaret Connelly of Arkansas, who was in her nineties and made whiskey during Prohibition.

Many women became master smugglers. They transported booze beneath their skirts, in baby carriages and inside their blouses—places where male Prohibition enforcers wouldn't search. In some states, male agents were not allowed to search women at all, a rule which many smugglers took advantage of. Lots of smuggling rings specifically hired women because of this. One male Prohibition enforcer in Oklahoma declared, "We find the woman bootlegger the hardest to catch."

SCIENCE HISTORY IMAGES/ALAMY STOCK PHOTO

Women's clothes made for easy smuggling during Prohibition. Who needs pockets when you've got a bar under your coat?

By 1922, two years into Prohibition, female agents were finally being hired to counteract the problem. But it wasn't until seven years later in 1929 that the United States at last put a female officer on the Canadian border patrol who was able to search women entering the country. Within her first three months of work, she had uncovered almost seven hundred bottles of alcohol from under dresses and long coats.

A woman could make a lot of money with illegal booze in the 1920s. Some female bootleggers made $30,000 a year, which is about $450,000 in 2020. Women were so good at transporting booze that some authorities worried that they would develop a monopoly on the market. Those long, cumbersome dresses were finally good for something!

Women, especially if they were working-class, were specifically targeted by Prohibition enforcement agents. They were the ones most likely to be arrested over small amounts of alcohol. Most women who illegally distilled, transported and sold booze were working-class mothers trying to feed their families. But if they were white, these women were also the ones most likely to be pardoned or to receive reduced sentences because they pleaded for their children's welfare.

Like most women who got into the trade, Gertrude "Cleo" Lythgoe didn't set out to be a bootlegger, much less the queen of them.

After losing both a lot of money in the stock market and her job working for a liquor exporter with the passing of the Eighteenth Amendment, Cleo saw Prohibition as an opportunity. In her memoir, *The Bahama Queen*, she wrote, "I felt this was the only door of opportunity open... I couldn't lose any more and had everything to gain." She decided to get into the bootlegging game.

Over land, alcohol was usually smuggled with cars and trucks. Bootleggers traveled by night and concealed their cargo in trunks, under false seats and behind door panels. To get alcohol into the country in the first place, most of the time it was smuggled in by boat.

The islands of the Bahamas played a crucial role in the alcohol smuggling industry during Prohibition. For one thing, alcohol was still completely legal there. For another, it was very close to Florida, making it an ideal spot for rum-running. Nassau, the capital of the Bahamas, quickly became a bustling hub of booze smuggling.

Now, the definition of *booze* got a bit loose during Prohibition. With all the legitimate American breweries and distilleries shut down and there obviously being no regulation or official oversight for illegal alcohol, a lot of the booze that was available was only booze in a technical sense. Bootleggers often used denatured industrial alcohol, which was intended for things like antifreeze, not drinking. Denatured alcohol is mixed with chemicals that make it unfit for human consumption. Some bootleggers redistilled this industrial alcohol to get rid of the harmful elements, but even then, the moonshine sometimes still held poisons. It's estimated that at least ten thousand people died from drinking bad moonshine over the course of Prohibition.

Even if it wasn't poisonous, lots of the alcohol being poured in America during the 1920s was truly awful. There was no time to age it, and aging for years in wooden barrels is what gives good whiskey its color and much of its taste. Many bootleggers opted to artificially color their booze to make it look like decent scotch or whiskey. Just like the Gin Craze in 1700s England, it was easy to make ersatz gin by taking raw alcohol and flavoring it with juniper oil. Alcohol was sometimes watered down to make it go further.

This is what set the Queen of the Bootleggers apart.

Cleo Lythgoe did not smuggle fake whiskey. Her buyers could count on her to sell them the real deal. As she put it, "Everyone knows my liquor is the very best."

After Prohibition went into effect in America, the English liquor company Cleo worked for (she never revealed their name)[111] tapped her to keep the business going. They wanted her to help them supply alcohol to the United States through the Bahamas. Realizing that this might be the opportunity of a lifetime, she agreed to the venture and traveled down to Nassau from New York City.

Cleo set up shop on bustling Market Street and oversaw the establishment of the company's wholesale liquor business in Nassau. She organized all the shipments, found the buyers and managed the financials. When a ship arrived from Europe with her cargo, Cleo was there to supervise the off-loading and make sure the liquor was of the highest quality.

She moved into a room in the Lucerne Hotel, a place known as a bootlegger's headquarters. The place was always filled with both criminals and the journalists writing about them. Since it was a hotspot for bootleggers and smugglers making deals, incredible amounts of money flowed in and out of the hotel lobby. All the cash on hand certainly made the bartenders happy.

Right off the bat, Cleo ran into some trouble in the Bahamas. She was the first white woman with a wholesale liquor license there, and not everyone was happy about it. And at first, she found that there were distillers and businessmen who refused to work with her because she was a woman. It wasn't unusual to see bars and clubs in Nassau with *No Skirts* signs out front. To discourage people from working with her, Cleo's competitors spread rumors that she was an undercover agent with the Internal Revenue Service.

But Cleo refused to be intimidated. She tracked down one man who was bad-mouthing her products, pulled out the pistol she always carried and threatened to shoot him if she heard any more from him. As she says in her memoir:

---

111 It is believed that she worked with two scotch brands, Haig and McTavish. If this is true, then Cleo helped keep American drinkers sipping on two of the finest brands of scotch available at the time.

Well, I found him in a barber's shop with his face lathered and I just walked right in and told him I wanted to talk to him. I fetched him along to my office, and there I just warned him. I told him I'd put a bullet through him as sure as he sat there. He went away mighty quick.

Between her top-shelf liquor and her no-bullshit policy, before long, Cleo was a formidable figure in the smuggling industry.

While the temperance movement was spreading throughout the world, there was also a widespread effort to shake things up. In many different countries during the 1920s, *modern girls* (a term like America's *flapper girls*) were stepping out.

Japan had its own version with *moga* girls, women with bobbed hair, shorter skirts, cigarettes and cocktails. During the Taishō era in Japan, a brief period of liberal movements from 1912 to 1926, many women worked jobs outside the home and toasted to their newfound independence with a drink or two. The moga or modern girls were living symbols of Westernization, urban women who lived for themselves.

Modern girls also appeared in Germany and France, while China had the *modeng xiojie* or *modern miss*. In Scotland, while many men left to fight in the trenches of World War I, women replaced them both behind and in front of the bar, much to the chagrin of local officials. With their husbands away, women had more money and freedom to visit pubs.

In Mexico, women were taking up arms and joining the revolution—a decade of armed struggles that resulted in social reform and a new political system. Across the world, Russia was experiencing its own revolution and then a civil war, where the monarchy was overthrown and eventually replaced by the Soviet Union. Women joined the new Soviet workforce in the 1920s. They also joined the new urban drinking culture—legally and illegally.

The colossal shift to widespread industrialization in the previous century brought about a modern, urban drinking culture. In
the new Soviet regime, drinking was equated with masculinity.
Young boys were encouraged to drink because it was believed
that alcohol helped them develop their masculinity.

Drinking was equated with a man's status as a worker. But
even if she was also a worker, the ideal Soviet woman's domestic responsibilities required that she stay sober. The now
age-old idea that a drunken woman was a sexually promiscu-
ous woman meant that alcohol threatened female chastity and,
consequently, the structure of the working-class Soviet family.
Alcohol was thought to make the weak bodies of women even
weaker, something that could be passed on to their children.
(Despite the fact that many state distilleries employed children
and paid them in alcohol!) The Soviet regime was not prepared
to condone women drinking because it was not prepared to accept that women were deserving of equal rights as men.

The connection between drinking, masculinity and the status of a worker continued to depreciate working women, even
after the Bolshevik revolution established legal equality between
men and women in 1917.

However, this image of the chaste, sober Soviet mother was
not an accurate reflection of the lives of real Russian women
in the 1920s. With more money and freedom than their rural
counterparts, female factory workers were apt to be enthusiastic
social drinkers. Lower female literacy rates mean far less source
material to tell us the habits of women drinking (something that
was true in almost every country in the world). However, we
do know about some all-women drinking rituals during Slavic
holidays like *Semik*, where mill and factory workers got together
on the seventh Thursday after Easter to drink, sing and adorn
themselves with ribbons and flowers.

One of the new holidays in the revolutionary state was International Women's Day on March 8. The opportunities for

sanctioned drinking for women were few and far between, but
that day in particular was a highlight. There was a lot of drinking and a lot of dancing. Some women even smuggled alcohol
in their skirts to bring to work that day. A worker named Nata-
lia Nikolaeva was toasting and dancing in her apartment when
her downstairs neighbor marched up to knock on her door and
complain about the noise. She informed him that "This is none
of your business. Today is a woman's holiday; I will drink and
carry on and no one will forbid or do anything."

So despite what the government wanted them to do, Russian women were still drinking alcohol in the 1920s. And despite what the law allowed, Russian women were still making
it. The tradition of female bootlegging from the 1800s was still
going strong. By 1922, nearly every single rural household in the
country made some sort of illegal alcoholic beverage, whether
it was fermented or distilled. During World War I, cloth exports were suspended, which devastated the local textile and
flax trade, of which women were a large part. Jobless, many
women took their small-scale home brewing or distilling and
turned it into a business.

With a home still, a Russian woman could take thirty-five
pounds of flour and make about a gallon of *samogon*, which
meant *home brew*, at 25–30% ABV. One more distillation could
bring that percentage up higher. Samogon is very similar to
vodka. It was Russia's version of moonshine and made from
whatever ingredients were lying around a woman's kitchen.
Flour was common, but women also used other grains, potatoes
and beetroot, and sometimes flavored it with fruit or honey.

Throughout the 1920s, women made samogon and sold it out
of their homes and small stands to local restaurants and cafés.
Some even sold it covertly in factories to the workers. It is estimated that seventy percent of the Russian population drank
homemade booze during this time. Female bootleggers were
all over the country, selling their wares.

It was an appealing way to make a living for a lot of women. Disabled women were especially attracted to the trade, as it was something that could easily be done in the home with a minimum of heavy equipment.

Women in Russia at this time, even if they worked for a wage, were not considered real workers, which was the optimal thing for a person to be. Men were the real workers. *Samogonshchikis*, home brewers, were considered the enemy of real workers. Most female bootleggers were impoverished, single women trying to feed their families, but they were considered treacherous, degenerate and, worst of all, capitalistic.

In 1922, the Russian government launched an official campaign against the samogonshchikis. Bureaucrats exaggerated the purported threat that they posed to both the economy and the morality of Russian society. Tens of thousands of women, from teenagers to elderly grandmothers, most of whom were poverty-stricken, were arrested for either selling or distilling. For the economic crime of bootlegging, these women faced criminal consequences like fines, forced hard labor for up to a year, imprisonment and confiscation of property. There were so many arrests of poor women that, eventually, the law was eased for samogonshchikis who were just trying to feed their families.

Here's the thing. Yes, women were part of the temperance movements that were happening all over the world. But most of the women that were rallying for the end of alcohol were upper-class women. The lack of middle- or lower-class female support became one of the movement's biggest problems.

In Canada, the *Vancouver Sun* reported that "women cannot be counted upon for an instinctively prohibition vote." Canada had a brief wartime prohibition from 1918 to 1920, but without widespread female support, temperance activists never managed to get it reinstated.[112] Just like it did for American drinkers, Canada's Prohibition forced drinking into the home, where it was almost impossible to exclude women. Canadian speakeasies or *blind pigs* had lots of female customers, which fostered a slowly widening acceptance of women drinking in public.

Afterward, during the postwar years of the 1920s, many Canadian women were rethinking their role within the country's drinking culture. Influenced by glamorous American Hollywood role models like Marion Davies, more and more women—especially working-class ones—went to beer parlours (Canadian bars or taverns). But they weren't always allowed in. Many hotels and beer parlours still excluded single women as customers or servers. Ontario women were prohibited from serving drinks, even if they owned the place.

Women were still interested in drinking at home, too. In 1924, the first person out the door of Edmonton's new government liquor store was a woman with six bottles of Guinness tucked under her arm.

By 1923, Cleo Lythgoe was selling millions of gallons of whiskey a year.

But that was just a start. Cleo wanted her business to keep growing. In one of the smartest business moves she ever made, she decided to partner with another famous bootlegger, the legendary Bill McCoy. The phrase *the real McCoy* comes from the satisfaction that his customers had knowing that the booze they received was real whiskey, not nasty industrial alcohol mixed with artificial coloring in a moldy bathtub somewhere. A lot of that whiskey came from Cleo.

---

112   For nonnative people, anyway. Indigenous women in Canada were still subject to the atrocious Indian Act of 1876, which included a group of racist prohibitory alcohol laws. If you wanted to drink or possess alcohol, you needed to be a Canadian citizen. To be eligible for citizenship as an Indigenous person, you needed to demonstrate sobriety. Some sections of the Indian Act were not repealed for over a hundred years, until 1985.

She partnered with McCoy to smuggle enormous amounts of her whiskey (rye, scotch and bourbon) into the United States. The two usually took a ship from Nassau to Florida, where they commissioned small speedboats to transport cases of booze, between five and two hundred at a time. The United States had a three-mile jurisdictional limit from the shore, so three miles out, boats waited to be loaded with booze. Sometimes, Cleo accompanied McCoy and his crew all the way up to New Jersey.

McCoy recalled how hardworking Cleo was, describing to English reporter H. de Winton Wigley how she nearly ran him "ragged." Despite how much she demanded from him, McCoy greatly admired her. He told Wigley:

Nassau was not the best place in those days for attractive unprotected women, but though she was the former, she certainly was not the latter. Members of the rum mob who drew their own conclusions concerning her and then tried to operate accordingly, probably will recall the breath-taking fury she could show, and one or two must remember the pistol jammed into their ribs by way of making things clear. An able thoroughly competent girl was she; no twittery jane at whom one could make passes with impunity. She expected others to mind their own business as she attended to hers.

More than the government authorities, Cleo and McCoy were afraid of fellow bootleggers. Hijacking among smugglers was commonplace. For her own peace of mind, Cleo was never without her huge pistol. But all their risks paid off big, and both bootleggers amassed vast fortunes as a result of their partnership. Toward the end of her career, it's believed that Cleo was worth millions. (In the mid-1920s, one million dollars was the equivalent of nearly fifteen million dollars in 2020.)

Cleo Lythgoe was not only one of the most successful booze smugglers of the Prohibition era, she was also the most famous. Reporters claimed that she ran the world's largest international whiskey business (which was probably true). In 1923, that British reporter Wigley finished his interviews about her in Nassau and ran a story called "Cleopatra, Queen of the Bootleggers," and the name stuck.[113] By the autumn of that year, every reporter in the world wanted to interview her. Cleo became a media darling. New York journalist Robert Wigley (no relation to the English Wigley) described her as "...truly a wonderful personality. A woman of cultivated tastes, who can talk on books and who travels with the best music in her trunks, and shows such artistic taste in dress..."

PUBLIC DOMAIN

The Queen of the Bootleggers.

---

113   More than a dozen other women were given this title in various American newspapers, including another Cleo, an infamous Oklahoma bootlegger named Cleo Epps. You'll meet her in a couple chapters.

Cleo might have been forthcoming about her literary tastes, but she was elusive about more personal information. The newly crowned bootlegging queen was known for offering a different story about her upbringing whenever she was asked. Despite being born to English and Scottish parents, people who met her immediately wondered about her racial identity and wanted to know what part of the world she came from. Cleo indulged them all, concocting stories about being from countries like Greece, Russia, India or Egypt.

Cleo Lythgoe's face graced the pages of newspapers like the *Los Angeles Times*, the *New York Times* and the *Chicago Tribune*. Despite her being one of the world's most successful alcohol smugglers, reporters asked her the type of asinine interview questions women are still asked today. Instead of inquiring about her whiskey, they wanted to know why Cleo was single and what her love life was like. Silly reporters. Girls don't like boys, they like whiskey and money.

Cleo received droves and droves of letters, professions of love and marriage proposals from all across the globe. People adored her. They wrote to invite her to parties, express their admiration and even ask if she would like to meet their sons.

Soon, Cleo had reporters and photographers following her around all the time and recording her exploits. This attention was a huge pain in the ass for someone whose livelihood relied on stealth and secrecy. Besides being a target for mothers with lonely sons, Cleo was now a target for the authorities.

Where did Cleo's whiskey go when it reached the United States?

Wherever it went, there was a good chance that the person drinking it, serving it, singing about it, fighting for its legality or even confiscating it was going to be a woman.

The whiskey might have ended up at El Fey, a luxurious, upscale speakeasy located in Midtown Manhattan. El Fey was one of the most successful speakeasies in all of America during Prohibition, all because of its firecracker hostess.

Texas[114] Guinan was the most famous and popular speakeasy hostess in all of Prohibition New York City. In 1923, she was working as a Broadway actress when she attended an industry party at the Beaux Arts Hotel. Like many industry parties, it was boring as hell. To liven things up, somebody asked her to sing. She was so fun and entertaining that the manager of the hotel offered her a job as the mistress of ceremonies. Guinan accepted. Soon, she met businessman (and racketeer) Larry Fay. Larry wanted Guinan to host at his new speakeasy, El Fey Club.

She was an immediate hit at El Fey. Texas Guinan had found her calling.

As an ace hostess, she knew just who to invite to the club. The most important, rich, famous (or some combination of the three) personalities of the era came to have a drink with her. Mobsters, artists and high-society patrons rubbed elbows as they drank and watched the show. El Fey often featured beautiful dancing women, which helped to distract from the exorbitant prices of whiskey and champagne.[115] The Vanderbilts, the Morgans, the Chryslers, and celebrities like Rudolph Valentino all loved to drink there.

Guinan was all sass and sarcasm as she traded barbs with patrons and fostered an environment of mischievous camaraderie that customers adored. Heckling was tolerated and even encouraged. A constant stream of wisecracks, jokes, whistles and quips flowed forth from her painted lips. She was an expert at not only making her patrons happy and comfortable with their very illegal activity but also willing to be overcharged for just about everything.

---

114 So named because of her incredible riding and roping skills. Born in Waco, Texas, she had a great career starring in westerns as a female gunslinger before Broadway called to her.

115 Texas was known for concluding the dance performance by yelling, "Give the little girl a great big hand!"

Patrons could easily pick Texas Guinan out of the crowd. She was a striking white woman with a big, bleached coiffure, glittering dresses, mounds of pearls and, to top it off, a gleaming white smile. The hostess was usually found perched upon a tall stool in the center of the club's main room, making a lively racket with a noisemaker or a whistle. She greeted everyone with her loud and cheerful trademark line, "Hello, suckers!"

Texas Guinan had competitors named Helen Morgan and Belle Livingston, who were also white hostesses at glamorous speakeasies. But instead of an air of rivalry, many female speakeasy owners and hosts fostered fellowship and friendship with each other. When Belle Livingston was arrested for selling alcohol, Guinan sent an armored car to escort her home from jail.

El Fey was a huge financial success for Larry Fay, earning about eight million (in today's dollars) in the first seven months it was open. Guinan's speakeasy was so successful that she declared she'd be "nothing without Prohibition."

There were women who owned their own speakeasies, as well. In 1927, businesswoman, philanthropist and leader of the Harlem Renaissance A'Lelia Walker[116] converted one floor of her Harlem town house into a nightclub. This club (which was gay- and lesbian-friendly) became one of the city's hottest spots for artists, writers, actors, activists, politicians and musicians to drink, socialize and generally have a blast. Langston Hughes called her the Joy Goddess of Harlem.

If Cleo's whiskey wasn't served at Texas's club or A'Lelia Walker's town house, it might have filled the glass of Bessie Smith, one of the most famous Black performers of the era, as she traveled the country in her seventy-two-foot-long railroad car.

Bessie Smith, the Empress of the Blues, sang about women's

---

116   The only daughter of America's first self-made Black woman millionaire, Madam C. J. Walker. Walker developed a line of cosmetics and hair products specifically for Black women with her company, the Madam C. J. Walker Manufacturing Company.

freedom to drink, express their sexuality (she herself was openly bisexual) and, most importantly, still be worthy of respect. Respect was something Smith struggled to get, as many people in the industry considered her a bit too rough (meaning working-class).

"Big, brown and built high off the ground," as described by NPR writer Gwen Thompkins, Smith was a beautiful, tall woman. She earned her title as empress with her legendary voice and touched people with songs about everyday experiences and feelings. In an era where American women were actively participating in and shaping public drinking culture, Smith was the voice behind it.

One of her songs (that is still popular today) was originally titled "Me and My Gin." It's now known as "Gin House" or "Gin House Blues."

Stay 'way from me cause I'm in my sin
Stay 'way from me cause I'm in my sin
If this place gets raided, it's me and my gin

Don't try me nobody, cause you will never win
Don't try me nobody, cause you will never win
I'll fight the army, navy, just me an' my gin

Any bootlegger sho' is a pal o' mine
Any bootlegger sho' is a pal o' mine
'Cause a good ol' bottle o' gin will get it all the time

When I'm feeling high ain't nothing I won't do
When I'm feeling high ain't nothing I won't do
Keep me full o' liquor an' I'll sure be nice to you

I don't want no clo's an' I don't need no bed
I don't want no clo's an' I don't need no bed
I don't want no pork chops, jus' gimme gin instead

Despite being one of the greatest singers of the era, Bessie Smith did not get to perform as widely as she rightly should have. While Prohibition caused many social boundaries to dissolve, speakeasies were strictly segregated. There were exceptions, clubs in places all over the country that welcomed a mixing of races, and these were sometimes called *black and tan* clubs. Overall, however, most clubs catered to either an exclusively white or exclusively Black audience.

Prohibition coincided with a rise in white Americans' interest in Black entertainment and music, especially jazz. Many Black musicians and singers were asked to perform in white clubs, even though those same clubs would never welcome them in as a customer. Bessie Smith was passed over by the first wave of white establishments looking for Black entertainers. She did not strive to be palatable for a rich, white audience. Smith came from the working class and sang about the working class. According to womenshistory.org,

> Her "look" did not conform to the period's popular standard of prettiness. She was full figured and dark skinned. Her interpretation of the blues was deeply rooted in the African American culture that created it, imbuing it with an unmistakable authenticity. A little too authentic for early cross-over audiences.

By the end of the 1920s, however, Smith was the most successful Black performer in the country.

One unfortunate possibility for a bottle of Cleo's famous whiskey was confiscation under the direction of America's most powerful woman.

Cleo Lythgoe was a favorite target of Mabel Willebrandt, the United States' assistant attorney general. She was the highest-ranking woman in President Calvin Coolidge's administration, and it was essentially her responsibility to enforce Prohibition.

A small, white woman with dark hair, Willebrandt started out her career as a lawyer. Besides the fact that she was extremely qualified for the job, her appointment as assistant attorney general was widely believed to both reward American women for supporting Prohibition...and hold them accountable for it if it didn't work out. When she accepted the job, Mabel Willebrandt ended up as the public face of Prohibition. She had not been a part of the temperance movement before, but Willebrandt took her job seriously and set out to aggressively uphold the new law of the land. The *Washington Post* called her the "Fountainhead of Prohibition."

Just like that, Willebrandt was in charge of the drinking behavior of the nation. This duty was what millions of women were responsible for in their own homes, but for her it was on a federal, countrywide scale. And just like those women, Willebrandt was not given enough influence or resources to do it. Despite being the highest-ranking woman in the federal government, she had no official control over the budgets for Prohibition task forces or over their agents.

In order to arrest someone for violating the Eighteenth Amendment, an agent had to catch them in the act of making, selling or smuggling alcohol fit for consumption (again, the consumption itself wasn't a crime). After the amendment was passed, many states handed the responsibility to enforce it over to the federal government. This made it part of Willebrandt's job to stop smuggling and rum-running. The government struggled with Prohibition enforcement, and she knew why. The federal agencies tasked with it were wildly inefficient and barely coordinated with each other. Many local communities were not interested in cooperating with them.

Willebrandt pushed on, constantly asking for more resources

and help. She told a reporter, "Give me the authority and let me have my pick of three hundred men and I'll make this country as dry as it is humanly possible to get it." The reporter believed her, claiming that Willebrandt was the one person in Washington, DC, who could handle the task, calling her "the first legal lady of the land."

One of the institutions she bolstered specifically to combat Prohibition violations was the Coast Guard. Willebrandt coordinated busts on rum-running and bootlegging operations, which made Cleo Lythgoe's life a lot more difficult. Every smuggler had to concoct complicated new strategies.

Another female smuggler, and one of Cleo's competitors, was a woman named Marie Waite. The daughter of a Swedish father and a Mexican mother, she was called Spanish Marie. Waite was an imposing figure at six feet tall who ruthlessly commanded a flotilla of fifteen boats on her regular runs between Havana, Cuba, and Key West in Florida. To avoid the Coast Guard, Waite employed a convoy system. Four boats went out at a time, but only three held their precious liquid cargo. The fourth boat was loaded with guns and meant to hold off the Coast Guard while the others sped off into the night. All her boats were equipped with radios that picked up a signal from her (unlicensed, of course) radio station in Key West. She designed a code in Spanish to get information to her boat. Waite was said to be the fastest in the business.[117]

If they were caught by the Coast Guard, a bootlegger like

---

117   Eventually, the Coast Guard broke her code, and she was apprehended with her crew in March of 1928 in Miami. They caught her unloading 5,526 bottles, including whiskey, rum, gin, wine, beer and champagne. After her arrest, Marie pleaded with authorities that she needed to go home to take care of her children. She promised to return to court the next day. They agreed, though they didn't know that Waite had no children. She was never seen again, having disappeared along with her boats, her pistol and a whole lot of money.

Cleo or Marie Waite was not above trying to bribe her way out of trouble, a method that was often successful.

Willebrandt also organized countless raids on speakeasies. Texas Guinan was another favorite target of Willebrandt's agents. El Fey was raided so many times that Guinan capitalized on the publicity by wearing a necklace of gold padlocks and a diamond handcuff bracelet to her court appearances. Guinan considered herself a pawn for Prohibition politics,[118] and despite enjoying the publicity, she worked hard to fight the legal consequences and protect her staff of dancers and waitresses. When El Fey eventually got shut down, Guinan opened up the Del Fey only two blocks away. When that was busted, she opened the Texas Guinan Club on West Forty-Eighth Street. Raids were such a regular occurrence for her that Guinan wrote a song to serenade her patrons with after each one.

The judge said, "Tex, do you sell booze?"
I said, "Please don't be silly.
I swear to you my cellar's filled
With chocolate and vanilly!"[119]

Try as she might, Willebrandt had a tough time keeping Texas Guinan down. In 1926, Texas opened the 300 Club at 151 West Fifty-Fourth Street in Manhattan, which was immediately successful and became one of the most glamorous speakeasies of its time. The place was packed with beautiful showgirls, glittering socialites and well-appointed celebrities of the day. Dorothy Parker and Mae West were regular customers there. Champagne, laughter and diamonds sparkled in every corner.

Whenever she was arrested, Guinan's explanation was always

---

118   She liked to say that "some people are so narrow-minded that their ears touch in the back."

119   From Glenn Shirley's biography of Guinan, titled *Hello, Sucker!*

that her customers brought their own alcohol and that she was not in control of them drinking their personal supply. According to her, the staff of the 300 Club never touched booze. It was a ridiculous claim, but one that was tough to disprove. Guinan never personally had to pay any fines or spend any time in jail. About a year after it opened, however, the 300 was raided by Willebrandt's agents for the last time. Guinan escaped charges, but the club never recovered.

Mabel Willebrandt eventually caught up with Cleo, too. She didn't have to work too hard to track the Queen of the Bootleggers down. Thanks to the relentless paparazzi who were desperate to see what Cleo was up to at all times, her whereabouts and travel plans were rarely a secret. This forced Cleo to work extra hard to keep her operations unseen. In 1925, some of her workers were caught and arrested for smuggling. Authorities nabbed Cleo herself in Miami shortly afterward. She was transported to New Orleans and arrested for violating the Eighteenth Amendment.

Cleo had her own creative excuse for the authorities. She claimed that the whiskey those workers had was hers, yes, but that it had been *stolen* by them. Her story posited that she was not a smuggler, but an innocent *smugglee*. Cleo's laughable explanation was not as successful as Texas Guinan's was, though. Prohibition enforcement agents did not believe her and, worse, could prove that she was guilty. The bootlegging queen was finally caught. She decided to make a deal.

Cleo's offer to the Prohibition agents was that if they let her go, she would turn witness against other smugglers. Cleo's deal was accepted, although historians don't know who she ratted out. The Queen of the Bootleggers was free.

Instead of heading back to the Bahamas to pick up where she left off, Cleo Lythgoe decided to retire. Bill McCoy pleaded with her to reconsider. He wanted her to run away with him, but she refused. Cleo told reporters asking about her retirement in 1926, "I've stood on my own two feet, and I'm ashamed of nothing. I don't need a man to tell me what to do... I'm not getting married."

By the end of the twenties, many of America's most important pro-alcohol female players were off the board. In the face of widespread calls for Prohibition Repeal, temperance organizations worked to project the idea that women were still universally against alcohol.[120] Many politicians supported Prohibition and counted on women to continue to uphold it. But America was getting rather sick of being a dry country, and one woman was getting rather sick of temperance organizations being the mouthpiece for female politics.

When Prohibition was passed, Pauline Sabin was a fabulously wealthy and influential official with the Republican Party. She was the founder of the Women's National Republican Club and had always publicly supported Prohibition. As the years went by, Sabin, along with many of the rich, white Republican women in her social circle, realized that the promises of Prohibition were not being kept. Organized crime rates were up, and so were alcohol-related deaths. Prohibition did not stop people from drinking. It stopped many people from drinking *safely*.

In 1927, the Women's National Republican Club surveyed its members for their opinions on Prohibition. The overwhelming majority of the women were against Prohibition and unhappy

---

120 Even Mabel Willebrandt, after helping bring down infamous boot-leggers like Al Capone and Roy Olmstead and overseeing tens of thousands of convictions, retired in 1929. She caused quite a stir by subsequently taking a job as a lawyer representing Fruit Industries, a group of California's biggest grape-growing companies. One of these companies' most popular products was grape concentrate, used by many to ferment into wine. For the next few years, Willebrandt defended Fruit Industries' right to sell such a product. She then moved on to defend other, non-alcohol-related companies and clients.

with the way it had changed the country. Many, including Sabin, were concerned about their sons drinking bad bootlegged liquor and falling ill.

While there were many women across the country who supported Prohibition (the WCTU was still going strong), it was becoming apparent that the majority of women in any class did not. The idea that American women were a political bloc of temperance idealists was completely removed from reality. Most women who drank did so in moderation, which infuriated temperance activists. These female drinkers proved that alcohol wasn't inherently addictive or ruinous. Sabin herself was a light drinker, with quite an impressive repository of high-quality wine and liquor at her home in New York City.

She decided that things needed to change.

In 1928, a year after the Women's National Republican Club realized that most of their members didn't support Prohibition anymore, Sabin shocked the country when she publicly announced her mission to get the Eighteenth Amendment repealed.

Sabin declared that, besides the risk that poisonous moonshine posed to her teenage sons, Prohibition encouraged a disregard for the law and the enforcement of it infringed on American civil rights. A year later, in 1929, she surprised everyone again with her resignation from the Republican National Committee. The next day, Sabin launched her campaign to end Prohibition.

Along with a group of fifteen other women, she outlined a plan. Sabin used her considerable network of contacts across the country to drum up support and publicity for the cause. She wrote pamphlets to distribute their mission, which promoted respect for the law and moderation with alcohol, instead of complete abstinence.

Her group became the Women's Organization for National Prohibition Repeal, or WONPR. (Another organization whose name I will shorten for both my sake and yours.) In a battle of the initialisms, WONPR went head-to-head with the WCTU. Sabin and her colleagues were dedicated to showing that the WCTU did not—despite their claims—speak for all American women.

Sabin realized that anti-Prohibition women were a silent majority and crusaded for them to get politically active and use their new right to vote. She encouraged women to get involved and informed at a time when women's votes were wanted but their opinions weren't. At this time, while women were allowed to vote, they were not allowed to serve on juries. Women were expected to lend their political support for things, just not have a hand in them once the laws were enacted. But Sabin insisted on having a hand in things. She wanted an organization that welcomed women's opinions and ideas.

Soon, WONPR was nationwide. Never underestimate a group of well-off and pissed-off mothers. They formed a national advisory council of women from every state, and each state had an advisory council that directed local campaigns. There were no dues in WONPR, as everything was run by volunteers. Politically neutral, it had a single focus: end Prohibition.

That's right. It wasn't a group of hard drinkers, bootleggers, smugglers or cocktail enthusiasts that had suddenly become Prohibition's most powerful opponents, it was a legion of mothers. Alcohol's greatest ally was now a formidable and elegantly coiffed host of mostly middle- and upper-class housewives.

Within a year, WONPR had written and advanced a series of proposals to amend the United States Constitution that stipulated regulation of alcohol instead of abstinence. In February 1930, Sabin appeared on the first day of a series of congressional hearings about alcohol laws to, in her words, "refute the contention that is often made by dry organizations, that all the women of America favor national Prohibition."

She spoke passionately about the increases that the Eighteenth

Amendment had brought to crime, the exorbitant cost of inefficient enforcement, the growing prison population, the death rate from poisonous alcohol, rising rates of teen drinking and increased dissatisfaction with the law. Sabin made a great case that total abstinence from alcohol was an impossible thing to ask from the country. She even detailed personal experiences she had with politicians who drank in private and supported Prohibition in public. As a prominent member of the New York City elite and as a woman who had been involved in politics for over a decade, Sabin had a lot of experience to draw from. She argued for an end to the ridiculous hypocrisy and for a sensible set of regulations to replace it.

After the hearings, WONPR took on the WCTU directly, using verified statistics to disprove what the WCTU claimed about the ostensible successes of Prohibition. By the end of 1931, WONPR had over 400,000 members, more than the WCTU had ever had in its fifty years of existence. They came from every single state, and most of them were completely politically inexperienced.

WONPR was not advocating for a boozy free-for-all in the streets; they were more pro-alcohol-legislation than they were pro-drink. But they wanted full Repeal. WONPR was not interested in modifying the Eighteenth Amendment at all. They wanted it gone, completely.

Sabin traveled all over America to give interviews and speak on the radio. She cited facts and figures to make her case, detailing how between 1920 and 1930, federal spending increased from 3.7 million to 29 million dollars because of Prohibition enforcement, and how alcohol-related deaths had increased three hundred percent. Sabin also made sure to travel to areas known for Prohibition support and open a WONPR chapter there. She was even seen in movie theaters all over the country, declaring her mission in the newsreels.

Sabin also worked hard at something no male politician could compete with: social lobbying. She weaponized female socializing and the fancy dinner party. Members of WONPR held receptions, afternoon teas and formal dinners for the wives of congressmen. Many an influential political wife was convinced of the case for Repeal over plates of tiny sandwiches and cookies.

WONPR also went to work on the congressmen themselves. At their 1930 convention, the WONPR members voted unanimously to mail their thoughts to President Herbert Hoover and the leaders of Congress and each major political party. The next year, WONPR sent a letter to every single senator and congressman. This letter asked directly if the recipient would vote for a bill to send the question of Prohibition Repeal to state conventions. WONPR was savvy: they didn't ask if the recipient was wet or dry (shorthand for whether or not you supported or opposed Prohibition), only if he would allow the American people to decide. Almost sixty percent responded that yes, they would. The other forty percent were named at the WONPR executive committee meeting, which was sort of like being called out on Twitter, just much, much slower. WONPR members were directed to vote against the men that were named in the upcoming 1932 elections. These men now had a political target painted on their backs.

WONPR rallied the support of the American public, as well. In November of 1931, they founded the Anti-Prohibition Institute and an associated school with the goal of educating speakers on the mission of Repeal. With this institute, WONPR launched a lecture series to carry the Repeal movement to organizations and clubs all over the country. WONPR also formed alliances with other groups that supported Repeal, like the American Hotel Association and the American Federation of Labor.

Sabin understood the power of branding and merchandise. A woman could buy a WONPR-branded pin, matchbook, silk scarf, thimble, powder puff case or even a cover for her spare tire.

Well-designed merchandise made supporting Repeal look cool.

WONPR was extremely effective, and their movement spread like wildfire. Soon, WONPR was the loudest voice for women in America. In order to change their image of a group for elite society women, they conducted a survey to show that WONPR members were thirty-seven percent housewives, nineteen percent clerical workers and fifteen percent industrial workers.

After her old friends in the Republican Party refused to include Repeal in their platform, Sabin appeared at the 1932 Democratic National Convention.[121] The Democrats went on the record for outright Repeal, and soon, Franklin Roosevelt was nominated as the party's candidate. WONPR urged their mas-

---

121   But did not get to speak there.

sive membership to only vote for congressmen that supported Repeal, no matter what their party.

That year, Pauline Sabin made the July 18 cover of *Time* magazine. The article's author doubted Sabin's ability to bring about Repeal, but she wasn't finished yet.

As the 1932 election neared, Sabin pulled a masterful maneuver and undermined the WCTU at their own game. She declared it was WONPR that supported temperance, not the WCTU. True temperance, not unrealistic abstinence. Sabin positioned Repeal as the position for the reasonable American citizen.

Roosevelt won the election in a landslide. After the election, wet politicians had a majority in both the House and the Senate. WONPR didn't let up the pressure, though. Some members of Congress supported changes to Prohibition, not full Repeal.

In 1933, the Senate proposed a modification to the Eighteenth Amendment. Pauline directed all the WONPR members, who by now numbered a million and a half women, to contact their senators and insist that they vote against it. After a political battle, the Senate finally passed the bill of Repeal, and the House soon followed.

On December 5, 1933,[122] American Prohibition was finally over.

Texas Guinan did not live to see it. She died a month earlier, still declaring it was Prohibition that had made her career. A'Lelia Walker also passed away before Repeal, surrounded by champagne at a Long Island birthday party in 1931. Bessie Smith's career was dwindling in 1933, although just a couple of weeks before Repeal, she recorded the song "Gimme a Pigfoot and a Bottle of Beer."

Send me 'cause I don't care,
blame me 'cause I don't care
Gimme a pigfoot and a bottle of beer

---

122   Now known as Repeal Day, a holiday celebrated at many bars even today.

It was one of the last songs Bessie Smith recorded before she died in a car crash in 1937.

After Repeal, Mabel Willebrandt ended up in private practice, never again defending (or prosecuting) anything alcohol-related.[123] WONPR had a final celebratory dinner two days after Repeal, and Pauline hopefully toasted her own victory with a glass of hard-won champagne.[124]

And what happened to the Queen of the Bootleggers, the woman who made sure cocktails could still be poured during America's dry years?

Cleo Lythgoe spent the rest of her life enjoying the fortune she'd amassed. She avoided the public eye as much as possible and lived alone in various luxury hotels all across the country. After years of being hounded by the press, Cleo wanted to tell her own story. Her memoir was published in 1965.

Her favorite hotel was the glamorous Hotel Tuller in Detroit, and Cleo ended up staying there for twenty-five years. In June 1974, she passed away in Los Angeles at the age of eighty-six. It is said that the flags in Nassau flew at half-mast for days to commemorate her.

After Repeal, some American states continued to enforce their own Prohibition, and the country wasn't entirely free from it until 1966.[125] But thanks to the tireless work of over a million WONPR members, the United States could drink again.

Because of women, drinking culture survived thirteen years of Prohibition.

In most books about the history of alcohol, women are only mentioned in reference to the work of the temperance move-

---

123   She spent the rest of her career working with aviation companies. This sparked a passion for flying, and she eventually became a pilot. Willebrandt mentored and supported young female pilots, including Amelia Earhart, whose round-the-world flight Willebrandt helped sponsor.

124   Their one goal achieved, WONPR dissolved after 1933.

125   Mississippi was the last state to repeal their prohibition laws.

ment, the WCTU, and how they supported abstinence. Many people still blame Prohibition on women. Over a hundred years after the WONPR fought to show that temperance was not the preference of most American women, that is still the story being told. But in reality, women were the ones who kept drinking culture alive, whether it was at-home cocktail parties or speakeasies, and expanded who was welcome in it. Women won Repeal.

Whether they were drinking it, singing about it, serving it, rallying in favor of it or supplying the entire country with it, women were alcohol's greatest ally during Prohibition.

Over the next two decades, there were still many alcohol-related cultural and political battles. Women fought them in beer halls, behind the bar and, in the case of the next woman you'll meet, up onstage.

10

TEQUILA, TROUSERS AND THE LEGACY OF LUCHA REYES

The 1930s and 40s

In the 1930s, Mexican women were enjoying more freedom outside the home. One thing they were still not allowed to enjoy outside the home, however, was a drink. Which is especially unfortunate, because after the Mexican Revolution of the next-to-previous decade, they really deserved one.

Female contributions to the revolution, which lasted roughly from 1910 to 1920, were some of the catalysts for a shift in women's rights. Their work as soldiers, activists and journalists helped push the country to treat them more equally. In 1922, they were given the right to vote in local elections, and by the 1930s, women could finally sign legal documents and contracts on their own.

The Mexican Revolution prompted the advancement of women's rights, but Mexican women were still clashing with repression and societal double standards in the 1930s and 1940s. This gender disparity was easy to spot in the country's public drinking culture, where women, whether they were single or married, were not welcome. Their drinking culture was largely a private one.

Alcohol was closely associated with masculinity in Mexican

culture. The local bars, called cantinas, were important community spaces reserved for men. Sometimes implicitly, sometimes
explicitly. Up until the 1980s, the owner of a cantina could legally prohibit women from stepping foot inside.

Women did work in cantinas as servers, food vendors or entertainers. But they were not encouraged to actually hang out there
and drink. Cantinas were not places for *proper* or *good* women
to go. An autonomous, drinking woman was thought to indicate a lack of male control over his household. Drunkenness was
considered to be shameful for Mexican women, mostly because
it might disrupt their domestic responsibilities as mothers and
wives. Sound familiar yet?

There were some cantinas owned and operated by women (in
the tradition of the pulquerias that came before). Overall, however, they were a masculine space, and the beverage of choice
there was a masculine drink: *tequila.*

Tequila is a distilled spirit made from the agave plant. Just as
champagne can only be made in the Champagne region of France,
tequila can only be made in the Mexican state of Jalisco.[126] And
as we've seen with so many other cultures and their respective
types of booze, tequila was closely associated with the Mexican
idea of manliness. Both in real life and in the movies, it was the
drink for tough guys.

In alcohol advertisements, however, it was women holding the
bottle. Whether it was beer or tequila, beautiful women were
used to sell booze. Their accommodating smiles were featured
in magazine ads for beer brands and graced the months of tequila calendars. Women were not pictured drinking the alcohol, just holding it or offering it to a man (or men). There was

---

126   Mezcal, another spirit made from the agave plant, is similar. It can only
      be made in certain designated regions of Mexico, though most of it
      is made in Oaxaca. Both spirits are made with agave, but the kinds of
      agave used and distilling processes are very different. Mezcal is characterized by a smoky flavor that tequila does not have, which comes from
      roasting the agave in underground pits.

one type of woman in particular that was regularly featured in these ads: the *china poblana*.[127]

First appearing in the 1900s (around the same time as women began to be used as props in booze ads) the china poblana was quiet and obedient, and she certainly did not drink. She was the counterpart of the *charro*, a sexy and rugged horseman character that frequently appeared in Mexican films in the 1930s and 40s. He fought bad guys, saved the day and celebrated it all over some tequila with his buddies. The china poblana, wearing a beautifully embroidered blouse and skirt, was his companion. She didn't say much, instead communicating in a silent language of adoring looks and pleasant smiles. In these alcohol ads, the china poblana chuckled over the charro's drinking adventures, but she did not partake in them. She happily served the booze but did not drink. Soon, the china poblana would be the ideal of Mexican femininity.

This ideal did not quite match up with reality, though. Women in Mexico, as they had in every country since that jackass Hammurabi came up with his code, clashed with the expectation to be quiet, compliant and sober. No one exemplified this struggle more than Mexico's greatest singer, Lucha Reyes.

Lucha was born May 23, 1906, in Guadalajara, Jalisco, the tequila capital of the world. Today, she is known as the queen of mariachi music.

Born María de le Luz Flores Aceves, her family moved to Mexico City when she was seven years old. Her mother had taken care of Lucha and her siblings by herself ever since their father had died when Lucha was a baby. By the time she was thirteen, Lucha was singing and performing in theatrical revue shows to help her mother support the family. The next year, in 1920, Lucha moved north to Los Angeles to develop her talent as a soprano singer.

---

127   This originally referred to a style of dress worn by women in the state of Puebla.

She developed her skills at the same time as a new entertainment medium was gaining in popularity: the radio. The rise of radio caused the demand for singers and songwriters to grow rapidly. This, combined with an emerging sense of national identity and new respect for the peasant class in the wake of the Mexican Revolution, formed a market for music about the everyday, working person.

Enter *canción ranchera*.

Canción ranchera was a Mexican genre of music with lyrics that focused on rural, working-class life. Before the revolution, the songs were usually only heard in cantinas and pulquerias. After the revolution, the genre became hugely popular. With the spread of radio, professional canción ranchera singers began to appear. They were seen as heroes, adored for their ability to sing the heartaches and hardships of the common people. They were also all men.

While canción ranchera was gaining popularity in 1920s Mexico, Lucha was touring the United States as a part of a traveling musical Mexican tent show with fellow singer Nancy Torres.[128] After nine years of performing in America, one abusive marriage and a miscarriage, Lucha was ready to return to Mexico City and try her hand at something new.

In Korean homes for centuries, making alcohol was women's work, as was the fermentation of all kinds of things like kimchi and soy sauce. Advances in distilling and brewing technology were all driven by women.

Ūmsik timibang,[129] which was the very first cookbook penned by a female author in the history of East Asia, featured detailed

---

128   Some historians suggest that Nancy and Lucha were lovers. Even if they weren't, most historians agree that Lucha was bisexual and that she did not attempt to cover up this fact about herself. There is speculation that she had an affair with legendary artist Frida Kahlo.

129   *Recipes for Tasty Food.*

alcohol recipes. Written by Korean noblewoman Chang Kye-hyang in 1670, this book is particularly special because, thanks to a Confucian patriarchal culture that discouraged women from reading or writing or doing anything of note, finding published work by women during Chang's time is rare.

There is a whole family of Korean rice alcohol, and most of them start the same way: with women washing, soaking and steaming rice. *Makgeolli* is the oldest of such drinks. It's a cloudy, fizzy liquid, with a tart taste and a creamy mouthfeel that's similar to horchata. To make makgeolli, women steamed the rice, then mixed it with water and *nuruk*, which is a wheat cake that acts as a fermentation starter. Once the ingredients were all mixed, the resulting liquid was left to ferment.

If the women stopped there, they had a batch of makgeolli. But if they filtered the makgeolli, it became clear and refined *yakju*. If the yakju was distilled, it became *soju*. Soju is clear and completely colorless and can end up being anywhere from 17–53% ABV. Rice can really do it all. Makgeolli, yakju and soju fall under the umbrella of *sool*, the Korean word that represents all the country's different types of booze.

Fermenting and distilling sool was a long-standing female tradition in many Korean homes. Often, women made alcohol to sell outside of the home, too. *Jumo* was the Korean word for a woman who ran a makgeolli shop. But as the Japanese Empire gradually took over Korea starting in the 1900s, female domestic brewing and distilling was soon under assault. By 1934, making alcohol at home was banned outright.[130] Legal brewing had to take place in a factory, and all alcohol was taxed.

That didn't stop Korean women. Like their counterparts all over the world, women kept making alcohol, even when it was illegal to do so. Sometimes, they kept it for family use or gave it away to neighbors. Often they sold it, turning their kitchens

---

130   This ban wasn't lifted until 1990.

into Korean shebeens. If the police caught on, the women bribed them with money or with some of their delicious, illicit booze.

Meanwhile, in South Africa, female brewers were also dealing with legal trouble as the result of colonization. As in Korea, it too was a bunch of bullshit.

In 1908, nine years after the 1899 law prohibited the sale of liquor to native Africans, the Native Beer Act was passed. The 1899 act had still allowed the sale of native beer (sorghum beer, utywala) by native women, but the new Native Beer Act completely monopolized the sale of this, too. In urban areas, the only place any beer could legally be sold and consumed was in a white-owned beer hall. To top it off, only men were allowed inside. Now, native African women were totally forbidden access to all alcohol and places that served it.

Another liquor act was passed in 1928 that extended government control over the alcohol industry into the countryside. Starting in January 1929, all home brewing and drinking of utywala—a dietary staple for many rural people—was prohibited. As per usual, white authorities believed brewing and drinking beer made women less controllable and caused them to neglect their domestic labors. A woman *might* be able to brew on private land…but only if she had the permission of the white man who occupied it.

By 1929, the only place a native African man could legally get a drink was the beer hall, the profits from which were largely being channeled into the salaries of white bureaucrats, which fostered more oppression of Black workers. It was a vicious system that managed class, race and gender oppression in one fell swoop.

Black women in South African provinces no longer had any control over the beer industry at a time when brewing and selling beer was one of the only options for a woman to support herself. Those living in places like Natal (a southeastern coastal province) in the 1920s had no rights to private property and were largely excluded from the political process.

These women continued to brew in secret but quickly became targets for the police. White officers often came to homes and broke down doors in the middle of the night. They dug up floors and damaged furniture and houses, all while sexually harassing the women who owned the homes in the process. Thousands of gallons of illegal alcohol were seized this way and destroyed.[131]

Before long, the beer hall became a symbol of Black female oppression.

In the spring of 1929, a beer boycott began in the harbor city of Durban. The movement spread into the countryside, supported by thousands of Black male migrant workers sick of being forced to drink in beer halls. By May, scores of native women joined in, and the rage that had been—ahem—brewing for decades spilled out. Women marched down village streets while chanting war songs before they raided the beer halls. The female protesters sometimes even fought the men inside who were drinking or serving.

The Industrial and Commercial Workers Union (founded in Cape Town in 1919) was a trade-union-based political movement that was extremely popular in the area. They had a women's auxiliary, and its members gathered in Durban to throw stones at the beer hall there. They armed themselves with *sjamboks* (heavy leather whips) and clashed with police officers.

The protests continued into June and kept escalating. Thousands and thousands of people joined in. Ma-Dhlamini, one of the organizers of the women's auxiliary, terrified police officers with her ferocity as she protested and fought. By the end of the

---

131   The only support those who were raided got came from other women. Brewers, especially single ones, were often part of mutual aid networks where they coordinated prices with one another and exchanged information about customers. When a woman was busted by the police, her fellow brewers supported her in the aftermath.

month, six Africans and two white officials were killed. One hundred and twenty people were injured.

As the situation grew in intensity, gatherings of the Industrial and Commercial Workers Union were banned by officials. But the protests and boycotts successfully continued for the next *eighteen months*. They kept spreading. Soon, the protests reached farther out into rural areas, and the task of maintaining them fell entirely to the women's auxiliary.

In September, the women's auxiliary members collected funds from the Industrial and Commercial Workers Union and left Durban. They used the money to travel around the area, marshaling and organizing support for the beer protests. Thanks to their efforts, protests in rural towns and villages communicated and organized with each other. Demonstrators across the area unified under one ideology: legalize home brewing, and close those goddamn beer halls.

Acute economic pressure contributed to the unrest. Many men did not earn enough to cover their family's needs even before they stopped off to overpay at the local beer hall. Some spent half of their daily wages on beer that their wives could have brewed at home for a small fraction of the cost.

To make matters worse, an awful drought caused the 1929 harvests to be abysmal. Many working-class people fell into dire financial straits. The areas hit the hardest were where protests sprang up the fastest. In the town of Glencoe, protesting women mixed their cries for the right to brew with cries of starvation. When these laws were passed, beer was still an essential part of the diets of many native South Africans, especially those living in rural areas. It was as if the government told native women that they could no longer make bread.

The beer hall protests ignited anger over other economic cruelties that native women were facing. Their wages—when they could find a job at all—were far, far smaller than men's, yet feeding a family was seen as a female responsibility. As we've seen in cultures all over the world, women were given responsibilities but not the power or resources to tend to them. Many protesting women stressed that the money they made from brewing was what fed their children and sent them to school.

Not all women were fighting for their families, though. A portion of the protesters joined in the raids on the beer halls to fight against sexual discrimination. They didn't just want to brew. These women wanted to be able to drink and, more importantly, be allowed into these community spaces. Drinking meant social power. One raid in the town of Ladysmith consisted of female protesters forcing their way into the beer hall and seizing all the alcohol inside.

No matter what they were protesting, women of all ages were involved. Teenagers and old women alike stood together to fight for their rights. In fact, there were quite a lot of elderly women involved. Many of them organized and discussed their protesting plans in church and at prayer meetings. Some women gathered to pray and sing hymns before they raided the beer halls. If any preachers disapproved of their activities and tried to preach sobriety to these women, well, they got protested, too.

As the movement continued to spread, women who participated in them prepared to battle. Days after the first protest in the town of Weenen (which was two hundred strong), four women were sent to meet with the local authorities at the beer hall. The magistrate was horrified when he saw they were all armed with spears. The meeting did not go well. Unhappy, a group of around seventy women returned ten days later for a raid on the Weenen beer hall.

The authorities were not dismayed simply because they were afraid of getting hit with a spear. (Although, that was certainly a concern.) This was a time when femininity for a woman of any race meant being obedient, submissive and demure. Militarism was a male pursuit, just like drinking. Seeing a huge group of armed women ready to battle was a shock. The beer hall protesters were defying every expectation of female behavior.

And these women weren't just armed. Most of them had
thrown off all symbols, traits and behaviors that marked them
both as sexual inferiors and as colonized people. Many were
wearing *mtshokobezis* (cow tails), feathers and men's loin cover-
ings while they held a stick or spear in each hand. They chanted
war songs, shouted, used weapons, mustered and marched in formation. So much of drinking history all over the world shows
men seizing control of alcohol and the spaces it was drunk in.
The women of these towns were seizing it back.

And yes, it was the women doing it. Men, white or Black,
did not overtly support the protests in any of the rural towns
where they took place. One protest leader shouted, "The men
have failed, and we women will show them what we can do."

The protests lasted for months and months. Women picketed
the beer halls, physically preventing men from entering them.
Sometimes the protesters broke in, marched through the hall,
smashed the windows and attacked the men inside. In these
cases, the protesters sometimes succeeded in driving the men
out. When authorities in Newcastle brought out a fire hose to
clear the protesters with, the women seized the nozzle and directed the spray back at the officials.

When authorities tried to meet with them, the women refused
to give their names, only referring to themselves as Trouble or
Drink. It was unprecedented to have a group of native women
confront white authorities en masse, especially without a male
chief or representative to speak for them. A protest leader named
Matobana Majora declared, "We are now the men."

Two days after women in Estcourt were arrested, protesters
swarmed the prison to break them out. White residents nearby
reported that the force of the marching, stamping and dancing
from the protesters shook the ground. Women in some towns
created organizations whose members all contributed money to
pay the fines of any who were arrested.

Through all of this, women kept brewing. Many made mead,
which wasn't technically included in the legal description of na-

tive beer. Beer made from honey could be brewed and drunk openly. But many, many more kept brewing utywala. In Ladysmith, police who attempted to raid brewers were tackled by women as they seized and loaded casks of beer into trucks.

The protests finally forced beer halls in towns like Weenen and Ladysmith to close. Brewing permits were issued to some women, but this did not solve the problem nor address their demands. Repressive policies were still in place, and police enforcement of them intensified. Protesters were threatened with guns and attacked with tear gas—the very first time it was used in the history of South Africa. But the women did not stop.

Eventually, they wore the authorities down. By the 1940s, illegal brewing by women in these areas had not been curbed. They still faced police harassment, but it became less and less frequent. Many native Africans completely ignored the alcohol laws, and authorities grew more and more reluctant to enforce them.

Things didn't really change for good, however, until the next decade. There was one final clash with authorities on the horizon for female brewers.

Women who drank and brewed had a much easier time in countries that were not colonized. In pre-WWII Japan, rural women had a robust alcohol culture that included and even fostered all-female drinking.

Kumamato, an area of the southernmost Japanese island of Kyushū, had a long-standing tradition of moon viewing parties. The women of the village gathered together to drink and watch the full moon rise. They continued to stay out until nearly dawn, eating cakes and candy. As they prayed to the moon and thanked it, the women usually tipped back some homemade shōchū. Most women in this area made, sold and drank shōchū, a distilled alcohol usually made from rice, sweet potatoes, barley or soba (buckwheat). Saké was also common.

People in rural Japan during the 1930s were always ready to party. Most celebrations, which might be for a birth, a harvest or a holiday, involved dancing, singing, eating and drinking. Some-

times, they were for women only. These all-female drinking
parties were particularly notorious for ending with the drunken
singing (and sometimes acting out!) of ribald songs. Another
favorite party activity was *dō age*, when two people grabbed a
third person by the arms and legs and swung them back and
forth, which was probably more thrilling the more shōchū you
(or the people swinging you) had.

Well into the twentieth century, women across the globe who
wanted to make and drink alcohol were still being persecuted
and oppressed. But many of them still found ways to brew, distill, drink and, sometimes, even party.

Upon her return to Mexico City in 1929, Lucha Reyes was
offered a contract by the radio station XEW. By then, radio was
absolutely booming. There were more and more radio stations,
and more and more radios. For the first time in history, musicians and singers could instantly reach listeners in even the most
rural communities. She said yes.

Now, despite the genre's popularity, Lucha was not singing
canción ranchera during this time. Canción ranchera was performed by mariachis, all-male musical groups. It was not a genre
for girls. A woman performing with mariachis was a transgression of a gender boundary, just like drinking tequila.

But something was about to happen that would completely
change both Lucha's career and the future of Mexican music.

After a run of performances in Mexico City, Lucha joined a
traveling musical group and, with them, embarked on a tour of
Europe. During the course of her travels, she was plagued with
throat infections and respiratory illnesses that badly affected
her voice. Things got worse for her on the overseas trip back
to Mexico, and by the time Lucha got home, she was in serious condition. The infections caused permanent damage to her
vocal cords. For an entire year, she didn't speak. Her normal
soprano range went down an octave, and she emerged from her
illness with a brand-new voice. What could have been a disaster

for her career instead became an incredible opportunity. Lucha embraced singing in a robust, husky style.

A style that was perfect for canción ranchera.

Soon after her recovery, Lucha returned to performing and became a regular singer for *La Voz de América desde México* (The Voice of America from Mexico), a popular radio show. Audiences found that it was not only her voice that had transformed but her entire persona.

Lucha had bobbed her long, dark hair, which by now was a symbol of modern, independent femininity the world over. On stage, she moved with extravagant gestures and a kind of bravura that, up until now, had only been seen in male performers. And she did all this wearing the clothes of the china poblana. Performers who wore these clothes rarely even spoke. Now Lucha was swaggering and swirling around the stage in them, as bold as the red, green and white of the material. She tossed all expectations of demureness right out the window.

Lucha Reyes.

With her new hair, new voice and new audacity, Lucha stepped further across the gender boundary and began to perform with mariachis. Although many conservative people were shocked by and disapproved of her, Lucha Reyes soon became a household name. She signed a record contract with RCA, sang in theatrical productions and had many radio hits. Between 1935 and 1943, she appeared in nine films.

As her career progressed, she pushed the envelope further. Sometimes, Lucha eschewed female clothing altogether and opted instead to wear trousers on stage. These were elaborately embroidered charro trousers, the counterpart to the china poblana outfit she regularly wore. By strutting across the stage in these extremely cool pants, Lucha openly scoffed at male privilege and gender expectations.

Soon, her subversions included drinking tequila.

Drinking tequila, especially in public, was the ultimate symbol of machismo. Lucha incorporated it into her act. A woman drinking tequila in public while passionately and boldly performing? Lucha Reyes became a human middle finger to ideals of femininity.

In 1941, Lucha Reyes released one of her most popular songs, "La Tequilera" ("The [Female] Tequila Drinker"). Even the name of the song was subversive. In Spanish, tequila is always preceded by *el*, the masculine pronoun.

Drinking itself was a taboo for women during this time. An unashamed public expression of a woman's desire to drink, even to get drunk, was completely unheard of.

My soul is always
drunk with tequila…
Like a good Mexican woman
I will suffer the pain tranquilly
since after all tomorrow
I'll have a drink of tequila

Before audiences even heard the lyrics, the title made sure they knew this song was about a *woman* drinking. "La Tequilera" is not a lighthearted drinking song: it's a heartbreaking tale about a woman using alcohol to cope with the cruelty of her lover. She sings about drinking too much so she can handle her pain "like a good Mexican woman."

The message of "La Tequilera" deeply resonated with women all over Mexico. Recording the song in the canción ranchera style only underscored how transgressive it was. Lucha used societal associations with tequila to confront tradition and reveal truths about the lives of everyday women. Like Li Qingzhao a thousand years before, Lucha Reyes wielded alcohol to publicly subvert ideas about female desire and pain and the expectation that women must conceal their emotions.

In the words of another female singer, Barbara Perry,

Why should we have to do all the cryin' at home?
Why can't women have a good beer drinkin' song?

Women in America also needed a song like "La Tequilera," especially the ones struggling with alcohol abuse. In the 1930s and 40s, women were being excluded from treatments for alcoholism. There was a fear that allowing women into programs would somehow corrupt the men who were attending. It was bad enough to be a man suffering from alcoholism, but a woman? She must be some kind of sinful, morally bankrupt creature who would influence those around her.

Fear of the shame and judgment around female alcohol abuse kept most of those suffering quiet about it, until a woman named Marty Mann pushed the medical community to finally help them.

In the early 1930s, Mann was a successful businesswoman working in London. She came from an upper-middle-class white family in Chicago, was educated in private schools and had traveled extensively. Mann was the picture of female success and fortune for the time. She was even a debutante. Underneath the veneer of her flourishing career, however, Mann struggled with alcohol abuse. When she sought help for it, the London doctors were indifferent toward her. She finally traveled back home to the United States to seek treatment.

In 1938, Mann checked herself into Blythewood Sanitarium in Connecticut. When she was released fifteen months later, she was not only determined to keep herself healthy but also to help other women who were struggling. Mann set off to eliminate the stigma around female alcoholism.

To maintain her sobriety, she decided to start attending meetings of the newly founded Alcoholics Anonymous. AA was initially a group made up solely of men. At first, many male members of the group were wary and even hostile to her. Since its inception in 1935, only two other women in the entire country had joined. Mann was the third.

The men in her group had doubts about Mann's ability to follow the program. Some objected to her being there and wanted her thrown out. But she persisted, becoming the first woman to achieve long-term sobriety in AA history. Mann went on to write the chapter "Women Suffer Too" in the Big Book of AA. She even met the love of her life in the program, a woman named Priscilla.

Marty Mann wanted more public education on alcohol abuse and was determined to spread the message that alcoholism was a disease, not a moral failing. In 1944, she founded the National Council on Alcoholism and later organized the National Committee for Education on Alcoholism. She was also adamant about making AA and alcoholism treatment more open and inclusive. Mann was responsible for starting AA groups specifically for the gay and lesbian community in New York City, where she lived with Priscilla.

Thanks to the work of Marty Mann, the public perception of alcoholism, especially of alcoholic women, slowly began to change.[132]

During this time in the United States, everything about alcohol was changing.[133] After thirteen long years of being underground, American drinking culture emerged blinking and bleary into the light. Distilleries dusted off their stills (at least the ones that hadn't been used to make industrial alcohol during the dry years), and breweries refilled their vats. Liquor companies needed to figure out how to market to this modern world, and reopened bars needed to figure out how to handle their modern customers.

One of the biggest differences after Repeal was the presence of women in drinking culture. Prohibition brought it into the private spaces controlled by women. Now that it was back in public again, women were going out there with it.

The first order of business for the new 1930s drinking culture was to figure out how to keep women segregated, even if they were allowed in.

Before Prohibition, men were absolutely happy to drink sweet, fruity cocktails with extravagant garnishes. It was common to see them tipping back cobblers and punches and juleps topped with a whole bouquet of fruit and herbs. Men loved a drink to give them the ol' razzle dazzle.

After Prohibition, those cocktails just wouldn't do anymore. If men could no longer gender the space where they drank, they started gendering *what* they drank.

This trick was thousands of years old. It was used all the way back in ancient Rome, when the women who were allowed

---

132   She was a prominent speaker on alcoholism education up until her death in 1980.

133   In 1933, Alma Fullford Whitaker released a guide for "polite" drinking that actually urged women to get hammered with their sweethearts before they got married. She thought it was a good idea for couples to see what the other was like when they were drunk.

into the convivium had to drink passum instead of wine. Generally, the gendering of alcohol is only found where women have access to a drinking space. If you can't keep women out of the space where drinking happens, you keep them out of the drinks themselves.

Austere martinis and highballs became the drinks for men. Sweet cocktails like gin fizzes and Bee's Knees were now considered drinks for women. Girly drinks were generally the same strength as the other drinks, the big difference being sugar content, a bright color and the presence of a pretty garnish like a sprig of mint or a slice of fruit.

In reality, however, girly drinks were not actually the most popular drinks with girls. Right after Repeal, in December of 1933, bartenders at the Biltmore Hotel in New York City found that the most popular cocktail with women was the old-fashioned, a drink made with whiskey and a little bit of sugar and bitters. D. G. Lam, manager of the Lotus Club in Washington, DC, said "Women patrons at [my] place order Old Fashioneds more often than any other cocktail."

If they didn't order a cocktail, women were more likely to order just a whiskey and soda. Bartenders everywhere were surprised to see that the new female drinkers across the bar from them were particular about their cocktails. More particular, in fact, than their typical male customers. Many women emerged from Prohibition with discerning tastes in booze. The next year, in 1934, the *New Yorker* reported that many women were now ordering their old-fashioneds with no sugar at all.

Positive economic shifts for American women in the 1930s and 40s gave many of them more freedom to go to a bar and have a drink. Cheers to higher employment rates and greater access to birth control and divorce! Lots of new bars opening up around America were even affordable for working-class women.

(The word *saloon* was rarely used anymore. From here on out, a place to drink was usually referred to as a *bar*.)

Women enjoying a drink in a bar after Repeal.

Huge numbers of male drinkers across the country bitterly complained about the loss of their men-only spaces. In fact, these guys didn't even want women allowed in to serve them. Some higher-end restaurants and hotels heard their lamentations and decided to institute men-only policies. This was around the time that women were finally being hired to serve customers in these places (although, of course, getting paid less than men). The union for male waiters petitioned politicians to prohibit women from handling liquor. A New York tabloid called the *Troy Record* reported, "Who wants the hand that rocks the cradle mixing whiskey sours?"

Then World War II threw those men-only policies a curveball. With many male bartenders now off serving in the military, *somebody* needed to serve those martinis. Women took up shakers all across America. Rosie the Riveter has a lesser known sister: Bessie the Bartender.[134]

In Brooklyn, the Bar Maids Local 101 was formed. The women's union had certain rules for its members that bent to social fears around women in bars, such as not working past midnight and not giving out their last names to customers. By the end of WWII, there were thousands of female bartenders in the United States, compared to the hundred and forty-seven female bartenders fifty years before in 1895. There were a hundred in Brooklyn alone.

Even with so many women bartending in America during WWII, there were lots of places where female drinkers were not allowed into a bar unless they were escorted by a male date. A year before the war started, Kentucky passed a law that women could only be served liquor at a table where food was also served. Women were not allowed to order or drink at the bar.

In 1945, when the war ended and the men came back home, women were expected to put down the shakers and get out from behind the bar. Many refused. Thanks to unions like the Bar Maids Local 101, they were able to keep their jobs. But sometimes, things got ugly.

Male bartenders unwilling to work side by side with women picketed bars that kept their female bartenders. Despite the fact that they successfully worked as bartenders during the entirety of the war, these idiots argued that women couldn't handle the job because of the barroom violence and the complicated cocktail recipes. Hopefully Ada Coleman read some of these articles and got a good laugh.

That same year, Michigan instituted a law prohibiting women from bartending. The only exception was for the wife or daughter of a *male* owner. Even if you were the owner yourself, if you were a woman, you could not tend the bar. Female bar owner

---

134   Sadly, she did not get any cool illustrations like Rosie did. Although, artists of the world, there's still plenty of time to correct that!

Valentine Goesaert challenged the law in 1948. She wanted to bartend in her own establishment, and she wanted her two female employees to be able to, as well. Michigan's law was upheld by the Supreme Court, and Valentine lost her case. The ruling encouraged other institutions around the country to pass similar laws, and this law wouldn't get changed for almost thirty years.

Just like the years before Prohibition, American women in the 1930s and 40s were tasked with buying beer for their families. The vast majority of alcohol sold for home consumption was bought by women.[135] Beer advertisements were aimed at mothers and wives. Both magazines and newspapers were full of ads that featured beautiful women—or even just their beautifully manicured hands—serving drinks to men in their homes. Brands wanted women to think that if they brought home a pack of their beer, they too could have a smiling husband and an idyllic home.

Besides advertisements, women also influenced the newest innovation in beer technology: the beer can.

Beer cans made their debut in 1935 and were a modern version of rushing the growler. Instead of walking down to the local saloon to get a bucket of beer to serve with dinner, women now picked some cans up at another brand-new innovation for the 1930s, the supermarket. Cans were lighter and easier to open than bottles, and soon they were the preferred way for wives and mothers to buy beer. That year, over two hundred million cans were sold. Soon, major beer brands like Anheuser-Busch, Schlitz and Pabst were scrambling to get their beer canned.

Metal rationing put the production of canned goods on hold during WWII, but afterward, it was clear the can was here to stay. Instead of picturing a toga-wearing frat boy when you think

---

135 Something that is still true today, yet alcohol companies usually do not feature women drinking in their ads.

of a beer can, picture instead a 1940s housewife. Although, she was probably far less likely to crush one on her forehead.

The success of "La Tequilera"[136] was one of the many achievements that cemented Lucha Reyes's place in the hearts of the women of Mexico. It became her trademark song.

However, it also affected her legacy.

While she deftly used tequila as a means to subvert gender roles, her tequila drinking was also used against her. Lucha would forever be associated with the song's heroine, a tragic, hard-drinking woman. Rumors proliferated that her husky voice came from alcohol abuse, despite collaborators like her friend Nancy Torres swearing otherwise.

On June 25, 1944, after a lifetime of turbulent personal relationships, three marriages and a struggle with depression, Lucha Reyes died by suicide with an overdose of barbiturate pills. (People rumored that this was accompanied by an overdose of tequila). She was only thirty-eight years old.

Lucha passed away the same year that Marty Mann assembled her national council for alcohol education to combat the harmful idea that alcohol abuse was a moral failing, especially for women. Lucha Reyes's tremendous artistic legacy is still being overshadowed by rumors of alcohol abuse (that were never confirmed!) because she sang about drinking tequila.

Negative portrayals in magazines, newspapers and even the 1994 biopic *La Reina de la Noche (The Queen of the Night)* depict Lucha as a self-destructive alcoholic and a heartbroken, fragile woman. She is considered a tragic figure, while many notable male singers and artists who had close associations with alcohol are remembered with admiration and respect. Ernest Heming-

---

136   Many believe that, although the credit for writing this song is given to composer Alfredo D'Orsay, it was Lucha herself who wrote it. Before 1937, women in Mexico were not allowed to register copyrights as composers. Even in the 1940s, it was not out of the ordinary for female singers to write songs without registering their copyrights.

way's famous drinking (there's even a daiquiri named after him) is glamorized, even though he also died by suicide. He's romanticized, as if he died from an excess of manliness. Cause of death: his chest was simply too hairy.

In Los Angeles, in Mariachi Plaza, there is a statue of Lucha Reyes in bronze. She stands proudly with her hands on her hips and her shoulders thrown back. This is the way Lucha should be remembered, as an independent feminist icon and the bold queen of mariachi music.

Despite the constraints of a patriarchal society, women were still a major influence on the modern world's alcohol culture, from South African beer halls to American beer cans. In the coming decade, it was the female drinking experience that would become the force shaping the next huge booze craze.

11

SUNNY SUND THE BEACHCOMBER

The 1950s

When World War II ended in 1945, many American soldiers returned from the South Pacific with a taste for tropical flavors, and many civilians developed a sense of wonder and curiosity about Polynesian aesthetics. This combination gave birth to one of the biggest and most enduring drinking phenomena the world has ever seen: tiki culture. Tiki mugs, those loud shirts your uncle always wears, cocktail umbrellas, mai tais and bamboo galore.

Tiki culture really began in 1934 with the opening of Hollywood's Don's Beachcomber, a tiki-themed restaurant and bar. But it wasn't until after WWII that America developed a ravenous thirst for it. Tiki culture might have stayed in Hollywood if it wasn't for the business savvy of one brilliant woman.

A quick note first, though.

Tiki culture is a fantasy. It's a uniquely American blend of cultural appropriation, racism and exploitation that features Polynesian-inspired decor, Cantonese food and American cocktails based on Caribbean drinks and flavors. There are no *authentic* tiki bars. Tiki culture today is still reckoning with the issues that make up its core and how impossible it is to excuse sipping rum out of a mug made to look like an important religious and cultural symbol for many Maoris, Hawaiians and Samoans. A good analogy would be a Catholic-themed bar, where people did shots out of glasses sculpted to look like the Virgin Mary… if Christian countries had ever been exploited and colonized.

Despite the fundamental problems woven into tiki culture, it is undeniable that it became an American craze, one that reached its most frenzied peak in the 1950s. So let's go to that first tiki bar, off a side street in Hollywood, California.

Don's Beachcomber (which later became Don the Beach-comber) was a small bar in a corner of the ground floor of a hotel, a stuccoed and unassuming spot for cocktail history. It only sat twenty-five people. Don himself, born Ernest Gantt, was a gifted bartender. At this time in America, cocktails were mostly made with gin or whiskey. Thanks to the founding fathers taxing it to encourage growth in the American whiskey market, rum hadn't been a widespread, popular drink in the United States since the colonial days.

Don actually had traveled through the Caribbean and the South Pacific and picked up a lot of cocktail knowledge. This included how to use different types of rum in tandem with each other, mixed with fresh fruit juice, to create delicious drinks. Don called them his Rhum Rhapsodies and opened a little bar to serve them to people. The cramped space was filled with pieces he picked up while overseas: fishing nets, Oceanic art, bamboo furniture, shark jaws.

The biggest problem was that Don was a terrible business-man. He was as bad at the business side of running a bar as he was brilliant at standing behind it. Lucky for him, and for thousands of tiki fanatics across the country, a young waitress from Minnesota walked into the Beachcomber one day and imme-diately saw potential.

Don the Beachcomber is the father of the tiki bar: that fact is undisputed. But the creator of the Beachcomber tiki em-pire? That was a woman named Cora Irene Sund or, as she was known, Sunny. And part of what powered that empire was that Sunny knew how to create a bar for women.

Sunny Sund did not set out to become the queen of a tiki kingdom. At seventeen, she started work as a schoolteacher in a small Minnesota school. In the winter, Sunny had to ski nineteen miles round trip every single day to teach all grades. Eventually, she realized that she wanted a more glamorous (and perhaps warmer) life than this. After saving enough money for the train fare, Sunny bought a one-way ticket to Los Angeles to stay with her sister who lived there.

Sunny, a white, long-limbed blonde, was employed as a waitress at the Tick Tock Tea Room when she first walked into Don's Beachcomber. At the time, the tiki bar hadn't been open for very long. Sunny quickly offered to buy the place and Don—surprisingly—said yes.

Her first order of business was getting some money together. Sunny started moonlighting as a model in a department store, borrowed some cash from her sister and got a loan from a bank. Soon, she had enough to purchase the bar. The contract was signed, and while Sunny kept Don on as a managing director, she became the president and CEO of Don the Beachcomber. At some point, Sunny decided that she liked the charming, extroverted bartender as much as she liked his bar, and the two started dating.

Sunny had big plans for the Beachcomber and put them into motion immediately.

In the aftermath of World War II, American drinking habits shifted again, especially for women. The new ideal of female domesticity included cocktails. Beer was still considered a family drink and a companion for meals, but stirring up a good martini was part of the necessary skill set for the 1950s housewife.

The postwar push for prosperity included a new social pressure to drink, especially for middle- or upper-class married women. The stay-at-home mother, who had once been discouraged from drinking, was now *expected* to. Just not too much. Wives and mothers were still responsible for the drinking behavior of everyone in their home. If a woman drank too much, it was probably because she wasn't fulfilling all her domestic duties. If a man drank too much, it was probably his wife's fault for not fulfilling all her domestic duties. American pop culture in the 1950s stressed the importance of conformity and traditional gender roles. Many so-called experts of the 1950s believed that alcohol abuse was a manifestation of failed gender performance. Which almost shakes out, considering that trying to conform to the role of a perfect 1950s housewife would make any woman want to have a drink.

This thinking was reflected in the alcohol advertising of the time. Advertisements in magazines and newspapers emphasized a woman's expected role as a good hostess. The at-home cocktail party craze that started during Prohibition continued in a more open way throughout the 1950s. One classic image of white, suburban, American prosperity is the beautiful housewife making cocktails for and serving beer to her husband and his friends. Countless ads depict this exact scenario: an elegant woman being almost psychotically thrilled to get her husband a beer.

Women were not the ones drinking in these ads. Just like it was in the 1930s and 40s, they were still only ever seen serving alcohol. Advertisements showed liquor in a domestic setting, but the Distilled Spirits Institute imposed a code for its members: no women in print ads. Beer companies, which again claimed to make a family drink, could do so, but not liquor companies. In 1958, the Distilled Spirits Institute became the Distilled Spirits Council of the United States and agreed not to include women in commercials on television, either. This ban was not lifted until 1987.

Across the pond, however, things were quite different. In England, a company called Francis Showering was getting ready to make history by advertising the very first alcoholic product on English television. The product was something new and unexpected: it was a drink for women.

Babycham is a light, sparkling *perry* or pear cider that is approximately 6% ABV, about the same as your average beer. Perry was not a popular drink in England at the time, but it certainly was about to be.

Babycham launched in 1953, a time when *girly drink* options were quite limited. Women were more accepted in England's bars and pubs now, but none of the beers there were marketed to them. The world loves to make fun of women for drinking girly drinks, but why on earth wouldn't someone want to try something advertised as specifically for them? Especially when nothing else is?

This brand-new beverage came in adorable, small baby bottles adorned with a cutesy little cartoon fawn on the label. At three and a half ounces, the contents of the bottle fit perfectly into a champagne coupe.[137] Babycham was considered posh, and it was advertised as a sophisticated drink, with commercials that featured sexy, chic women who purred, "I'd love a Babycham."

Babycham advertisement.

---

137   Babycham was sued by French champagne producers for leaning too hard into the illusion that it was champagne. For a while, Babycham called itself a *champagne cider* or *champagne perry*. But Babycham won the legal battle.

Babycham became *the* drink for the post WWII English woman.

The teensy bottles were hugely popular in pubs and bars because they wasn't competing with beer. Beer companies didn't feel threatened by the cider's meteoric rise in popularity since it didn't cut into their target audience.

Something similar happened in Australia, with the Gramps wine company introducing Barossa Pearl in 1957. In the 1950s, there was an increase in nonnative Australian women drinking in pubs, so companies wanted to create something for them to buy. Barossa Pearl was a light, sparkling grape wine meant to be a feminine alternative to beer. The taste was a bit like a weak, poor-quality champagne. Barossa Pearl, like Babycham, took off. It was especially popular with young women there who, like English women, had never had alcohol marketed to them before.[138] Many Australian grandmothers of today have a story—good or bad—about Barossa Pearl.

Women were still making their mark on the whiskey world during the 1950s, in both legal and illegal ways. In America, lots of them continued to work at distilleries as bottlers, but they were now slowly breaking into other departments, as varied as barrel making and marketing. One woman, named Marge Samuels, changed the bourbon marketing game forever.

If a woman walked into a liquor store in the 1950s to buy a bottle of whiskey, she'd better know what brand she wanted, because the bottles were almost identical. Almost all whiskey, no matter the kind (rye, bourbon, etc.) came in a clear, glass bottle about a foot high with a slender neck. There was no variety—no brightly colored labels, interestingly shaped or colored bottles, and definitely no gimmicks.

Marge Samuels took advantage of that.

Her husband, Bill Samuels, was a sixth-generation whiskey

---

138   You can still buy Babycham and Barossa Pearl today. I can't promise they'll be good, but you can certainly buy them.

distiller. When he finished his time in the military, Bill wanted
to continue the family tradition. In 1953, the Samuelses bought
a distillery northeast of Loretto, Kentucky.

Founded in 1805, the building had previously housed the
Burks Spring distillery. Samuels was excited by the site's historical significance, and instead of tearing down all the old buildings, she convinced her husband to restore them all. She spent
time interviewing her new neighbors about the old distillery's
significance to the community. It took almost thirty years, but
Samuels succeeded in getting her application for a National Historic Landmark approved through the National Park Service,
making it the first distillery in the country with that distinction.

The husband and wife team collaborated to make a smooth,
sweet bourbon that used wheat instead of rye as a secondary
grain. Samuels baked different loaves of bread with a variety
of types of grains and had him taste-test each loaf. Eventually,
the two decided on a red winter wheat for their bourbon. Red
would soon be a significant color for the distillery.

As a woman with both a chemistry degree and an interest in
calligraphy, Marge Samuels had a uniquely balanced talent for
art and science. In 1956, she became a one-woman research and
development department for bottling the bourbon. Sitting in her
kitchen, she experimented with designs for the bottle and the
label. Samuels wanted the whiskey to look more handcrafted
and less mundane than everything else on the liquor store shelf.
Her bourbon bottle needed to be eye-catching.

Inspired by the look of cognac bottles that used wax to seal
the alcohol instead of a cork, Samuels decided to test out something new, something that had never been done with a whiskey
bottle before. She hauled her deep fryer out of her kitchen and
down into the basement and spent seven months experimenting
with different types and colors of wax. Samuels finally settled
on red. After successfully achieving the look that she wanted—

red wax covering the top of the bottle and dripping down the side—she christened it Maker's Mark.

Maker's Mark launched in 1959 and was an immediate hit. Not only was it good bourbon, but with its bright red wax, the bottle stood out on every shelf the sat on. Other brands set out to copy Samuels's work. Over fifty years later, they're still trying. In 2012, tequila juggernaut Jose Cuervo tried to copy the dripping-wax look of a Maker's Mark bottle, and a court ruled that they infringed on Samuels's design. It was a landmark trademark law that completely changed liquor packaging.

Maker's Mark's wax seal.

LUC NOVOVITCH/ALAMY STOCK PHOTO

Maker's Mark's historic distillery became the first in what is now known as the Bourbon Trail, a group of bourbon distilleries in Kentucky sponsored by the Kentucky Distillers' Organization. Tourists are encouraged to take a trip down the Bourbon Trail by stopping at each distillery (for their liver's sake not all on the same day) and taking a tour. In 2014, almost thirty years after her death, Marge Samuels was inducted into the Kentucky Bourbon Hall of Fame. She was the first woman with a distillery to be inducted. Maker's Mark is still one of the most easily recognizable bottles of whiskey in the world.

American women were very much involved with 1950s *illegal* whiskey production, as well.

After Prohibition, there were still many dry areas of the country. Lots of states had dry counties—where the sale of alcohol was forbidden in various degrees of severity, from every day of the week to only on Sundays. (Some states still have dry laws today.) Many women picked up bootlegging as a side hustle, buying legal booze and bringing it over the border into a dry town to sell.

Oklahoma was almost completely dry—the saltine of states. The only alcohol allowed to be sold there was low (3.2% or less) ABV beer. Female bootleggers distilled and sold illegal liquor all over the state. The most famous of which was Cleo[139] Epps, who ran moonshine during the 1940s and 50s. She was beloved in her community and even helped many buy their own homes with the millions she earned from bootlegging. The police knew about her and mostly turned the other way, so well was she loved. Epps kept selling illegal booze until her death in 1970, even after Oklahoma finally repealed Prohibition in 1959.[140]

Sunny's first order of business for the Beachcomber was expansion; seating only twenty-five people didn't cut it for her.

After some local reconnaissance, Sunny realized that the apart-

---

139   Yes, so many Cleos in this book. If you want your daughter to be a famous drinker or bootlegger, name her Cleopatra.

140   Epps was murdered by the local mafia for testifying against them in court.

ment building across the street from the tiki bar was abandoned, and she bought it. This building became the new site of the Beachcomber, with two stories and upper dining alcoves.

Even in the new location, the Beachcomber still looked nondescript from the street. The entrance was obscured in a bamboo thicket, and the sign out front was small and hard to read from far away. Taxi drivers had a difficult time finding the place. This might have plagued some bar owners, but the secluded location of the Beachcomber worked perfectly with her plans.

Sunny wanted her new bar to be a special place for her customers. It wasn't a dive bar to pop into for a quick drink after work. The Beachcomber was a place to go for, as she put it, "a big night out." She instituted a dress code and insisted that all her male patrons wear suit coats.

Not happy with the quick stir-fry Don had previously cooked up for his customers in the tiny, dingy kitchen in the original location, Sunny changed the menu. Leaning into the idea of the exotic that her patrons were expecting with the Oceanic decor and the Caribbean-inspired cocktails, she hired a Chinese-American chef to cook Cantonese cuisine. She imported ingredients like bamboo shoots, water chestnuts and oyster sauce directly from China. For the final culinary touch, anticipating white American hesitation, Sunny hired a full-time menu adviser to walk around the dining room and help guests understand what was being served.

She also knew it wasn't enough to have a bunch of dusty decorations strewn around. Sunny flew in massive shipments of fresh flowers and plants from Hawaii and real fruit to put around the Beachcomber. The bar looked like a Hollywood set from a South Seas film, with patrons sipping Don's famous concoctions out of coconuts and pineapples.

Music was piped in to play softly in the background, since Sunny never wanted live music in her bar. From the start, she wanted this to be a romantic spot. It was her idea to keep the lights dim because, as she said, it would "make every woman look lovely and mysterious."[141]

What made the Beachcomber stand out and become successful was that it was designed by a woman for women. With every new addition and expansion, Sunny was thinking about the experience her female customers would have at the Beachcomber. She was so innovative and conscientious about the creation of her bar because she herself loved bars. She loved to drink and have a good time, and she understood what made a bar appealing for women. Sunny designed the type of bar that she, too, would want to drink in.

Around the same time, right before WWII, the first major sociological study of drinking among American youth in college was being conducted. More than half of young women reported drinking regularly, most of whom did so for the pure enjoyment of it. When asked why, they gave answers like "to be gay" or "for enjoyment of taste" or "to relieve tension." The results were clear: young women in America wanted to participate in drinking culture.[142]

All of this meticulous thought and attention to detail worked. Within six months of Sunny taking over, she said that "everything was paid for…except the icebox and the cash register." By 1937, the Beachcomber was serving around six hundred people every weeknight it was open, and nine hundred on Saturdays. Sunny relied on word of mouth to drum up excitement for the Beachcomber. What made her bar truly successful was that the mouths the praise was coming from were famous.

Don the Beachcomber became one of the regular haunts for

---

141   She said in an interview with the Saturday Evening Post in 1948, "We think it has helped a lot of romances."

142   These were mostly white women who were polled. It wasn't until 1953 that Prohibition was repealed for the Native population of the United States. Jim Crow laws of racial segregation were enforced until 1965, meaning there were many bars where young Black women were not welcome.

the Hollywood set. Female celebrities like Greta Garbo, Joan Crawford and Marlene Dietrich fell in love with the place. Joan Crawford was known to regularly come in for her favorite meal of egg rolls, fried shrimp and spare ribs. She said that "drinking a piña colada was better than slapping Bette Davis in the face."[143]

It was this star power that helped kick off the tiki craze. Sunny was sensitive to the wants and needs of her famous clientele and made sure all her staff looked out for them and kept fans and photographers away. She leaned into the idea of the Beachcomber being an exclusive, out-of-the-way place. People always want whatever is hard to get. Sunny installed a velvet rope in front of the entrance and sometimes instructed her staff to turn away customers, even if the restaurant was not full.

Most of these customers—even Hollywood icons—had no idea that Sunny even existed. Don, ever the extrovert, loved being among the guests. But Sunny intentionally stayed behind the scenes. Although this "long gammed, deep bosomed blonde" (as described by the press) was the driving force of the business, she was happy to let Don be the face of the bar. By now, the two were married. The staff adored her, and most of them called her Mama CI for *Cora Irene*.

Her only indulgence was the Queen's Table, her own personal dining area. The table itself was massive, bean-shaped and polished to gleaming. The wood was sliced from a tamarind burl and protected under plate glass. At the head of the table was the Queen's Chair, a fan-shaped lattice chair that was unique, the only one of its kind in the entire bar. No one was allowed to sit in it but Sunny Sund. And she sat in it often.

---

143 Joan was extremely particular about her booze. She was known to travel with the brands that she liked, but she also had a rider in her contracts that stipulated that Smirnoff Vodka, Old Forester Bourbon, Chivas Regal scotch, Beefeater Gin and Moët champagne be available for her.

Sunny in her Queen's Chair.

Dr. Nicola Nice is the owner of Pomp and Whimsy liqueur and also a sociologist by training. She's adamant about remembering how important contributions like Sunny's are to the history of cocktails. "Bartending is about *hospitality*. Women care about other people's experiences."

Some rich and famous folks were familiar with tropical flavors from the years of Prohibition, when it became fashionable for those who could afford it to fly down to Havana for a drink. After Repeal, Havana continued to be a hot spot for drinking tourists, including stars like Rita Hayworth, Elizabeth Taylor and Josephine Baker.[144]

Even some leaders of the temperance movement couldn't re-

---

144   Baker even had a cocktail named after her.

sist a rum cocktail. Los Angeles gospel preacher Aimee Semple McPherson was famous for her temperance sermons that she broadcast on the radio. Once when she arrived at a bar in Havana under a fake name, bartender Max Bilgray nevertheless recognized her. After her visit, amused by McPherson's hypocrisy, he had postcards printed up and distributed around the world with the recipe for the cocktail he created for her.

A special concoction invented by M. Bilgray
in honor of the visit of Aimee Semple McPherson

Hallelujah Cocktail

Babylonian Grape Brandy
Ice from the crest of Mount Sinai
Lemon from the Desert of Sin
Gomorrah and Sodom vermouth
Rum aged in Noah's Ark
Add Cain's syrup from the Garden of Eden
You then give it the Hebrew shake, and
Say "Hallelujah" after drinking[145]

For many of Sunny's customers, however, her bar was the first place they ever encountered cocktails with these types of flavors and liquors. Don was an alchemical genius. Instead of just lemon or lime, he used fresh pineapple, grapefruit and orange

---

145 The recipe comes out to be
     1 oz brandy
     ¾ oz rum
     1 ½ oz sweet vermouth
     A dash of grenadine
     And 4 drops of lime
     As a cocktail, it isn't great. But then again, neither is jet-setting off
     to have cocktails in Havana while you're imploring the people of
     America to stop drinking.

juices. Instead of plain simple syrup, he tried mixing honey, maple syrup or different spices like vanilla, allspice or cinnamon with the sugar.

The cocktails, the ambience, the air of secrecy and the exclusivity proved to be an unbeatable combination. Sunny opened a gift shop,[146] a rum shop and a grocery store but soon needed to cannibalize the space for more seating.

Then, two big changes occurred. Sunny and Don divorced in 1940, and soon after, Don left to fight in WWII in Italy. The two continued to be business partners while Don was off in the service. Many written histories of tiki culture paint the situation as if Sunny took the business away from Don in the divorce, looking to make money while he was being a hero in Europe. But the Beachcomber was Sunny's bar, even before they got married.

Now, she had her sights set on the rest of the country.

In 1950s South Africa, women were still fighting for their right to make booze.

This decade saw a rapid spread of home distillation technology across the entire continent. Women were always looking for ways around the laws that banned the brewing and consumption of fermented drinks, and distillation fit the bill. *Waragi* was a generic term for all distilled liquor, most of which was made by rural women. African women were now in on the moonshining game, and shebeen queens added waragi to their menus.

Brewing and distilling was a secret source of money, independence and power for women during the apartheid years in South Africa. Starting in 1948, apartheid was a system of institutionalized racism and racial segregation that lasted until the

---

146 She was adamant about maintaining the romantic, no-distractions atmosphere. So, instead of having young women walking around the restaurant selling cigarettes and souvenirs, she opened the gift shop for customers to buy things like fresh leis after they had eaten.

1990s. As they had for decades, shebeens served as hubs for both Black resilience and rebellion against white supremacy. Female brewers took drums of their alcohol and buried them, either to leave them to ferment or to hide them. Their family members, friends and neighbors served as lookouts as the huge drums were being buried or dug back up.

Among the tensions and terrors of apartheid, native women were still battling against the oppression of the white-run beer halls. In 1959, there was a long string of raids and busts on female brewers and distillers in Cato Manor, a working class neighborhood in Durban. The women in the area finally had enough, and on June 17, there was a massive demonstration.

The protesting women forced their way into the Cato Manor beer hall, led by Florence Mkhize and feminist activist Dorothy Nyembe. The protest—two thousand strong—was eventually broken up by police. Mkhize and Nyembe tried to express their grievances to the authorities, but it all fell on uncaring ears.

The next day, instead of dying down, the protest spread throughout Durban. The women organized a larger protest and a boycott of all the local beer halls, which soon were forced to temporarily close. Throughout the rest of the year, over twenty thousand women protested. Over a thousand of them were arrested and convicted in court.

Still, the laws did not change.

But the efforts of these women were not totally in vain. The next decade would finally bring about some change for the female brewers of South Africa.

Looking at the history of bars and public drinking spaces, it's easy to see their importance to women's livelihoods, political power, independence and community involvement. In the 1950s, they also became increasingly important to women's social lives. This is especially true for one particular part of the female population: the lesbian community.

Before the 1920s, in America lesbians usually partied in private homes. But just as Prohibition brought women into the fold of drinking culture, it also allowed for more gay and lesbian nightlife. Drinking had to happen somewhere safe and secret, just as lesbian parties did.

Harlem in particular was a hub for gay and lesbian partying. On 126th Street in Manhattan, there was a gay bar called Wellsworth. Wellsworth was one of those old saloons that featured a side entrance for women, so the bar owners took advantage of it and dedicated the back area of the bar to lesbian customers. It was a gay and lesbian mullet, with gays in the front and lesbians in the back. The back area of Wellsworth was a hot spot for the Black lesbian community during Prohibition.

By the 1950s, almost every lesbian bar in New York City was owned and operated by the Mafia. Now, please don't think this was because the members of the New York City Mafia were staunch believers in gay rights. It was more that anytime anything illegal was happening and money was being made from it, the Mafia wanted in.

The LGBTQ community was targeted by authorities during the 1950s, and it was illegal for bars to even serve them. Patrons drinking and dancing at a gay or lesbian bar were at risk of being arrested, which led to the risk of being outed, losing their job, their family, everything. This was the era of McCarthyism, and the LGBTQ bar scene was rife with undercover cops trying to infiltrate it. The New York City Police Department had a so-called vice squad that conducted violent (sometimes sexually violent) raids at these bars.

Which is where the Mafia came in.

Mafia-owned bars could afford to pay off cops and offer their customers a slightly heightened amount of security. Most gay or lesbian bars, Mafia-owned or not, were hidden and had blacked-out windows to offer protection from outside eyes. Women looking to drink there had to know where to go and who to talk to.

These bars were not exactly great places to drink, since the booze was usually wildly overpriced. But the women who drank here were not looking for quality mixology. These bars were the only place for them to be out in public and meet other lesbians. Some women were looking for babes, but many were also looking for a community. Community was (and is) absolutely vital for LGBTQ folks, who are far less likely to have the support of family, coworkers or neighbors. These bars were the only gathering places for lesbians outside of private homes.

Besides being special places for the lesbian community, lesbian bars are special in the history of female-centric alcohol culture because, besides the beefy mafioso bouncers, everyone inside was usually a woman. All the customers were women, and so were the waitresses and bartenders.

But they weren't always welcoming to everyone. These bars, especially the ones owned by the Mafia, were mostly frequented by working-class white women. Legendary Black writer and activist Audre Lorde wrote about her difficulty fitting into the New York lesbian bar scene because of the racism that was rampant there.

One of the most important and popular bars in the city was the Sea Colony in Greenwich Village. It was more friendly to all women. Audre Lorde and other writers like Ann Bannon were regulars there. Historian Joan Nestle talked about the Sea Colony in a 2001 interview with *Ripe Magazine*:

The Sea Colony was basically two rooms, in the front room was the bar and tables for tourists, the back room was where the illegal activity took place which was called dancing. A red light flashed to alert us when police were coming so we could sit down at our tables and not touch each other. Another image I keep alive is the bathroom line, before Stonewall there was the bathroom line. These bars were run by organized crime who made lots of money off of us so the bars had to negotiate legitimacy with the police. They created a rule—we'd only be allowed into the bathroom one woman at a time. Because they thought we were so sexually depraved, if two of us went in we'd probably make love, and that could bring the vice squad.

Every night, a short, handsome, butch woman with toilet paper wrapped around her hand had a job to allot us toilet paper. The bathroom line went from the back room through a narrow hallway to the front room to the toilet which was behind the bar. This butch woman would stand at the front of the line and we each got two wraps of toilet paper. When I stood on that bathroom line, I could've been drunk and when you drink you have to pee a lot... It took me a long time to realize that while I was fighting for all these other causes, that it wasn't okay for me to get my allotted amount of toilet paper... That image, of this allotted amount of toilet paper is at the center of my life's work—paying homage to that community of women who stood on the bathroom line, the mix of desire, politics, oppression, and resistance.

Sunny Sund didn't let the divorce from Don get her down... or get in the way of her plans for the Beachcomber.

In 1940, the same year she got divorced, Sunny opened another Don the Beachcomber location in Chicago. Despite a blizzard howling across the city, the opening night was absolutely packed. The fervor kept up, and the bar was full every single night afterward. Sunny saw a return on her investment within eight months, truly a miracle for a new bar. Most bars and restaurants don't make it past their first year.

To ensure the quality of the new location, Sunny shuttled key members of her beloved staff via airplane between her original

Hollywood location and the new spot in chilly Chicago. For the first two years it was open, she joined them on the trips and split her time between the two cities. Meanwhile, she continued to plan and expand.

Don the Beachcomber eventually became a coast-to-coast affair with sixteen different locations across America, including a second one in Los Angeles and one nearby in Palm Springs.[147] It wasn't easy to do, since this was a time when a woman could not legally secure a line of credit without a man to help her. But Sunny was determined. Eventually, she successfully drummed up more investors for her tiki kingdom.[148]

And a kingdom it was.

Rum experienced a colossal comeback thanks to the tiki craze, which was spurred on by Don's cocktails and Sunny's business smarts. By 1945, hundreds of thousands of cases of rum were being sold to American bars every year. Not just to Don the Beachcomber locations, either. Sunny's bars and Don's drinks had inspired hundreds and hundreds of imitators across the country, the most notable of which was Trader Vic's.[149]

Trader Vic became Sunny and Don's biggest competitor over the years, even though Vic admitted he got the idea to make his restaurant into a tiki bar after seeing the Beachcomber in the late 1930s. Trader Vic is lauded by tiki historians as being another king of the tiki bar. Sunny is cast as the villain who stole the Beachcomber away from Don, even though it was *her* bar that Trader Vic walked into and got inspiration from.

As the 1950s came to an end, the tiki craze showed no signs

---

147   Per the terms of their contract, Sunny held dominion over the United States. Hawaii was not yet a state, so Don opened his own tiki bar in Waikiki.

148   It helped that she remarried. Her second husband was a prominent businessman in manufacturing from Ohio named William Casparis.

149   Trader Vic is known for inventing the mai tai, named by his white Tahitian friend Carrie Guild. When she tried the drink, she said, "Mai tai!" which is a Tahitian colloquialism that roughly translates to *Awesome!*

of stopping. Hawaii became an American state in 1959, and that only fueled the tropical fire. Suddenly, there were tiki-themed bowling alleys, apartment complexes, restaurants, songs, clothing and furniture. Disneyland even created the Enchanted Tiki Room, which you can still visit today.

Sunny died in January 1974 when she was sixty-three years old. To this day, Sunny Sund is the true queen of tiki culture. She understood that for many people, especially women, going out for a drink is about so much more than just going out for a drink. It's about atmosphere, it's about hospitality, it's about an escape from the everyday. Sunny understood what women want…from a bar, at least. That, combined with her keen business sense, gave rocket fuel to a brand-new type of bar and a new type of cocktail.

Tiki is America's longest-lasting drinking trend, with its heyday lasting from the 1940s until the 1960s. It is the only cocktail fad to have spawned a lifestyle, with people living in tiki-themed homes, wearing tiki-themed clothes and throwing tiki-themed parties. JFK celebrated his presidential election win in 1960 with a daiquiri made by Jackie herself from her own personal recipe.[150]

A drinking trend that was so maniacally popular with one generation of Americans was bound to face a backlash from the next one. Something different was in order for the next generation to drink. Fortunately, a bespectacled Scottish woman was there to show them the way.

---

150   Jackie's Daiquiri is two parts rum, one part lime, a few drops of Falernum (a liqueur made with ginger, lime and spices) and two parts canned frozen limeade.

12

LADIES NIGHT WITH
BESSIE WILLIAMSON

The 1960s and 70s

The 1960s and 70s are known as the years of free love and grooviness...but not for the cocktail. These decades were the dark age of drinks in America.

Baby boomers were completely uninterested in drinking the things their parents drank. Rum went from tiki to kitschy. Babycham became an old folks' drink.

To be fair, the cocktails their parents drank had become syrupy, overly sweet shadows of their former selves by the 1960s. Consumers were more interested in simple, sanitized drinks that reflected a culture that was hostile to eccentricity. Drinkers sipped on manhattans, gin and tonics, and dry martinis. Safe, conventional cocktails.

The 1960s saw the rise of two forces that devastated the spirits world. The first was the corporate cocktail, a recipe designed by a company to sell a certain type of booze. The second was the Cold War, which Russia won. Behind the bar, anyway.

Welcome to the age of vodka. Despite being a decidedly Russian spirit, it became all the rage in the United States during the Cold War. Vodka completely took over as a substitute for gin. Orange blossoms became screwdrivers. Martinis were now simply vehicles for vodka and olives.

The goal of vodka is to be as tasteless and clear as possible. It doesn't add anything flavor-wise to a drink—it's not supposed to.[151] The spirit doesn't have a strong, boozy smell or taste and can be poured into any mixer. All of this made vodka fit with a new American desire for sterility and cleanliness. People even believed that its so-called purity meant it couldn't cause a hangover. In 1968, for the very first time, vodka sales eclipsed gin. Bold flavors and novelty were out, purity was in.

But while vodka was leading America into a cocktail dark age, there was one woman reaching to turn on the light.

When you think of single-malt scotch, you probably think of an older white man, sitting in a study with a pipe while he strokes his large beard. Maybe you think of rich businessmen wearing expensive suits. You might even think of *Parks and Recreation* star Nick Offerman. Whatever you're imagining, remove the suit, the beard and the pipe. Add a pair of cat's-eye glasses, a cozy cardigan and a pair of sensible heels. The person you should be thinking about is Bessie Williamson, the First Lady of Scotch.

Bessie was born Elizabeth Leitch Williamson on August 22, 1910, in Glasgow. After graduating from Glasgow University in 1934, this young, bespectacled woman decided to see her country for the first time. Bessie embarked on various plane trips before she finally stopped to vacation at one of the most popular Scottish destinations at the time: the beautiful, temperate island

---

151   Because of this, it's usually looked down upon in the world of cocktails. Listen, I'm not telling you not to drink vodka. If you do, you can toast to all those badass Russian women who bootlegged the hell out of it and then tell cocktail snobs to go screw.

of Islay.[152] It's a small island on the southern end of the country, and it had a population of less than four thousand in the 1930s. What it lacked in size, it made up for in scotch.

When Bessie first arrived at the island, Islay shipped about eight million pounds worth of untaxed whisky back to the Scottish mainland every year. It was sent in bulk and used for blending in with other scotches. Why? Because there's something special about an Islay scotch.

Scotch is just whisky from Scotland. Not all scotches are heavy and smoky, but Islay scotch sure is. Whisky from this little isle is known for being the heaviest, smokiest scotch in the world. Most folks at that point in history were drinking blended scotches, mixes of different scotches from different distilleries, whereas a single-malt scotch is just scotch from one distillery.[153] There wasn't a huge consumer demand for single malts or for Islay scotch, which was considered too powerfully smoky to be bottled on its own. That is, until Bessie came to Islay.

During her vacation, Bessie fell in love with this gorgeous island. So, when she chanced upon a job listing in a local newspaper, she applied. The ad was for a shorthand typist at one of the local scotch distilleries, Laphroaig. Bessie got the job, only planning to stay for three months.

Bessie's new boss adored her. She had both a sharp mind for business and a natural way with people. The owner admired Bessie's smarts and her work ethic and decided to offer her a full-time, permanent position at the distillery. She stuck out a bit there, since Laphroaig mostly employed men at the time. Out of everyone, it was soon Bessie whom the owner trusted with

---

152   Pronounced *EYE-la.*

153   There's a whole lot of snobbery around single-malt whiskeys. That's all it is, though: snobbery. It's true that most lower-quality scotches and whiskeys on the market are blends. It's easier to hide poor quality or quickly made whiskey in a blend. But a scotch being a blend doesn't mean it's inherently bad, just like a scotch being a single malt doesn't mean it's inherently good.

the run of the place when he traveled. She was the one with the keys. When Bessie was in charge, she handled all the shipments and worked with the distributors. She didn't quite realize that she was being groomed for a new job.

When the owner of the distillery suffered a stroke in 1938, Bessie took on more responsibility. She was put in charge of business with America. This was an important gig during the late 1930s and 40s, when all scotch companies were desperately trying to regain their customers in the wake of American Prohibition. Soon, she took over as the manager of the entire distillery, becoming the only woman in Scotland with that title.

Bessie took the reins at Laphroaig just before the start of World War II. She handled the turbulent war years with skill and guided the distillery when the Scottish government used the Laphroaig facilities for military purposes, such as becoming a major ammunitions hub. Bessie made sure that not only were her equipment and her products protected during the military takeover but also some of her employees. She argued that the unique whisky-making ability of her warehouse manager exempted him from service, and she won. Bessie regularly negotiated with the military on a host of other matters, always allowing them to take over far less space than they requested. With a masterful combination of charm and strong will, she made sure her distillery got through the war unscathed.

In 1954, the owner passed away and left the company entirely to the most qualified person for the job: Bessie. She had big plans for her distillery and its smoky scotch.

The second wave of feminism hit America in the 1960s. It was time for birth control, the fight for equal pay, more reproductive rights and oh so many pairs of go-go boots. Along with boardrooms and federal courts, one place that became a feminist battleground was the barstool.

Although most bars now couldn't *technically* forbid a woman from entering, many states and establishments therein continued to employ some creatively misogynist workarounds. It had been thirty years since Prohibition was repealed, but men were still wary of letting women drink alongside them. There were still many men-only bars and clubs, and lots of places had rules limiting the hours that women were allowed inside, usually after three o'clock, when all the important work lunches and business meetings had already happened. Many bars only allowed a woman inside if she had a male escort. Discrimination of women in bars was universally accepted. Bars even coughed up a flimsy excuse for it: B-girls.

B-girls had been working in bars since the 1940s. They were women hired by the bar to dance with men and encourage them to drink. The practice actually dates back to far earlier than that, to the dance halls and saloons of the late 1800s. At first, they were called *percentage girls* because the bar paid them a percentage of the money they got men to spend on drinks. These women were (usually) not sex workers and did not go home with the men. They spent the night dancing and flirting and convincing men to buy booze. Because the women didn't want to become absolutely hammered, often bartenders secretly poured something nonalcoholic like iced tea in their glasses. These women became extremely skilled at covertly dumping drinks into the pots of nearby plants. Marilyn Monroe played a B-girl in the 1956 film *Bus Stop*, which features a scene where the legendary bombshell complains about having to drink fifteen fake cocktails a night.

Seems like a slightly exhausting but still legitimate way to make a living, right? Not to many male bar patrons. Now, please don't laugh, but men saw themselves as—wait for it—victims of these women. Men were incensed at the thought that women might have an ulterior motive for hanging out with them at a bar. Okay, now you can laugh.

B-girls, women just trying to earn a living, were seen as conniving predators, especially after WWII. The threat of B-girls became wildly sensationalized in the 1950s because of all the servicemen hanging out with them in bars. These women were a source of moral panic. They were an attack on the wholesome American way of life. A woman, in a *bar*, pretending to be interested in an innocent soldier so she can coax away his hard earned dollars? (Never mind the fact that a lot of these servicemen were probably happy for the company.) Clearly, if a man buys a woman a drink, she owes him, well, anything he wants. A lot of the outrage surrounding B-girls came from those late nineteenth century American traditions surrounding the obligation created when a man buys a woman a drink.

Well into the 1960s, the supposed threat of B-girls was used to justify excluding women from bars. Better ban an entire gender to protect those fragile male egos! Better to deny women access to a public space than have a man realize that the only way a woman would listen to his stupid work stories is if she's being paid!

Everything started to change one December evening in 1967.

On that night in Syracuse, New York, a young journalism student named Joan Kennedy had just finished Christmas shopping with her mother. After a long day of trying to figure out what different family members wanted in their stockings, the two women decided to go into the bar at the Hotel Syracuse. The bar, named the Rainbow Lounge, denied them entry on the grounds that they were without male escorts. Kennedy was furious.

Soon afterward, she approached Karen DeCrow, who was then a law student active in the brand spanking new chapter of the National Organization for Women (NOW) in Syracuse.

At first, NOW had a lot of internal disagreement about whether or not it should be a priority for the organization to make the barstool a battleground for the women's rights movement. Thanks to the thousands-of-years-old shadow cast over women who wanted to drink, some were reluctant. Equal pay seemed to be a lofty pursuit, but was the fight to have a beer in public just as lofty? Lots of members didn't think so.

Karen DeCrow, however, did.

She argued that going to a bar was a symbol of being a free person and a way to get women integrated into the workplace. DeCrow thought it was crucial for women to be able to leave the home and hang out in the public sphere, where important networking and business meetings happened. Since so many states, cities and towns allowed discrimination behind the bar as well, it also kept a lot of women out of a potential job. In 1964, twenty-six states still prohibited women from bartending. The rest of NOW eventually agreed with DeCrow. After she got everyone on board, DeCrow launched a plan.

NOW activists traveled from all around the country to participate in a sit-in that she organized at the Rainbow Lounge. But the hotel was ready for them, and the owners had taken precautionary measures. Right before the protesters arrived, the hotel staff changed the numbers on the occupancy limit sign in the bar from one hundred and ten to six. To top it off, they removed the seats from all the bar stools. It didn't deter the NOW protesters, though. They still entered the bar and just stood around. Afterward, DeCrow issued a lawsuit against the Hotel Syracuse.

The next year, after a few more sit-ins, DeCrow brought the issue of gendered bar discrimination to the 1968 NOW Convention in New York City. The convention was held at the Biltmore Hotel, which was perfect for the point DeCrow was trying to make: the hotel had a men-only bar. (She did not hold a protest there just yet.)

In February of the following year, DeCrow organized Public Accommodations Week with other members of NOW. Part of the week of activism and protests for women's rights involved drink-ins at men-only bars across the entire country. Sites for drink-ins included the Polo Lounge at the Beverly Hills Hotel, the Retreat in Washington, DC, the Berghoff in Chicago, and the Plaza Hotel's Oak Room in New York City, where Betty Friedan's party of three was refused service by the bartender.

McSorley's, a bar in Manhattan, had never served a woman in

all one hundred and fifteen years of its existence and was proud
of it. The bar sported a sign on its front door proclaiming *No
Back Room in Here for Ladies*. The owners were proud that they
had "thrived for over a century on good ale, raw onions and no
women." Nothing but grumpy men and the stench of raw onions. Sounds like paradise.

For DeCrow's drink-in that week, she marched unafraid into
the stinky atmosphere of McSorley's with a group of fellow
NOW members. Male bar patrons immediately began derisively
hooting and hollering at them. The women were ignored by
the bartenders, and when one man tried to buy drinks for all of
them, an angry crowd of men grabbed him and quite literally
threw him out the door. He staggered away covered in blood.
(None of the women were hurt.)

By the next year, NOW's protests and drink-ins had finally
paid off. In 1970, New York City law eliminated gender discrimination in all public places.[154] Some bars refused to comply
with the law and had to be forced to let women in. Some bars
welcomed their new customers. Some tried to turn the whole
affair into a publicity stunt, such as the Berghoff, which publicly invited Gloria Steinem (and a whole bunch of media) to
come and have a drink.

These legal gains were of course fantastic and long overdue, but
they didn't immediately change the reality of what it was like to
be a woman in a bar. Many women were still intimidated and uncomfortable walking into one, especially if they were alone. Just
because bars legally allowed women didn't mean that they always
went out of their way to welcome them in. Until some drinking
establishments realized that female customers could be a draw.

In the 1970s, many bars figured out that allowing female customers in also meant more male customers. Bar owners learned

---

154   McSorley's first female customer was Barbara Schaum, the owner of a
      nearby leather goods store. Let's hope she liked raw onions, too.

that women in bars attracted men *to* the bars. Can you believe it took them so long?

Singles bars took off in the 1960s and 70s. These were places where women were not simply tolerated but actively welcomed and encouraged to come. Drinking establishments scrambled to undo centuries of gender discrimination and draw in female customers.

Some bars were subtle and focused on making the place safer and cleaner and more appealing to women. Other bars were… not so subtle.

Ladies' entrance at a bar.

JONI2/STOCKIMO/ALAMY STOCK PHOTO

The 1970s saw the rise of the ladies' night. This was one night a week or a month, usually a weeknight, where women drank for free or very cheap. The hope was that a swarm of single men would descend on the bar, attracted by all the women, and buy enough booze to make up for all the free drinks the bar was giving out. The original New York City location for the restaurant chain TGIFridays was one of the first places to have a ladies' night. Unfortunately, they did not offer loaded potato skins back then.

But ladies' night was not designed as a perk for women. It was designed as an attraction for men. Women were commodified at ladies' nights. They were the bar's loss leaders, not the customers that the bar ultimately cared about.

Whatever the motive, the strategy was successful, especially in college towns where female college students were always looking for free stuff. In fact, ladies' night spread worldwide to cities like Hong Kong. The phenomenon lasted well into the 2000s, when people started challenging the legality of charging men but not women for drinks.

Another bar phenomenon spurred on by female customers was the fern bar. Fern bars began in 1970 at a place called Henry Africa's[155] in San Francisco. This bar catered to all genders, but it featured a bunch of feminine touches designed to attract the female customer. There was an abundance of plants (which is where the name came from), cozy booths, upholstered barstools and nicer glassware. It's hilarious that having a cushion on a barstool to make it more comfortable is considered a *feminine touch*, but there you go. Maybe it's a mark of masculine virility to have a sore butt.

Fern bars became popular places for young professionals who wanted to go have a drink, relax and mingle after work. Falling somewhere between a grungy dive bar and an expensive, upscale hotel bar, they filled a huge gap in the market. The bars on television shows like *Three's Company* and *Cheers* were modeled off fern bars.

Up in Canada, similar movements were happening in the bar scene. By the 1960s, some Canadian provinces were finally

155 The owner of the bar was named Norman Hobday, but he loved his bar so much that he had his name legally changed to Henry Africa.

allowing women to serve alcohol. There was a new category
of tavern to serve it in: the lounge. Cocktail lounges, dining
lounges, anything followed by the word *lounge* was liable to be
more female-friendly. Similar to a fern bar, lounges had more
feminine touches to attract female customers. They were so
female-friendly that they became the first type of Canadian bar
that women felt comfortable entering solo. The biggest problem
with the lounges was that they excluded working-class women.
Many had a dress code and required that you wear a skirt to
enter, meaning that the women knocking off from a day at the
factory and looking for a drink were not welcome.

In some American states, the laws concerning drinking ages
began to be less discriminatory, as well. For all genders, in
fact. In 1976, the landmark case of Craig v. Boren was decided
by the Supreme Court. The case started in Oklahoma, where
3.2% ABV beer was available for purchase by women at the
age of eighteen, but not by men until the age of twenty-one.[156]
This was a holdover from the practice of women buying beer
to bring home for their families. The thinking was that women
needed to be able to bring home beer for their husbands and
families to drink, but men only bought beer for themselves to
drink. A twenty-year-old man named Curtis Craig and a female liquor store owner named Carolyn Whitener agreed that
the law needed to be changed. The two teamed up to challenge
it in court.

The lawsuit was in rough shape until a brilliant legal counsel
at the Women's Rights Project at the American Civil Liberties
Union offered some assistance. It was a woman named Ruth
Bader Ginsburg, future Supreme Court justice herself. She wrote
to the lawyer on the case, saying that she was "delighted to see
the Supreme Court is interested in beer drinkers."

With Ginsburg's help, the case was argued successfully. The
Supreme Court ruled that the Oklahoma law made unconsti-

---

156 Women could not purchase anything stronger until the age of twenty-one.

tutional gender classifications. With this ruling, a new standard for review in gender discrimination cases was set.

Next time you have a beer, raise your glass to RBG.

Along with more generally female-friendly bars, lesbian bars flourished in the 1970s. The highest concentrations of them were found in big cities like San Francisco and New York City. In New York, there were as many as ten lesbian bars operating at a time. There were enough in 1977 to have the Women's Bar Awards, hosted by the very popular Bonnie and Clyde, one of the first women-owned lesbian bars in the city. The event featured awards for Best Barmaid, Best Waitress and Best Bouncer. It was the first female-centric alcohol industry awards in the country, possibly the entire world.

Sadly, most of them are closed today,[157] but there were many types of lesbian bars in the 1970s.[158] There were dive bars, swanky cocktail lounges and cozy pubs. One thing they all had in common, however, was that they were important community spaces, still the main public place for members of the LGBTQ community to meet and socialize. Gay and lesbian travel guidebooks printed in the 1960s—which were coded for safety— mentioned lots of these bars. By the 1970s, resources like *Gaia's Guide* were more open with their terminology and even started to feature advertisements for specific bars.

But it wasn't all sunshine and rainbows. Some lesbian bars in the 1960s and 70s shifted from denying entry to Black women to denying entry to trans women. (Although sometimes, the racism was still there.) Not all bars did this, but some featured signage and ads stating that only *biological women* were welcome.

It was a trans woman in a bar that helped start the gay liberation movement. In 1969, the Stonewall Inn, a men-only gay bar, finally began to let women (all women) and drag queens inside.

---

157   As of 2019, there were only three lesbian bars in New York City.

158   There were still far fewer lesbian bars than gay bars.

Marsha P. Johnson, a Black trans woman, made history with her involvement in the gay rights uprising there that June. Johnson was one of the most prominent figures in what are now known as the Stonewall riots. The riots started in response to a police raid on the bar, and Johnson is believed to be the one who lit the spark.

By the time Bessie Williamson had officially taken over as owner of Laphroaig, she had about sixteen years' worth of experience managing the company and developing strong business relationships with other distilleries. Now that she was in charge, Bessie was ready to change the world of whisky.

Laphroaig, with its powerful and distinctive flavor, was one of the most coveted whiskies to use in blends. But Bessie believed that drinkers were ready for straight Laphroaig in all its bold and smoky glory. Instead of watering it down in a blend, she wanted to push the idea of a single malt, of selling a bottle of Laphroaig that was just Laphroaig.

Bessie also wanted to develop the concept of an Islay whisky. As the new distillery owner, she didn't just push Laphroaig, she pushed the island itself. The characteristically full flavor and smoky taste was supposed to evoke a trip to Islay. Her goal was for customers to think of a bottle of Laphroaig as a bottle of salty ocean winds, wool sweaters, rolling green hills and peat smoke. Peat, a deposit of decaying vegetable matter found in acidic bogs and fens, is traditionally cut, dried and used as an alternative to firewood in Scotland. The flavor that comes from making whisky with peat smoke is distinctive of Islay scotch, just like the scent of peat smoke is, for many, distinctive for Scotland.

In a television interview she gave in the early 1960s, Bessie proclaimed that "the secret of Islay whiskies is the peaty water and the peat, which we can get on the island that makes the Islay whisky what it is…"

During that same interview, she promoted the idea of scarcity and high demand. "There's an increasing market for the

Islay whiskies. We can't supply the demand that we have for our whisky." This eventually became the most successful marketing tactic for whisky all over the world. Consumers began to see a bottle of Laphroaig as something special to be snatched up before it was gone.

Impressed by her passion, enthusiasm and marketing genius, the Scotch Whisky Association wanted to tap into the power of Bessie Williamson. In 1961, they named her as their American spokesperson, and later that year, Bessie was off to the States to convince the country to drink single-malt scotch.

COURTESY OF LAPHROAIG

Bessie Williamson at her beloved distillery.

On her tour throughout the United States, she met with bar and liquor store owners. During these meetings, Bessie did what she did best: express her passion and love for scotches, for Islay scotches in particular. She convinced these owners that drinking a single-malt scotch was drinking something high caliber, something their customers would shell out for.

For the next three years, Bessie blazed through America on her scotch crusade. With her plaid skirts, cozy sweaters and huge smile, she was the perfect ambassador for Scottish whisky. You've seen wine moms. Well, Bessie was your whisky aunt. She had an unbeatable combination of charm and conviction, which made it easy for people to share in her love of scotch.

Her campaign worked. By the mid-1960s, American tastes began to change. Blends fell out of favor, and consumers now wanted single malts, at home and at the bar. Liquor stores and bars started carrying more single malts and recommending them to their customers.

The press took note of Bessie and her crusade. What interested them the most wasn't her movement to promote scotch but that she was a woman. This often put her on the defensive. She didn't want to talk about what it was like being a woman in the world of whisky, she wanted to talk about the whisky itself. "Yes, it is odd for a woman to be a distiller of whisky, but you don't have to be an odd woman to be a distiller," she told an AP reporter in 1962.

While she was away from Islay often, Bessie didn't stop developing things back home. She continued with her plan to push Laphroaig ahead of all other scotch brands.

Up until the 1960s, there were basically no women working in the world of American wine.

There were some wine widows in the late 1800s, mostly in California, such as Kate Warfield, who ran the Ten Oaks Vineyard in Glen Ellen with great success. Her neighbor Ellen Good ran the winery at the Glen Ellen Ranch at the same time. Overall, though, it was a man's world.

Finally, in 1965, Mary Ann Graf earned a bachelor's degree in fermentation science from the University of California, Davis, which is a good place to start for a woman who wants a career focused on brewing or wine. Graf was passionate about the latter and got a job working as a winemaker at the Simi Winery in Sonoma County. She was the first woman to be awarded such a degree, but it didn't take too long for other women to join her.

In 1970, Zelma Long also attended UC Davis for a master's degree in enology (study of wine making) and viticulture (study of grape growing). She left before completing her degree and ended up becoming the first woman to take over senior management of Simi Winery. In 1973, Meredith Edwards followed in Graf's and Long's footsteps at UC Davis and is now the owner of two acclaimed vineyards in Sonoma County.

It was during the 1970s that the world finally started taking American wine seriously, Californian wine in particular. Up until that point, wines from the United States were considered inferior to wines from countries like Italy or France. On May 24, 1976, a tasting panel in Paris shocked the industry by ranking wines from California on par with ones from France. Suddenly, there was a spotlight on Californian wineries, especially ones in Napa Valley to the north and Sonoma Valley to the south. This resulted in an extraordinary boom in the California wine industry.

It was a great time to be a woman working in it.

New vineyards were popping up in California by the dozen, and they all needed staff. Because these companies were so new, they were not as entrenched in misogynistic traditions as many older wineries, like the ones in Europe. By 1985, the *New York Times* reported that America had over three dozen female winemakers, a huge leap from the zero of twenty years earlier.

Dr. Ann Noble went one step further. She became the one giving out those degrees at UC Davis. In 1974, Dr. Noble was the first woman to be hired in the Department of Viticulture and Enology. Within a few years, she was joined by several more women in the department.

Dr. Noble was a sensory specialist with a PhD in food science from the University of Massachusetts Amherst, and she wanted to change the way people described wine. Before her, wine was described in extremely vague and misleading terms. Some wines were *feminine* and some were *masculine*. What does *masculine* wine taste like? Sweaty tube socks? Old Spice? Talking about wine like this is unhelpful at best and confusing at worst. Dr. Noble wanted to fix it by creating a food-based lexicon of wine.

Her aroma wheel featured twelve basic categories, including Nutty, Fruity, Spicy, Floral and Woody. Each category was a word that almost everyone can understand. You've probably seen some of them on wine bottles at the store. Dr. Noble pioneered the use of objective and clear descriptors to talk about wine. This made her system accessible to people of all classes, who might not have grown up around expensive wines. The Aroma Wheel opened up the wine industry and completely revamped the way people taste and talk about wine.

Meanwhile, on television, Julia Child was completely revamping the way people think about women drinking it.

Child was an American educator and chef with a wildly popular television show called *The French Chef*. It premiered in 1963, and she became an instant favorite among American audiences. While the show was incredibly influential in the world of cooking, *The French Chef* was also notable for its portrayal of female drinking. Child regularly sipped on wine while she was cooking, just as if it was a totally unexceptional activity. She loved to say, "I enjoy cooking with wine. Sometimes I even put it in the food."

Drinking wine on air simply was not done in the 1960s, especially not by women. Especially, *especially* not by a lovable housewife. *The French Chef* aired several years before second wave feminism built into a huge movement. This was a time when the issues and lives of housewives were largely ignored by television. Women had been drinking in their kitchens for nearly a thousand years by then, but now it was on display for the whole world to see. Julia Child showed people that it was normal.

This was also a time when Americans were drinking awful wine. Until the late 1960s, most Americans drank what was referred to as table wine. Table wine is a lower-quality and lower-priced wine. Remember how the Widow Clicquot made her magnificent champagne with juice from the first or second pressings of grapes? Table wine is the stuff that comes from a few pressings after that. Julia Child's enthusiasm for good wine played a huge part in reviving the popularity of drinking higher-quality wine with meals.

As much as she was an advocate for good wine, Child was a gin lover. She loved her upside-down martini, which was heavy on vermouth and light on gin. This chef did *not* participate in the new vodka martini craze.

What Julia Child was doing for wine on television, a bartender named Joy Perrine was doing for bourbon down in Kentucky.

During the 1960s and 70s in America, bourbon was considered a grandpa drink. It was old man booze. Young people didn't drink it much, and it was definitely not marketed to women. Bartenders didn't put bourbon in cocktails. The old-fashioned was a popular drink with female drinkers after Prohibition, but by this time, the cocktail lived up to its name. Until the self-dubbed Bad Girl of Bourbon came along, that is.

Joy Perrine began her career down on the island of Saint Croix in the early 1960s. Her parents were both rumrunners in New Jersey during Prohibition, so she had spirits in her blood. When she started bartending, Perrine was in her early twenties. She absolutely loved making drinks. As a part of the US

Virgin Islands, Saint Croix was a prime spot for rum cocktails, and Perrine learned the art of mixology by experimenting with rum. Eventually, she moved to Louisville, Kentucky, and left the Caribbean behind forever. It was 1978, only six years after the state had lifted the ban on female bartending.

Perrine's career behind the bar continued in Kentucky. In her new post, she found herself in love with a new drink: bourbon, the signature spirit of the state. She wanted to play around with it like she had with rum. While Perrine believed that the old-fashioned was the most important cocktail for a bartender to learn, she wanted to experiment and move beyond it. The problem was that most of her customers didn't like (and weren't used to) the taste of straight whiskey.

Perrine started experimenting with bourbon cocktails that featured flavored syrups and fruit infusions that she made herself. Her delicious concoctions immediately faced a backlash from the bartending community. To many traditional bartenders, it was sacrilege to mix bourbon with things like fruity syrups. What she was doing was taking a masculine spirit and using it to make girly drinks.

This is where her self-dubbed nickname, the Bad Girl of Bourbon, came from, breaking the rules of what you were supposed to do with bourbon. But Perrine didn't care. Sharing her love of bourbon was more important than following bartending traditions. In an interview in 2016, she said, "Hey, there are some people who just don't like the taste of whiskey straight. So if I make a cocktail and convert them to being a bourbon drinker, then who cares?"

Despite the industry criticism, Perrine's cocktails were a hit with local drinkers. Slowly, she converted her customers both to her new cocktails and to her beloved bourbon. By mixing it with flavors that were more widely palatable, like apple or ginger, Perrine turned many drinkers on to the spirit that might have never tried it. To show her haters what she thought of them, she got a black widow spider tattooed on her hand. It ensured, as she said, that "no one fucks with me."

By the mid-1980s, Perrine had worked her way up the bartending ladder. In 1985, she was hired at the bar of the venerable Equus Restaurant in Louisville, where she reigned until her death in 2019. (That bar is now known as Jack's Bourbon Lounge.) Her bartending career spanned over fifty years, and as Perrine said, she was "born a bartender and will die a bartender." Along with bourbon expert Susan Reigler, Perrine wrote two books of bourbon cocktail recipes, *The Kentucky Bourbon Cocktail Book* and *More Kentucky Bourbon Cocktails*. In 2016, she was the first female bartender to be inducted into the Kentucky Bourbon Hall of Fame.

Joy Perrine really was onto something.

Around the same time Perrine was enticing drinkers to bourbon, whiskey juggernaut Wild Turkey was trying to do the same thing. In the mid-1970s, the company's master distiller Jimmy Russell declared that he believed women found bourbon to be too strong. (Never mind that bourbon was not marketed to women in any way.) Apparently, he never met Joy Perrine.

To capture the modern market of drinking women, in the late 1970s Wild Turkey released their now infamous American Honey. American Honey is a liqueur, a sweet blend of bourbon and honey. The company marketed it as bourbon...for *ladies*.

American Honey was a massive hit (and still sells well to this day), but Wild Turkey eventually was forced to admit that just as many men drank it as women did.

During the 1960s and 70s, there were still women in many parts of the world fighting for their right to make and drink alcohol. Yes, still.

Women in Nepal have a long-standing tradition of making and drinking *raksi*. Raksi is a distilled alcohol that's made from either millet or rice. It's strong and clear and tastes a bit like saké. Raksi was an important part of village communities, not just

as recreation but as a part of people's diets and medicine. In re-
mote villages, alcohol might be the best available painkiller for
someone undergoing a medical procedure, or it could be served
to birthing women to keep their strength up. Some communities featured raksi as an important part of religious ceremonies
and rituals.

But most importantly, raksi served as a key source of income
for women, especially for Thabangi women living in the district
of Rolpa, in the province of Lumbini. Money made from making raksi was special. This income was (and still is) considered
to be a woman's property, not the property of the household,
and was usually used for children's school fees and clothes. The
sale of raksi contributed to the slight redistribution of wealth
between men and women. For many women, selling raksi was
an important part of their livelihood and their identity.

In the 1970s, the industrialization of the alcohol industry
had finally hit Nepal. There was a movement to take alcohol
production out of the kitchen and into the factory—which
meant out of the hands of poor women and into the hands of
men. Male village leaders proposed a ban on home brewing
and wanted to substitute locally made raksi for licensed liquor.
This went over with the women of Rolpa about as well as it
did for the women of South Africa. In the early 1970s, there
was a women's uprising.

The women in Rolpa protested. They marched to the meeting place of the village council and obstructed the council
proceedings. Afterward, they organized a group of women to
persuasively argue their case. This group put together a strong
argument and presented it to the council. They won their case
and kept their right to make and sell raksi.

To this day, raksi remains a vital source of income for women
in Nepal. Many young daughters keen on modern life look
down upon the tradition, but distilling raksi still brings great
pride and power for the older women.

★ ★ ★

What about those South African brewing women who had been fighting for decades?

In 1961, South Africa became a republic. What followed was widespread demand for the lifting of the legal alcohol restrictions, not for social reasons but for economic ones. The beer hall monopoly was not making the government enough money to justify it. Plus, the police finally had to admit they could not control the shebeens or the shebeen queens that ran them. People were going to make, drink and sell beer, whether it was illegal or not. So the government might as well find another way to make money off it.

By the next year, the Liquor Act was amended. On August 15, 1962, the ban on drinking for native Africans was lifted. No more beer hall monopolies. Home brewing was legal again, although a woman now needed a license to sell her product. But apartheid had not yet ended and wouldn't for several decades. Native Africans still had to enter liquor stores through a non-European entrance at the side.

Through all the years of oppression, women in South Africa never stopped brewing. In the following decades, they would finally get to flourish.

While she was creating a market for it, Bessie Williamson made sure her scotch was the finest around.

In 1961, the same year she was hired by the Scotch Whisky Association to be their American spokesperson, Bessie launched big plans for Laphroaig. She wanted to expand, and she wanted new equipment, the best she could buy for her distillery. In order to get the funding, Bessie decided to sell some of her shares in the business. It cost her some power at the company, but the sales resulted in her getting the money that she needed to revamp her Laphroaig.

Bessie soon bought a brand-new warehouse, an additional still and a boiler so huge that a landing craft from the Scottish military had to be used to transport it over to Islay from the mainland. She got the distillery's property renovated, too.

Thanks to her marketing genius and increased output from all the new equipment and space, Laphroaig soon became one of Scotland's top whisky brands.

But Bessie wasn't doing it all for the money. She loved her distillery and especially the people working in it. The First Lady of Scotch was known for taking extremely good care of all her employees. The distillery actually would have been a lot more profitable in the 1960s and 70s if she didn't pay her employees so well and donate so much money. Bessie also made sure that Laphroaig was a positive force in its community, opening the distillery buildings for public use during seasonal celebrations. She did so much charity work that Queen Elizabeth gave her a medal for it.

In 1972, at the age of sixty-one, Bessie Williamson finally sold the rest of her Laphroaig shares and retired from the scotch industry. She passed away in Glasgow ten years later. The Laphroaig distillery has not had a female manager or owner since.

Bessie heavily contributed to the success of Islay scotch. She laid the groundwork for the success of other whisky distilleries on the island that are operating today, such as Bowmore, Lagavulin and Ardbeg.

Bessie Williamson is proof that a glass of neat, single-malt scotch is, in fact, a girly drink. And you can thank her for its popularity in America. It was a woman who believed that consumers of all genders were ready for its powerful taste. Bessie argued—and successfully made her case—for *not* watering down your whisky or making it sweeter.

It's okay to make it sweeter, though, if you want. As the Bad Girl of Bourbon[159] Joy Perrine herself insisted, any way you take

---

159 She also called herself the Bar Belle.

your whiskey is the right way. Whiskey is for everyone and every taste, whether it's scotch, rye or bourbon.

In recent years, an interesting ideal has developed, probably in response to centuries of straight whiskey being considered a man's drink: the whiskey-drinking woman. She's a cool girl because she likes guy stuff, not girly stuff. She's sexy and tough because she's drinking a *man drink*, not a girly drink.

This weird subgenre of the cool girl is just a new type of male fetishization of women. It developed from advertisements designed to sell whiskey to men and what's called *aspirational drinking*. The idea is that if a man drinks a certain brand of whiskey, a cool, sexy woman will want to drink it with him. What's extra frustrating is that many women bought into this idea, that *cool drinks* and *girly drinks* were mutually exclusive categories of beverages. She's not like other girls because she drinks whiskey. And yes, whiskey is cool. Whiskey is awesome. But drinking it doesn't make you cooler or more awesome than someone who drinks wine or beer or, yes, even vodka. Don't let the patriarchy influence your drink choices. Drink what you want! Plus, if someone wanted to be a true whisky woman like Bessie Williamson, she'd grab a pair of vintage glasses, put on a frumpy, wool cardigan and twist her hair into a sensible updo.

After all these groundbreaking female distillery owners, bartenders, scientists and activists, it was finally time for the world to get its first female master blender.

13

THE JOY SPENCE
ANNIVERSARY BLEND

The 1980s and 90s

After hundreds of years of being pushed out of and excluded from alcohol industries that they either invented or were crucial in developing, the 1980s and 90s saw women finally—officially, legally—back in the world of brewing and distilling.

One woman paved the way for the entire industry and cleared a path for scores and scores of women after her. The world's first female master blender—of any type of spirit—was Joy Spence, known as the Queen of Rum.

Now, in the twenty-first century, rum gets a pretty bad rap. Unless they're a craft cocktail geek, most people only encounter rum when it's on fire in the center of a scorpion bowl or when it's mixed with cola in a red plastic cup. After rum's revival during America's tiki craze, it sank back into the depths of spirits obscurity. By the 1980s and 90s, most consumers associated it with cloying cocktails or questionable decisions during college parties.

But rum is a spirit with depth and a complex flavor profile

on par with the world's finest whiskeys. To make a good rum (and believe me, there's a lot of excellent rum in the world) requires extraordinary skill and experience. Joy Spence has plenty of both.

Born in 1951, Joy grew up in Jamaica's capital city of Kingston. At the age of thirteen, she began to develop a passion for chemistry. Her love was kindled by her beloved chemistry teacher, who passed away while Joy was still finishing high school. Although Joy was absolutely crushed, she was determined to make her teacher proud and continued to teach herself chemistry.

She graduated with First Class Honors from the University of the West Indies in 1972 and, several years later, went on to earn her master's in science in analytical chemistry from England's University of Loughborough.[160] Joy returned to Jamaica and eventually landed a job as a research and development chemist at Tia Maria, a company that produces a liqueur made with coffee beans.

After a couple of years, Joy got bored. She felt like she wasn't getting challenged enough at Tia Maria. Luckily for her (and all of us), next door was legendary Jamaican rum company Wray and Nephew. Joy kept looking across the way and trying to see what was going on over there. Making rum looked like a lot of fun. She finally decided to send over her résumé.

What came of it was booze history.

By the 1980s, the dream of second wave feminism was still not fully realized. There were many gains made by women in the Western world, yes. In 1984, forty-nine percent of bachelor's and master's degrees in America went to women. There was now a woman on the Supreme Court and, soon, even one in space. The Supreme Court ruled that sexism in a work environment

---

160   Joy's final exam scores still hold the record for the highest ever achieved by a student at Loughborough.

was hostile and abusive. But there was still a lot of work to do. That same court also ruled that states could deny public funding for abortions and prohibit public hospitals from performing them. Though women now made up half of the workforce, they were still paid less and dealt with a lot of bullshit.

Women were still not totally accepted into public drinking culture, either, in America and beyond. Many non-Western countries which adopted Western alcoholic beverages and practices excluded women. In Japan, male drinkers were happy to try American drinks like bourbon, but they discouraged women from doing the same. Women were expected to be the ones serving alcohol, not the ones drinking it.

In fact, the 1980s were a time of medical panic about women drinking. Studies conducted during the previous decade discovered fetal alcohol syndrome, where heavy drinking (eight to ten drinks a day) during pregnancy could cause congenital malformations in a fetus.[161] By 1982, the FDA commissioner issued a suggestion that all types of alcoholic beverages should contain warning labels for pregnant women.

European health professionals felt a little differently. They thought that the risk of fetal alcohol syndrome was small, especially when compared to the health benefits a pregnant or nursing person might get from a glass of beer or wine. In Germany, a glass of beer was recommended if you were breastfeeding.[162]

In 1989, a bill requiring warning labels on bottles and cans of alcohol for pregnant women (and warning of the danger posed by alcohol for any person driving or operating heavy machin-

---

161 What they discovered was that alcohol is a *teratogen*, a malformation-causing substance. Atomic weapons and some viruses like rubella are also teratogens.

162 This divide exists today. In the United States, the Center for Disease Control's official stance is that there is no way to safely drink any alcohol while pregnant. A study done from 2004 to 2011 in Ireland, England, New Zealand and Australia concluded that minimal- to low-alcohol consumption during pregnancy did not negatively affect the baby.

ery) was signed into American federal law.[163] While this bill was undoubtedly a good thing, it contributed to the belief that a mother who had a glass of wine while she was pregnant or breastfeeding (or even after that) was a bad mother. It was a new justification for an age-old belief that mothers did not belong in drinking culture. The intense panic around mothers having a drink persists to this day.

The new generation of women growing up in the Western world in the late 1980s and early 1990s were ready for rebellion. Mirroring the American flappers of the early 1900s, many young (and usually white) women started going wild.

In 1990s England, ladette culture sprang up. It was a direct response to the rise of the lad subculture, which featured mostly middle-class young men who shunned intellectual pursuits in favor of heavy drinking, shouting and being sexist. It was all sort of a drunken ouroboros. Ladette culture formed in response to lad culture, which was formed in response to men feeling threatened by feminism, which spread in response to sexism. You'd think it would be easiest to just cut to the chase and get rid of the sexism, but here we are.

Ladettes were trash-talking, heavy-drinking young women who wore scant clothing and were out to prove that whatever lads could do, they could do better. Or at least the same. Ladettes liked to binge-drink, flash passersby and pick up men while chugging pints of beer.

Although ladettes could come from any economic class, many of them were young professionals with money and decent jobs. They were usually college educated. That's part of what shocked society: that ladettes were so-called good girls.

Many ladettes were also figuring out what it meant to be

---

163   This was actually a victory for the alcohol industry. Pregnant women were never a substantial part of their market, and the drunk driving warning absolved alcohol companies of all liability.

modern, career-focused women. They bucked both housework and having children. Ladettes occupied a space that was completely outside the sphere of traditional feminine expectations and behavior. There were no blueprints, no widespread examples for them to follow. So, ladettes did what the lads did. And because they weren't starting families yet (the average age for that was on the rise), these women had more money to spend. And they wanted to spend it at bars.

In a cloud of fruity body spray, ladettes descended upon England's bars like a navel-pierced battalion. English media celebrities like Zoe Ball, Sara Cox and Denise van Outen were famous and very public examples of ladette culture. The media went into an absolute frenzy for depictions of these wild, sloppy, drunken women (even if they were alongside equally wild, sloppy, drunken men). A woman unleashing a powerful beer burp while standing on top of a bar wasn't quite the face of female independence that many second wave feminists dreamed of.

America's version was the annual televised *MTV Spring Break* special and "Girls Gone Wild" videos that every kid saw in between infomercials at two in the morning when they had the flu. Both featured candid footage of college-age, usually white women drinking, partying and, sometimes, exposing themselves. They put a spotlight on the raucous college and spring break binge-drinking culture that women were participating in more and more.

The number of women binge-drinking (having five or more drinks in a single sitting) was sharply on the rise in the 1990s, but it wasn't even close to the number of men. A study in 1998 showed that thirty-nine percent of men aged eighteen to twenty-four binge-drank, while only eight percent of women did. Lads far outnumbered the ladettes, but the ladettes were much more notorious. Ladettes were blamed for a rise in alcoholism, car accidents and just about any social problem related to alcohol. Boys will be boys, yet girls partying like boys might bring down all of society.

Ladette culture finally burned itself out in the early 2000s. The panic about it really was a modern version of the now millenia-old horror over women acting like men. Ladettes were just ancient Greek maenads who wore tank tops and chunky heels and worshipped Dionysus with shots of peach schnapps.

Beanie Babies, grunge music and lesbian bars: they all had their heyday during the 1990s.

This decade had the highest number of thriving and inclusive lesbian bars of any decade in America. Being out as a lesbian in public was a little safer, which was a breath of fresh air after the 1980s, where cities like New York still had a morals division in their police department, which enforced homophobic regulations. The morals division squads specifically targeted bars that were frequented by Black and Latinx women. Racist and homophobic neighbors used the police to harass these bars by reporting noise complaints. Some bars, like Duchess in Manhattan, got in legal trouble for refusing to sell drinks to men. But by the 1990s, things were looking up for the lesbian bar.

Scores of inclusive bars opened up in big cities. Crazy Nanny's in Manhattan was known for being a bar that welcomed trans women. Two different Latinx lesbian bars opened up in Queens. Henrietta Hudson's (near the Stonewall Inn) opened up in 1991 and is still open to this day, making it the longest-standing lesbian bar in New York City. (Maud's, which was located in San Francisco and opened in 1966, claimed to be the oldest lesbian bar in the United States, but they closed down for good in 1989.)

Sadly, it did not last. After the 1990s, there was a sharp decline, and by 2010, lesbian bars were closing in droves for a myriad of reasons. There were now many other gathering places for members of the LGBTQ+ community and brand-new dating apps to meet people with. Many traditionally gay neighborhoods, especially ones populated by the BIPOC (Black, Indigenous, and people of color) gay community, were gentrified. Overall, there was less interest in specifically lesbian bars and more preference for generally queer-friendly spaces that welcomed the entire spectrum of the LGBTQ+ community.

No matter what their sexual orientation was, a lot more women went to bars in the 1990s. More women worked as bartenders and waitresses, which meant more job opportunities. More women joined in business meetings and networking events, which meant more power in the workforce. More women availed themselves of access to this part of the public sphere, which meant more opportunities to socialize and meet people outside the home and, depending on the type of bar it was, maybe even relax. More women were able to go enjoy a goddamn drink when they wanted to.

But after decades of fighting to be able to enter a bar, women began to worry about what was going to happen once they got inside. The 1990s saw the emergence of the what became known as the date-rape drug.

Fear of having someone put a date-rape drug in her drink became one of the biggest influences on women's drinking culture in bars and nightclubs. It completely changed female public drinking behavior.

Date-rape drugs incapacitate a person and make them vulnerable to sexual assault. The most popular ones can be secretly dissolved into a drink and have no smell or taste. It isn't the only drug in this category, but the most notorious by far is Rohypnol, also known as roofies. In the 1990s, Rohypnol was cheap to acquire. It became so infamous that the entire class of date-rape drugs was sometimes called roofies. *Roofied* even became a verb.

Rohypnol, also known as flunitrazepam, is basically a much stronger Valium or Xanax. It's a benzodiazepine that was first marketed in the 1970s as a treatment for severe insomnia and is part of a group of minor, psychoactive tranquilizers. Rohypnol also has the propensity to produce anterograde amnesia, which is the inability to form new memories while under its influence. (Some other drugs in this class, like GHB, also do this.) This side effect is particularly terrifying when Rohypnol is in the hands of a sexual predator.

National concern over these drugs emerged around 1995 and 1996. Newspapers and magazines began to feature reports on both the drugs and the vile way they were being used. Most of the scares centered around party venues like bars and nightclubs in the United States, Canada, Australia and the United Kingdom.

Desperate to avoid restrictions and regulations, Hoffman-La Roche—the manufacturer of Rohypnol—launched a campaign that would forever change the way women act when they go out to drink.[164]

The Watch Your Drink! campaign was part of Hoffman-La Roche's lobby for decreased regulation. Their approach was twofold. One, they insisted that alcohol itself was the real problem. Despite the fact that Rohypnol can be put into any drink, alcoholic or otherwise, Hoffman–La Roche declared that alcohol was the number one date-rape drug. Two, they put the onus on women to protect their own drinks and avoid assault. There was an air of *Well, if you left your drink unattended...* or *Well, if you didn't go out drinking...* as if sexual assault was not an intentional crime but rather some kind of arbitrary force of nature, like a heavy rain, that could be avoided with good planning. Spiking someone's drink sounds innocuous, but it is nothing short of evil.[165]

---

164   Rohypnol is actually illegal in the United States. It always has been. It's usually smuggled in from Europe or Mexico. In 1998, the company added a blue dye to make the drug detectable when dropped in a clear drink.

165   In 2004, the Safe Drinking Campaign was launched in North Wales that featured a cartoon hedgehog named Spike. Seriously.

Hoffman–La Roche did not, however, launch a Don't Assault Women, You Pieces of Garbage! campaign to go along with the Watch Your Drink! campaign. The responsibility of preventing date rape was placed on women's shoulders.

Nearly thirty years later, the campaign is still extremely effective.

An entire set of cautionary behaviors for female drinkers sprang up in the wake of Watch Your Drink! The first and usually the only thing that women are taught about drinking is to watch your cup. Don't put it down, stay in packs, only accept a drink from the bartender.

Bartenders eventually devised a special code to keep their female customers safe. Any mention of *angels* or *Angela* meant a customer was in trouble or she suspected someone drugged her drink. If a customer ordered an *angel's shot*, it was a call for help from the bartender. A woman who ordered an *angel's shot neat* was asking for the bartender to escort her to her car. An *angel's shot with ice* meant she was asking for a taxi or ride service to be called. An *angel's shot with lime* meant that the bartender should call the police.

As a cherry on top of the revulsive sundae, companies began developing and selling products to detect the presence of drugs in a drink, such as nail polish that changes color when exposed to Rohypnol. Many of these companies released inflated statistics of date-rape drug incidents in order to keep female fear high and sell more of their products.

To muddy the statistical waters, the rise of date-rape drugs went hand in hand with the rise of binge-drinking on college campuses. Now, binge-drinking was certainly not a newcomer to college students, but there was an uptick in the 1990s. Binge-drinking is usually defined as more than five drinks in a single episode. As we saw with the ladettes, men still drank more and binge-drank more, but in the 1990s there was a sharp increase among women. The *Journal of American College Health* reported that there was a one hundred and twenty-five percent increase in binge-drinking at all-women colleges from 1993 to 2001.

Some women became convinced that they had been given a date-rape drug, when in reality they had just had far, far too much to drink. Most people, no matter how old they are, underestimate how much they've had to drink. College-age drinkers are especially terrible at it. American society has an enormous amount of confusion surrounding what is meant by *a drink*, as in, a single serving of alcohol.

Party punches like jungle juice are a common drink of college parties. They're cheap to mix and serve to a ton of people. It's usually a mildly revolting mix of extremely high ABV grain alcohol, cheap vodkas, juices and sodas. The problem is that one full red plastic cup of this mix is usually six to seven servings of alcohol, meaning that drinking one whole cup already constitutes binge-drinking. Students, however, consider that one drink. So many parents and educational systems are resistant to teaching kids about drinking, but young people really should know this stuff.

The Watch Your Drink! campaign also created a discomfort surrounding sexual assault victims who were *only* drunk and not drugged. There was a thinly veiled suggestion that if a woman got too drunk at a party or a bar, she deserved whatever happened to her, even rape. As if she should not have *let* that happen. It was and still is the equivalent of thinking that a woman wearing a short skirt is *asking for it*.

America was not able to square itself with a woman's right to be intoxicated and not be assaulted.

In the pre-Prohibition days, the narrative of the good girl was used to discourage women from drinking. In the 1990s, a new narrative emerged: the smart girl. Responsibility replaced respectability. Smart girls know how to protect their drinks. Smart girls know that men are just, gosh, naturally sexually predatory when they drink and that they should be avoided. Smart girls know to always keep an eye on their friends and how much they're drinking, too. In fact, smart girls really shouldn't be at the bar at all. It's a man's place, and boys will be boys.

So, let's see here. Women are responsible for their own drinking and behavior, their friends' drinking and behavior, and the drinking and behavior of all men within a quarter-mile radius. Of course, it *is* a smart idea for a woman to know how much alcohol she's drinking and to keep an eye on her friends and to protect her drink. But the narrative of the smart girl was a new twist on a concept that had been weaponized against women for centuries: women have all the responsibility and none of the power.

Decades after it was launched, the Watch Your Drink! campaign is still working. Don't get me wrong, it's also still needed. While other date-rape drugs have replaced Rohypnol in popularity and then they themselves been replaced, men are still putting them into people's drinks. Decades after it was launched, there still hasn't been a campaign to convince them to stop.

The folks at Wray and Nephew, the Jamaican rum company next door, turned out to be just as interested in Joy Spence as she was in them. They were extremely impressed by her résumé, and although the company didn't have any vacancies, they still offered her a job. The salary was less than what she was getting at Tia Maria, but Joy said yes.

In 1981, she was hired as the new chief chemist of a rum distillery that Wray and Nephew owned called Appleton Estate. In this role, it was Joy's job to make sure the chemical specifications—such as the alcohol percentage—of the rum were met. Nestled in Jamaica's beautiful Nassau Valley, Appleton Estate is one of the world's oldest names in the rum industry. The distillery was established in 1749, and their sugar estate is the oldest in Jamaica.

During the 1980s in Jamaica, women didn't drink or go to bars. It was considered improper. Joy herself didn't drink at all before she got hired at Appleton. But once she got there, she fell in love with rum.

Joy started by working with Appleton's master blender, a man named Owen Tulloch. A master blender is someone who develops blends using a combination of spirits with different characteristics. They must be adept at both the artistry and the science of alcohol. Many types of spirit companies have master blenders, including those that make whiskey, rum, brandy, even vodka.

Perhaps the most important requisite for being a master blender is an impeccable set of sensory skills. Tulloch recognized right away that Joy was an organoleptic talent: that she had an extraordinary ability to detect, identify and differentiate between smells. She could sense over two hundred different aromas.

Seeing her talent, Tulloch got Joy involved in distilling.

To make rum, sugarcane[166] is harvested (in Jamaica, the harvest season is from January to May) and then crushed to release the juice. The juice is boiled until it becomes molasses. Using a centrifuge, crystals of sugar are separated from the molasses. The sugar is sold off, and the molasses heads to the rum distillery. Water and yeast[167] are added to the molasses, then the mixture ferments for about three days. Finally, it is distilled into rum. At Appleton Estate, the final product is sent in barrels over to a site in Kingston to age.

For seventeen years Joy worked closely with Tulloch. During that time, she developed a passion for the complexities of rum and how it was an expression of Jamaican culture. Because rums age three times faster in a tropical climate, the spirit

---

166   There are different varieties of sugarcane used, depending on what type of rum you make.

167   The particular yeast culture that Appleton Estate uses is a secret that's been handed down for generations. Joy holds the secret to recreating it, should a disaster strike the distillery.

quickly becomes as deep and complex as other dark spirits like scotch or brandy.

When it was time for Tulloch to retire, Joy was the natural pick for the job. She became the very first female master blender in the world—of any type of spirit. There were male colleagues who doubted her ability to do the job (despite her *seventeen years* of training), but her overwhelming competence and enthusiasm for rum eventually convinced all who needed convincing. Joy's first assignment was to create a special rum for Appleton Estate's two hundred and fiftieth anniversary. No pressure!

As the master blender, it was Joy's job to select from all the different rum barrels and batches which ones to blend. If the idea of walking through a gigantic rum storage warehouse to pick out, smell and taste different rums sounds like heaven, then Joy was on cloud nine. After selecting the potential components of a blend, Joy then analyzed it in her laboratory to make sure that the specifications (like the alcohol percentage) were met. Of course, it also had to taste right.

The Appleton Estate's 250th Anniversary Blend definitely tasted right. Joy knocked it out of the park. The commemorative rum was released in 1999 to high praise from the spirits industry. Only six thousand bottles were made, and they are now collector's items.

And that was just the *first* rum she made.

Joy Spence was the first, but over the next few years, she was joined by other female master blenders at distilleries all over the world. The 1990s saw a long overdue influx of women in the Irish and Scottish whiskey industry.

In 1995, Rachel Barrie was hired at scotch giant Glenmorangie and completely changed the whisky industry. She was trained as a chemist at the University of Edinburgh, and when she graduated, Barrie got a job as a research scientist at the Scotch Whisky Research Institute. There, she helped to develop the sensory science techniques that are used by modern distilleries to enhance the taste of scotch.

When she was hired at Glenmorangie, Barrie started to experiment with new malting procedures and with ways to age the spirit in different types of casks. No one had ever tested these ideas out on a large scale before, and Barrie's delicious results made huge waves. Soon, other distilleries were trying out her ideas, especially the experiments with different types of casks. Lots of scotch is aged in barrels left over from other alcohol industries. Used bourbon casks are very popular, but some scotch is now, thanks to Rachel Barrie, aged in used rum, sherry or wine barrels.

A couple of years after Barrie was brought onto the team, Glenmorangie bought another scotch company: Ardbeg. Glenmorangie is a Highland scotch company, and Ardbeg is an Islay scotch company, meaning that Ardbeg is much heavier and smokier. Highlands tend to be a little sweeter, spicier, maltier and even a bit fruiter than an Islay. In 1997, Barrie was charged with assessing their new distillery. She flourished there, and in 2003, Rachel Barrie became Scotland's first female master blender. Her ingenuity and brilliance supercharged Ardbeg. Along with her team, Barrie developed the Ardbeg Supernova,[168] which earned World Whisky of the Year awards in both 2008 and 2009. It's widely considered to be one of the greatest scotches of the twenty-first century.

The same year Rachel Barrie was hired, down in Ireland the chemist Helen Mulholland was hired at the Bushmills distillery. By 2005, she became Ireland's first female master blender. Along with her all-female tasting panel, Mulholland has created some of the best Irish whiskeys in recent history. Like Joy Spence, Mulholland was tasked with creating a special anniversary blend for her distillery. The Bushmills four hundredth anniversary blend—the Bushmills 1608—won the World Whisky

---

168   My personal favorite scotch.

Awards' Best Irish Blended Whiskey in 2008. She became the first woman inducted into the Whisky Magazine Hall of Fame in 2018.

In America, Kentucky bourbon finally got its first female master blender with Marianne Eaves at Castle and Key[169] in 2015. In the same year, Tennessee got its first female head distiller with Alex Castle at Old Dominick, who also became the first female president of the Tennessee Distillers Guild in 2020. Nowadays, no matter what type of whiskey you like to drink, you can find one created by a woman.

The world is still waiting, however, for a major whiskey brand named after a woman. Jack Daniel's, Jim Beam, Johnnie Walker, Pappy Van Winkle, Elijah Craig… Maybe someday we'll get a bottle of Rachel Barrie or Ol' Helen to join the boys' club on the shelf.[170]

Not to be outdone by the spirits world, the American beer industry got its first female brewmasters in the 1990s.

In 1995, Patricia Henry became the first female beer plant manager in the country at the Miller brewery. After getting her bachelor's in chemistry in 1969, Henry started working at Miller in 1977. She went on to become the first woman and first Black person to be a brewmaster for a major American brewery.

Anheuser-Busch got their first female brewmaster in Jill Vaugh, who started working at the company in 1992. Vaugh completed her master's in food and science technology that year. She saw a notice on a bulletin board for a job opening at Anheuser-Busch and decided on a whim to apply. Knowing absolutely nothing about beer, she went to the library and checked out a textbook on the science of brewing. Vaugh took the book on the plane with her when she flew out to get interviewed. She

---

169   Eaves left Castle and Key in 2019.

170   There are a few smaller brands with whiskeys named after women, but none of them are actually made by women.

deeply impressed the folks at Anheuser-Busch with her (new-found) beer knowledge.

Vaugh went on to work there for nearly thirty years. She developed the recipes for popular beers such as Bud Light Lime and Michelob Ultra. But her most famous creations are collaborations with fellow Anheuser-Busch brewmaster Rebecca Bennett, who joined the company in 2005. Vaugh and Bennett developed the recipes for such party staples as Bud Light Platinum, Shock Top and the Straw-Ber-Rita. Bennett is still at Anheuser-Busch, working with other veteran brewmasters like Jane Killebrew.

Most of the senior brewmasters at Anheuser-Busch are women, but this is an anomaly in the industry. According to the Pink Boots Society, a nonprofit organization of women working in the beer industry, ninety-nine percent of the brewmasters in America are men. In a 2014 interview with *Essence* magazine, Bennett said, "People have a perception that brewers are all guys with beards and are surprised when they see me, an African American female." Next time you see Beardy McFlannel droning on about beer while he dunks an orange slice into his glass of Shock Top, let him know what's up.

Along with beer, wine and spirits, a new alcohol category emerged during the 1980s and 90s. Like a demon flying straight out of hangover hell, the alcopop arrived to wreak havoc on the world.

It all began in the early 1980s, when wine coolers first came out. A wine cooler is a mix of poor-quality wine, poor-quality juice, sugar and soda. They caught on for many reasons. Wine coolers were inexpensive, and thanks to the fact that they had lower ABV levels than wine (sometimes even lower than beer) they were subject to less restrictive alcohol laws. They were brightly colored and barely tasted like alcohol so they appealed to a market that had never really been catered to before: new drinkers who weren't used to the taste of alcohol yet, and people who didn't like the taste of alcohol but still wanted to get drunk.

Wine coolers sold very well but ran into a huge problem in 1991. In January of that year, the United States Congress quintupled the excise tax on wine. Suddenly, wine coolers could not be made so cheaply anymore. At least, as long as they had real wine in them. Someone got the idea to replace the wine with cheap malt liquor and, boom, the alcopop (alcohol + pop) was born.

The rest of the decade saw a cloying, fizzy alcopop boom. Products like Zima, Mike's Hard Lemonade, and Smirnoff Ice became wildly popular beverages. Alcopops were not considered to be real drinks (even though they were sometimes higher in alcohol than beer) and didn't have the strong associations with masculinity that beer or whiskey did. They were sweet, they were candy-colored, and their commercials featured cool, sexy, young women drinking them. (The ban on featuring women in spirits ads on television had only just been lifted in 1987, and it was still a relatively new thing to see a woman drinking beer or liquor in a commercial.) Alcopops became girly drinks.

Customers didn't need a taste for or knowledge of alcohol to order an alcopop. They also didn't have to worry about making a face when they tried it and have people laugh at them. Alcopops were like sodas that made you drunk. They were also advertised to women in a market where few if any other products were, and women responded by buying them. Because of this, alcopops soon garnered misogynistic nicknames like Bitch Brew and Bitch Beer.

The sweetness and widespread popularity caused several serious problems with alcopops. Because they're brightly colored and taste basically like soda, alcopops were also appealing to teenagers. The Center for Science in the Public Interest conducted a poll in 2001 that showed that fifty-one percent of seventeen- and eighteen-year-olds had tried them, and thirty-five percent of fourteen- to sixteen-year-olds had. Not good! Some alcopop companies got in legal trouble for creating advertisements that catered too much to the teenage market. (These studies and complaints prompted the American Federal Trade Commission to investigate, but they found no evidence of advertising to those age groups.)

Alcopops are also, quite frankly, usually pretty gross. They are typically made with poor-quality malt liquor, artificial colorings and powerful sweeteners. Many children of the 1980s and 90s will visibly shudder when shown a bottle of Arbor Mist the same way cats do when shown a vacuum. If someone downs several of them at a party, the next morning they'll probably be woken up by the feeling of their brain trying desperately to escape their skull and crawl away to safety.

By the end of the 2000s, even teenagers thought they were uncool. Alcopops began to be seen not as a girly drink but as an immature drink that was unappealing to all age groups. All these reasons eventually led to the decline of the alcopops. But the desire for less boozy-tasting booze lives on. Recent years have seen the rise of alcoholic seltzers and canned, pre-made cocktails and wine spritzers. Instead of the syrupy sweetness of an alcopop, many of these products are made with more quality ingredients but are still designed for easier drinking.

Alcohol companies still haven't quite figured out how to advertise to women. Instead of just making room for them in their target audience, these companies usually advertise products to women that are sweeter, lower-quality versions of what they usually make. Even if, like Wild Turkey American Honey, more men than women end up drinking it, these types of products are still considered girly drinks.

After her success with the 250th Anniversary Blend, Joy Spence went on to create ten new rum blends for Appleton Estate. Many of the higher-quality blends that are sold today feature her signature printed on the bottle.

Joy was passionate about rum. She was also passionate about Jamaica and how rum was its signature spirit. Along with her duties as a master blender, she began to work as an Appleton Estate brand ambassador, traveling and educating people all around the world about Jamaican rum. Like Bessie Williamson, Joy Spence, a short woman with dark, curly hair, and an infectious smile, was the perfect person to convince someone to try her favorite spirit. Joy's speeches were full of expertise and enthusiasm, as masterfully blended as her rum. In 2005, the government of Jamaica awarded her the Order of Distinction in the rank of Officer for her service to the rum industry.[171]

Joy wanted to take Jamaican rum to the next level.

Along with a team of fellow experts and enthusiasts, Joy began the work to get geographic indication for Jamaican rum. Geographic indications are rules, agreements and laws regarding how products made in a country or region can be made and described, specifically when those products refer to the name of that country or region, i.e., Jamaican rum. They don't always refer to alcohol; sometimes things like cheeses or fruits have geographic indications, too. It's sort of like a place having a trademark on its products. Champagne can only be made in the Champagne region of France, and bourbon can only be made in the United States. Made anywhere else, these products would just be called sparkling wine or corn whiskey. Why does this matter? For someone buying it, it means that certain quality standards are met and that it's actually made where it says it's made. If someone buys a bottle of something labeled *champagne*, they know they're getting a bottle of sparkling wine made in Champagne.

The ability for beers, wines and spirits to get geographical indication is part of what makes them magical. It's one of the exciting things about drinking, being able to taste and smell the very essence of a place. The soil, the weather, the water, the dedication and skill of the people there. Maybe it's a place that

---

171 This was bumped up to Commander in 2017.

you love, or maybe it's a place that you long to see. Either way, while you're sitting down with a glass, you can experience that place in a small, yet intimate, way.

In 2008, Jamaican rum was deemed eligible for geographic indication. Joy was part of the group that helped determine what exactly the rules were to stipulate that a rum could be called Jamaica rum. Among other technical and ingredient requirements, such as using naturally filtered limestone water from certain regions of the country and having no additives, there was one important rule. The rum must be fermented and distilled in Jamaica. If all the right ingredients were flown over to the United States and made into rum there, it couldn't be called Jamaican rum.

Securing geographical indication was important for people who wanted to buy Jamaican rum, but it was also important for Jamaica. It meant that the industry and its jobs could not be sent anywhere else.

Finally in 2016, thanks partially to Joy's hard work, Jamaican rum was approved for geographic indication.

The following year, Appleton Estate released their Joy Anniversary Blend, which commemorated her twenty years as Appleton Estate's master blender. The Joy Anniversary Blend contained twenty-five- and thirty-five-year-old rums, along with some rums that had special significance to Joy's career: one from 1981 (her first year with the company) and one from her preferred type of still. It's her favorite rum out of all the ones she's ever made. The blend won Rum of the Year in 2017.

Joy Spence is still reigning at Appleton Estate; she's been there for nearly forty years. The distillery tours are named after her. In addition to her work at Appleton Estate, she offers free chemistry tutoring to students. Joy continues to foster the passion that she has for both rum and Jamaica itself in others.

That same year her anniversary rum blend was released, Joy won the Grand Dame Award at Tales of the Cocktail, at the time one of the world's biggest and most influential spirits trade conferences and festivals. The Grand Dame Award is given to the most influential woman in the cocktail and spirits community.

In her acceptance speech, Joy stressed the importance of women in the alcohol industry, saying that,

> In Jamaica, we say "big up to these ladies"…not just at distilleries. We're bartenders, we're bar owners, we're ambassadors, we're decision makers, we're trendsetters, we're mentors and most importantly, we are friends. We are united in making this industry an inclusive space for all, no matter our gender, color, heritage, sexual orientation or religion.

Joy Spence made history at Appleton Estate and opened doors for women at distilleries all over the world. As the 1990s came to an end, it was time for women to make history behind the bar again.

14

JULIE REINER BEHIND THE BAR AFTER THREE

The 2000s

By the year 2000, the cocktail had been stuck in the dark ages for decades. Things were looking particularly grim after alco-pops and Zima.

At the end of the millennium, there were very few bars around the United States making cocktails with fresh ingredi-ents, instead of heavily processed mixes from a bottle. Crafted cocktails were a thing of the past, a distant, uncool memory in America's drinking culture. If a customer wanted something like a manhattan, they were probably out of luck. Because there was no market for them, it was difficult—if not impossible—to even find the ingredients for these drinks.

That was all about to change.

In the late 1980s, Rockefeller Center in New York City got an enormous renovation. The Rainbow Room, a restaurant up on the sixty-fifth floor, underwent an expansion and a make-over to restore it to its 1930s glamor. The new head bartender,

Dale DeGroff, took inspiration from Prohibition-era drinks and began to lay the foundations for a cocktail revolution.

Throughout the 1990s, the Rainbow Room became the center of a movement. DeGroff was keen to share his methods and take bartenders who were passionate about their craft under his wing. He is now known as the father of the modern cocktail renaissance. Of his three most legendary protégés, two were women, and the one that was most successful and responsible for bringing the art of craft cocktails to the masses is named Julie Reiner.

Julie was born and raised in Hawaii. Her family eventually moved to Florida, where she later went to college. In 1994, Julie headed out west to San Francisco. After a few boring jobs, she realized that she didn't want to be behind a desk for the rest of her life and started work as a cocktail waitress at the bar of the Parc 55 hotel. The bar manager, a woman named Linda Fusco, taught Julie how to make drinks, and a star was born.

Once she developed her skills enough to make the move from server to bartender, Julie got a job at AsiaSF, a restaurant that featured drag shows by Asian performers. But New York City, the home of the burgeoning cocktail renaissance, beckoned.

Julie, along with girlfriend Susan Fedroff (a former bar manager herself), headed back east in 1998. When they reached New York City, Julie had a tough time finding a bartending job. In an interview with *Thrillist* in 2017, she said that she would walk in to apply for a job, and bar managers would ask her "Are you sure you don't want to cocktail waitress?" At each place she applied, there would be only male bartenders. She'd ask the managers for a chance, telling them that she could "bartend circles around" the male bartenders. But she still had no luck.

Luckily, soon Susan got a call with a tip that the bar inside the Washington Square Hotel needed a manager. Julie applied and landed her very first job managing a bar.

The bar was called C3, and it desperately needed some fresh energy. From the sidewalk, it was tough to tell there was even a bar there. Julie was the perfect fit for the challenge. She was filled with creativity and curiosity and used both to completely revitalize the drinks menu there. She experimented with her own twists on classic cocktails and tried out brand-new infusions. Her boozy adventurousness endeared her to the blossoming New York cocktail community. Julie shone: she was outgoing and talkative, with a big laugh to go along with her big personality. Under her management, C3 began to overshadow the restaurant it was connected to.

In 2000, the *New York Times* reported on Julie's apple martini. Rather than using a flavored vodka, Julie mixed the drink with a handmade infusion of vodka and Granny Smith apples. A few months later, one of her cocktail creations called the French 77 (a twist on the French 75 cocktail made with brandy and Chambord) made the *New York Times* again. After that, *New York* magazine wrote about her. That year, Julie eclipsed everyone else who worked at C3.

Instead of being excited about the attention she was garnering, those in charge at C3 were unhappy about their bar manager outshining the bar. They let Julie go.

It ended up being the best thing they could possibly have done for her.

The 2000s were the start of a brand-new millennium and a brand-new set of girly drinks. While Julie Reiner was emerging onto the New York cocktail scene, so was one of the most well-known and notorious girly drinks of all time: the Cosmo.

There are many origin stories for the Cosmopolitan cocktail,[172] but what we know for sure is that the drink was floating around various drinking communities across America in the 1980s and

---

172 The most credible of which is that the Cosmo was created by Miami bartender Cheryl Cook in 1985. She wanted to make a cocktail that went into a martini glass but had a taste that was more widely appealing than a martini.

1990s. The recipe calls for a mix of vodka, lime juice, orange liqueur (known as triple sec) and cranberry juice, which gives the Cosmo its famous pink hue. Madonna was photographed with one in 1995 at a Grammy party held at Dale DeGroff's Rainbow Room.

The Cosmo might have stayed within the purview of cocktail aficionados if it wasn't for one extraordinarily popular television show. In 1999, the cocktail made its first appearance on the second episode of the second season of *Sex and the City*. The show was a tastemaker among American women. It influenced young professionals about desirable products, such as designer shoes and bags. Cocktails were no different.

By 2000, the Cosmo was all the rage among women drinkers and became the signature cocktail of Carrie, one of the show's main characters, played by Sarah Jessica Parker. It was the perfect moment for the Cosmo. Sleek and polished in its martini glass, pink and glamorous, the Cosmo was a symbol of everything many young women wanted to be. It was the chic drink of success and freedom. It was also one of the most affordable things that was featured on the show. A woman might not be able to shell out a thousand dollars for a designer purse, but a Cosmo was probably within her reach.

It was also unabashedly a girly drink. Clear, sterile-looking martinis, the most popular cocktail of the time, were synonymous with businessmen in business suits doing business things. Cosmos were literally pink, the most identifiable—for better or worse—shorthand for *female* in American culture.

Up until the second season of *Sex and the City*, there were no female drink influencers, as we'd call them today. Women had no blueprint for what to order, besides maybe a vodka soda, the less interesting cousin of the vodka martini. When most customers walk up to the bar, they order what they know. Now, women could have what Carrie was having. If the martini was the drink for the male professional, the Cosmo was the drink for the female professional.[173]

Soon, bartenders were sick of making Cosmos. Even for male drinkers, it was one of the most popular drinks to order in the country, especially in urban areas. Within a few years, Cosmos went the way of all fads and lost their sheen. By the time the *Sex and the City* movie came out in 2008, they were seen as a cliché and basic drink order.

Another pink drink rushed to fill the girly drinks void: rosé.

Rosé is its own type of wine and not just a mix of white and red. It's actually one of the oldest types of wine and is made when some of the color of the grape skins is incorporated into the juice. In the mid-2000s, rosé became the hot new drinking fad for some of the same reasons that shot the Cosmo into the stratosphere. It was girly, it was new, and it sounded swanky. (The popularity might have been helped along by a record 2005 grape crop which resulted in a colossal amount of California rosé to sell for cheaper prices.)

A lot of groundwork for the popularity of wine among women was laid down by another female screen star.

Bridget Jones's Diary was released in 2001, a film adaption of Helen Fielding's 1996 literary reinterpretation of *Pride and Prejudice*. The main character is played by Renée Zellweger, and her drink of choice is white wine, chardonnay specifically. But Bridget has a very different relationship with chardonnay than Carrie Bradshaw has with the Cosmo.

While the Cosmo was the drink of success, chardonnay was the drink of the woman who couldn't quite get there. Bridget embodied the thirtysomething white working girl who can't get her shit together. She's trying to quit smoking, trying to lose weight, trying to get a better job, trying to find a man and

---

173 Julie Reiner had her own version of the Cosmo, made with blood orange instead of cranberry.

trying to drink sensibly, as she sees it. White wine became the booze of choice for stressed out, frustrated women in the United States and the United Kingdom.

Sales of chardonnay increased in the wake of the film's release. British yearly wine consumption nearly doubled in 2005 from what it had been in 1995. The so-called Bridget Jones Effect helped give the wine industry a jump, selling 703 million gallons of all types of wine in 2005, where it had been 464 million gallons in 1995.

What made on-screen drinkers like Carrie Bradshaw and Bridget Jones stand out was that alcohol was a regular part of their lives. The antics of the drunken women are not new to cinema or television (even *I Love Lucy* had an episode featuring a comically drunk Lucy). But rare was it to see the normal drinking lives of women as we saw it in the normalization of sitcom fathers having beers or drinking on fishing trips or heading out to the pub with their buddies after work. Bridget Jones struggles with overindulgence just as she struggles with all other aspects of her life, but the women of *Sex and the City* made going out to the bar with your lady friends seem like a regular, average thing. Even Kate Middleton, future Duchess of Cambridge, started an all-female drinking club when she was a college student at the University of St. Andrews in Fife. She did this not to get smashed all the time but to protest the fact that all the other drinking clubs at the college excluded women.

The changing norms of drinking culture were reflected in many of the party songs released by female artists during the decade. Writer Gabrielle Moss, in her 2011 essay "Party out of Bounds," wrote about songs from artists like Ke$ha, Katy Perry and P!nk. These songs, Moss says, epitomize the changing meaning of female pleasure, independence and body autonomy in the 2000s. Party-girl pop (which had a largely female fan base) wove a musical fantasy where there was no judgment and no danger for the drunk girl, a "drunktopia" as Moss calls it. It was a genre of party anthem with a narrative about women making themselves happy, not falling into ruin.

Unfortunately, drunktopia did not actually exist. Society's inequalities have always been reflected in its drinking culture, and 2000s America was no different. Women still faced a higher level of scrutiny than men over drinking and had less disposable income with which to do it. In every state in the nation, women made less than men, with BIPOC women earning less than white women. While white women were more generally accepted in bars and other drinking spaces, BIPOC women still statistically drank less, especially on college campuses. Things have been slowly getting better, but there is still a long way to go before we're all living in a Ke$ha song.

In the 2000s, a combination of decreased import duties on booze, lower taxes and shifting social attitudes led to an increase in Chinese women participating in drinking culture. As in America, China had developed an after-work drinking culture. More women entering the business world—and therefore having more money to spend on a drink—meant more women at the bar after work. In 2000, the male-to-female drinking ratio was 13 to 1. By 2010, it was 5 to 1.

The same shift was happening in other countries, like Korea and Singapore.

The 2000s saw more young Malaysian and Singaporean women drinking than young men. In Korea, makgeolli and soju companies started marketing new types of drinks to women. Fruit fusion makgeolli was made to appeal to female drinkers specifically and became quite popular. Soju companies changed their branding to seem less old-fashioned and more appealing to young drinkers. All over, young women felt less bound to traditions, and the long-standing societal disapproval of women drinking publicly was beginning to fade.

After getting booted from C3, Julie Reiner was now free to try whatever she wanted, and she knew that New York City wanted more craft cocktails. People wanted to drink them, and journalists wanted to write about them.

It was time for Julie to have her own bar.

In a wonderful moment of serendipity, Julie was approached by a trio of investors, all siblings, who wanted to open a bar in an area of the city that was a drinking dead zone: the Flatiron District. The Kossi siblings thought that if a good bar finally opened in the area, it would do very well. Her résumé and the press about her was impressive, but the Kossi trio wanted something else from Julie, as well: money. The one thing a bartender usually is in need of. So, Julie talked to her parents and borrowed sixty thousand dollars from them. This money went into a partnership with the Kossis.

After an eighteen-month-long building process, part of which involved finding an old art deco bar from the 1920s, Flatiron Lounge opened in May 2003. This wasn't a tiny bar making complicated, expensive cocktails for ten people at a time. It became New York City's first mass-appeal, high-volume craft cocktail bar.

They didn't have money for a PR firm, so to drum up excitement in the press, Julie called all the journalists who had ever written about her or her drinks. Soon, the bar was buzzing. Flatiron Lounge was in a bustling neighborhood filled with people working in the fashion and music industries. These customers descended on the bar en masse, thirsty for new, hip cocktails at this new, hip place.

Julie designed her menu to appeal to all these drinkers, and many of her famous infusions were featured. The drinks were light, breezy and not intimidating to those unfamiliar with cocktails. Julie wanted to win these customers over, not scare them off. Sure, a customer could get a Cosmo there. But Julie or one of her other bartenders might convince them to try something a little different.

Susan Fedroff, now Julie's business partner in addition to being her wife, came up with the brilliant idea of flights of cocktails.

Three tiny drinks featured spirits and flavors that customers might not normally try out or even know about. It was a genius method of welcoming the masses to the world of craft cocktails.

It was hugely successful.

Flatiron Lounge, more than any other bar, was responsible for introducing the general public to the art and delight of mixology. Cocktails featured in Fedroff's flights became popular favorites. Customers started bypassing Cosmos and martinis to try something new and adventurous. The Beijing Peach, one of Julie's creations that used jasmine-tea-infused vodka, became a menu staple.

Her bar also became a training ground for some of the industry's best bartenders. Julie welcomed and even encouraged female bartenders at Flatiron Lounge and trained women who had no experience mixing craft drinks.

In the early 2000s, most bartenders didn't measure anything. To be fair, there wasn't usually much to measure. Most bars didn't feature drinks that had complicated recipes. But at Flatiron Lounge, Julie made sure that all her bartenders poured precise amounts of each ingredient. Everyone had to use a jigger (a bartending tool that measures liquor). Each drink had to be made well and, just as importantly, needed to be made the same way every time. Drinks couldn't be different depending on which bartender made them.

In order to make a massive number of craft cocktails for a massive number of people, Julie and her team figured out ways to streamline the process. For their most popular cocktails, they created what they called cheater bottles, filled with a precise mix of the liquors and liqueurs that went into the drink. Flatiron Lounge's system ended up inspiring other craft cocktail bars and changed the way they did things behind the bar.

Soon after the Flatiron Lounge opened to huge success, the Kossi siblings wanted another bar. Julie and Susan knew just who to approach: Dale DeGroff's other female protégée, Audrey Saunders.

Saunders started bartending when she was in her early thirties. After taking a seminar from Dale DeGroff, she offered to work for him for free in exchange for training. He agreed, and by the next year, she was helping him with special events at the Rainbow Room. In 1999, he hired her to work with him at a bar called Blackbird in Manhattan.

During this time, Saunders was developing her own cocktail recipes, drinks that would eventually go on to become modern classics. She was a passionate advocate for gin, that clear, tasty spirit that had been largely abandoned decades ago in favor of vodka. In the 2000s, gin was very unfashionable. She wanted to make it cool again. Saunders featured it in her recipes, such as the Gin-Gin Mule. The drink became an Audrey Saunders signature creation, served in bars all over the world.

In 2001, she became beverage director of the legendary Bemelmans Bar at the Carlyle Hotel. Despite all her experience, she wasn't allowed to join the all-male bartenders' union, of which Bemelmans was a part. So Saunders couldn't actually make the drinks herself. She instead needed to convince the old-school bartenders to make her new-school cocktail recipes. They were extremely reluctant at first. But she charmed the hell out of them (so did the taste of the drinks), and the bartenders eventually agreed. Saunders turned Bemelmans into a cocktail destination.

One day, Saunders visited Flatiron Lounge and ended up in a conversation with Kevin, one of the Kossi siblings intent on creating a new bar. Two weeks later, Julie and Susan were over at Bemelmans to brainstorm with Saunders, and the idea for Pegu Club was born.

Julie felt like it was too soon after Flatiron Lounge had opened (it had barely been two years) to put her name on another bar, so they agreed that Saunders was in charge of this new venture. Saunders set up shop in the basement of Flatiron Lounge and started to plan an incredible menu. She left Bemelmans in January of 2005.

The new bar was named after a cocktail from the pre-Prohibition days, the gin-based Pegu Club. The name signaled to cocktail nerds what sort of place it was while also reflecting Saunders' favorite spirit.

In August 2005, Pegu Club finally opened. Excitement in the New York City cocktail scene over the new bar let Saunders have her pick of bartenders, and she assembled an all-star team. The group needed to be skilled: Saunders was known for being meticulous with her drinks. But unlike the Flatiron Lounge, customers couldn't get a Cosmo at the Pegu Club. It was a bar dedicated to serving craft cocktails and converting drinkers to something other than vodka. Some customers got mad when they found out they couldn't get a rum and coke, but many more were intrigued and wanted to learn more about what the bartenders were serving.

Within a year of its opening, Pegu Club was widely considered to be the top cocktail bar in New York City.

For Julie, it was time to think about opening yet another one.

In the wake of Joy Spence's work (and Rachel Barrie's and Helen Mulholland's), the 2000s saw scores of women joining the alcohol industry.

They were included on sensory panels: groups of people tasked with developing new products and giving feedback on new flavors and the performance of different blends and barrels. They were hired as master blenders and chemists. By the end of the decade, women were on nearly every spirits-tasting panel in the world.

Over in Japan, Emi Machida set out to change the world of saké.

Machida is a toji (master saké brewer) at the Machida Brewery in Gunma, Japan. Her family has owned the brewery for over a hundred and thirty years, but she is the first toji in the entire family. For a long time, the saké industry was made up of owners who did not actually get involved in the brewing of their own saké. Migrant brewers traveled the country to different breweries, where they made the year's saké and then headed to the next place. Machida's family decided to convert to being an owner–brewer company, and she, the oldest daughter, came home to help.

When she was a kid, Machida never dreamed of being a toji. Born in 1975, she grew up during a period when the number of saké drinkers was in decline. In her grandparents' time, women were still not allowed in the Machida brewery for fear that their supposedly unclean bodies would spoil the sacred space. But in 2000, at twenty-five years old, Machida was sick of her office job and joined the brewery. She never looked back.

Machida learned the craft by studying books and getting taught by older brewers. Soon, she was immersed in the back-breaking work of making saké. Hauling the rice and mixing it while it ferments was tough enough, but Machida also had to oversee all the employees and equipment. Male employees refused to listen to her, and some male customers refused to buy from her.

It didn't help that Machida liked to be unconventional in her saké brewing. While she respected the old ways of doing things, she wanted to experiment. She became incredibly passionate about the process and figuring out how to make the best saké she could. A year after she joined the brewery, she got married. Her new husband took her name and joined, too.

It only took six years for Machida saké to start winning awards. In 2006, the brewery got its first gold medal at the Annual Japan Saké Awards, and Machida became the first female toji to win it. In the coming years, Machida's premium saké won Gold seven times, something that had never happened before she took over the brewery.

Besides her own ingenuity and ambition, the key to Machida's success was support from other female toji. She joined the Women's Saké Industry Group (which now has over twenty members) and greatly benefited from being connected to other like-minded women.

There are about fifteen hundred saké breweries in Japan, and only about fifty of those have female toji. But their numbers are slowly growing. Emi Machida is at the forefront of the rising movement of female toji.

After the success of Pegu Club, Julie Reiner was ready to put her name on another bar. She and Susan had moved boroughs and found themselves living in the Cobble Hill neighborhood of Brooklyn. Despite being a perfect location for it, there wasn't a good craft cocktail bar around. A light bulb went on.

Clover Club opened up to immediate success in 2008. Julie drew inspiration from pre-Prohibition cocktail history for its menu and focused on making the place a more comfortable, neighborhood-type bar. The name itself comes from a pre-Prohibition drink, made with gin and raspberry syrup.

Within a year of its opening, Clover Club won Best New Cocktail Lounge in the World at the 2009 Tales of the Cocktail conference. The booming success of Clover Club brought Julie Reiner into the international community of spirits and bars. Four years later, it won Best American Cocktail Bar and Best High Volume Cocktail Bar. That same year, Julie won Best Mentor.

The award was well-earned. Julie Reiner has trained more influential female bartenders than any other New York City bar owner. In a 2015 interview with *Grub Street*, she described how she always wanted to create an environment that's supportive for women and make sure they had opportunities "to be behind the bar."

Some of the best evidence of Julie's philosophy is Leyenda, her newest bar venture.

Ivy Mix is one of the industry's most important new voices.

Her bartending career kicked off at Fort Defiance in Red Hook before she began working for and getting mentored by Julie at Clover Club. Mix, thanks to a trip to Guatemala when she was nineteen, has a deep passion for mezcal and Latin-inspired cocktails. She told Julie that she wanted to create a bar that showcased these kinds of drinks, but as a new bartender with no bar owning experience, Mix had difficulty finding investors. Julie agreed to partner with her in a space right across the street from Clover Club.

In 2015, Leyenda's doors opened and Mix won Best American Bartender of the Year at Tales of the Cocktail. In 2019, Leyenda was nominated for a James Beard award for its bar program.

Mix partnered with another of Julie's disciples, award-winning bartender Lynnette Marrero, to create the all-female bartending competition Speed Rack. Marrero was trained and mentored by Julie at Flatiron Lounge. Mix and Marrero, frustrated by the boys' club of bartending, wanted to establish an event that showcased the skill of female bartending and raised money for charity. Speed Rack started in 2012, a speed bartending competition that has several rounds in cities around the United States before the final round in New York City (where Julie has sometimes been a judge). Proceeds from ticket sales have raised over a million dollars for breast cancer research so far.

The same year Leyenda opened, Julie released her first cocktail book, *The Craft Cocktail Party*. The book is focused on making craft cocktails accessible for everyone, not just hard-core spirits geeks. Julie also started a company, Mixtress Consulting, that consults on bar programs and trains staff. She's helped the bars at some of New York City's biggest hotels, like the Hyatt in Times Square. Julie even started a brand of canned cocktails called Social Hour Cocktails with one of her Clover Club partners, bartender Tom Macy. Everything that Julie Reiner does is focused on making cocktails fun and welcoming to everyone.

Crushed by a massive rent increase, in 2018 Flatiron Lounge

closed its doors for good. But Clover Club and Leyenda live on, and so does Julie's mission to support women working behind the bar.

In 2019, the World's 50 Best Bars awards gave the International Icon award to cocktail expert and noted misogynist Charles Schumann. Schumann has gone on record about his views about female bartenders in multiple interviews over the years. He told German *Playboy*, "A bar is no place for a woman. The important characters are always men" and the *Japan Times* that women in bars "are not wanted." Julie had firsthand experience dealing with his bullshit. She appeared with him in a documentary about his career, and on camera Schumann explained to her that female bartenders should be out of the bar by three in the afternoon to make way for the "real" bartenders: the men.

After Schumann received the award, Julie immediately took to Instagram, making a post declaring that "Sexism is not iconic. Misogyny is not iconic. Stop giving awards to assholes. Achievements don't excuse misconduct. Do better." Julie included the hashtag #womenbehindthebarafter3.

The post and the hashtag immediately went viral, with female bartenders posting photos of themselves working behind their bars after three. Five days later, Schumann gave the award back, stating that he didn't want the award anymore and that he was "hurt" that his statements "were so misunderstood."

Julie also took the awards association to task, with many other female bartenders and bar owners joining in. A week later, the World's 50 Best Bars released an apology and declared that the 2020 awards would have gender parity in their judging pool.

We don't know yet how spirits industry awards will fare in the future in regards to gender representation. But we do know that Julie Reiner won't stop fighting for inclusivity in the world of drinking. She's a testament that if you welcome women to the bar—or behind it—they will come.

And they will shine.

15

APIWE NXUSANI-MAWELA'S BOLD BREW

The 2010s

So here we are.

Twenty-five thousand years after the Venus of Laussel was carved. About four thousand years after the world's very first brewers, those beer-loving women, sang to Ninkasi. All that time has passed, and women are still fighting to be part of an industry they created.

When it was discouraged, illegal, even punishable by death, women still made, served and drank alcohol, whether it was fermented or distilled. Against millennia of opposition, women have never stopped doing the very thing that started it all: making beer. Wherever Ninkasi is, she's toasting to the brewers who are keeping her legacy alive. Women like Apiwe Nxusani-Mawela, the first Black woman in South Africa to found a microbrewery.

Born in 1984, Apiwe grew up in the Eastern Cape in a small village called Mgomanzi. She had an early interest in both science and beer. Her parents wanted her to work toward a degree in medicine, but when she was in eleventh grade, she attended an open house at the University of Johannesburg and became fascinated with the science of brewing. Growing up, Apiwe had seen family members brewing and watched adults drink umqombothi (sorghum beer). Once she discovered all the technology behind beer, she was hooked. The biochemistry, the mathematics, the microbiology, the physics and engineering involved... Apiwe fell in love with the craft of brewing.

She went on to earn her bachelor's degree in science from the University of Witwatersrand, along with an Honors in microbiology from the University of Pretoria. As soon as she was out of college, Apiwe launched straight into the world of beer. In 2006, she joined South African Breweries through their graduate recruitment program. The next year, she started brewing.

After completing an eighteen-month internship program, Apiwe wanted to take it further and become a master brewer. While still working at South African Breweries, she got her diploma in brewing from the international Institute of Brewing and Distilling. Then, she got her Master Brewer diploma. She became the first Black African to become certified as a trainer for the institute.

To give thanks to their ancestors for guiding and supporting Apiwe on her incredible educational path and career endeavors, her father suggested that she come home for an *imcimbi*, a traditional ceremony. While she was there, Apiwe spent time brewing traditional umqombothi with her mother and her aunts. That's when it hit her. At South African Breweries, she had spent years mastering *Western* brewing techniques and recipes. Apiwe realized that her family had been making beer for generations and generations with their own techniques and recipes. Once she learned about the long history of African female brewers, Apiwe's work would never be the same.

The United States was well into the twenty-first century by now, yet most American alcohol companies were still figuring out how to market their products to women, if they bothered to at all. In the wake of the Cosmo, there was still a huge, girly-drinks-shaped void in the industry. That is, until a woman named Bethenny Frankel figured out how to fill it.

The work of women like Julie Reiner was slowly causing women around the country, especially in major urban areas, to feel both knowledgeable and comfortable with craft cocktails. But not everyone can afford a craft cocktail, and not everyone has a fancy cocktail bar in their town. Most people only encountered cocktails at chain restaurants, drinks chock-full of artificial syrups and an overload of sweeteners. Bethenny Frankel, of *Real Housewives* fame, started a female-focused line of bottled cocktails that would stand in opposition to those drinks. In a truly genius move, she combined the rarity of a female-focused drink brand with the one thing that every American woman is told she should be constantly trying to do: lose weight.

Skinnygirl launched in 2009 to overwhelming overnight success. The first kind of Skinnygirl bottled cocktail was the Skinnygirl Margarita, sold in a slim, opaque bottle adorned with a silhouette of a thin and stylish woman shaking a cocktail. The drink had every element needed for a booming success. It didn't need to be mixed with anything—the alcohol was included in the bottle. Perfect for busy women. It was only 150 calories per 6 ounces. Perfect for dieters. To top it all off, each 750 ml bottle was less than twenty bucks. Perfect for, well, everyone.

The Skinnygirl Margarita was soon followed by other drinks, including the Skinnygirl Cosmo and even Skinnygirl Wine. It started a wildfire in the alcohol industry. From 2010 to 2011, the number of drinks labeled *skinny* increased 533%. Cocktail books capitalizing on the trend were released, like *Skinnytinis* and *Skinny Jeans Cocktails*.

The problem with Skinnygirl—besides the fact that diet culture is a toxic dumpster fire that financially preys on the bodily insecurities of women that were manufactured by a society that profits from them—is that they don't actually save that many calories.

An old-fashioned is fat-free and usually clocks in around 176 calories. A margarita made with lime juice and not prebottled mix is about 153 calories. Skinnygirl Cosmo has about the same amount of calories as a regular Cosmo: 95. Skinnygirl Wine has 100 calories per 5 ounces, where red wine has 124 and white wine has 116. An ounce and a half pour of bourbon with an ice cube is usually about 124 calories. For reference, a large banana is about 121 calories. If this all sounds like splitting a pointless hair, that's because it is.

But Frankel's concoctions are quick to prepare, they are cheap, and more importantly, they were actually marketed specifically to women where few other alcoholic beverages were. The website even proclaims that *a lady knows about Skinnygirl Cocktails*. They flew off the shelves. Bethenny Frankel had succeeded in a market that nearly every other company in the industry didn't even try to touch.

Maybe someday, companies shilling *skinny* drinks will realize that the last thing a woman needs after a long day is to pick up a bottle that is going to body-shame her. Instead they might start using their enormous marketing and manufacturing power to sell women a drink that isn't infused with self-hatred.

The other major female drinking trend of the decade has been as maligned as it is lauded: the wine mom.

In the mid-2010s, the term began to spread virally on social media in countries like the United States, Kenya and the United Kingdom. #winemom appeared underneath the selfies of mothers as they finally stopped to relax with a glass of wine after a long day of working and momming and doing five million things. It quickly became a popular way for mothers to relate to each other and bond over the stresses and impossible demands of motherhood and careers. Talking about being a wine mom was a way for women to express that while they were dealing with it all, it certainly was not easy. Moms used GIFs of characters from television chugging bottles of wine and drinking from gigantic glasses to show their exhaustion and frustration in a way that was only half joking.

Wine mom quickly became a term of derision, but some women embraced the term, feeling like it gave them a little bit of an edge and a little more of their premom identity back. It became a way to remind people that there is more to a woman's identity than motherhood, that moms are people, too. A woman calling herself a wine mom was a sort of a rejection of traditional notions of homemaking that featured mothers as obedient, unruffled and unsexy. Wine mom T-shirts, wineglasses, coasters and decor sprung up in stores.

These modern women weren't actually doing anything that women hadn't already been doing for centuries. Alewives were doing it hundreds of years ago, decompressing in their kitchens with a tankard of ale. They just didn't have smartphones or Wi-Fi. Wine moms put what had been happening in private for generations on display for the world to see. As the term spread, a backlash built up.

Wine moms were accused of glorifying binge-drinking and disparaged for using wine as a coping mechanism. But there have been no studies that show binge-drinking is a problem specific to mothers or that the wine mom trend had caused any uptick in it. Women without kids still drink more on average than women with kids. Men, on average, still drink more than women do, but there is no *beer dad* scornful stereotype. For decades, lovable sitcom fathers who crack open a beer when they get home from work are seen as deserving of it. Since mothers are expected to be on call 24-7, there is no *after work* for them. Therefore, it's scandalous to see them openly and publicly do the same.

Many wine companies finally started aggressively marketing wine to women. In Kenya, wine-themed, female-centric events sprang up everywhere. All over the country, wine was added to regular activities like yoga and pottery classes in a bid to attract more women.

But just as alcohol is not the cause of capitalism's problems, it is also not the cure. Wine does not alleviate wage inequality or the lack of affordable childcare. If people mocking wine moms on Instagram were truly concerned about their health and welfare, they might instead try working toward getting women the support they desperately need.

After Apiwe's revelation about the history of female brewing in Africa, she was determined to include traditional African techniques and ingredients in her beer.

To learn more, she enrolled in a course at the University of South Africa called Thought Leadership for Africa's Renewal. The goal of the course was to train Africans for the "political, economic, social and cultural renewal of the African continent and its people." In an interview with *Food for Mzansi* in 2020, Apiwe said, "My heart started beating for Africa and I wanted to contribute to the development of Africa within the brewing industry. I asked myself, 'How can I elevate Africa in my own space?'"

In 2014, Apiwe left South African Breweries and found partners with whom to start her own brewery, Brewhogs, in Kyalami. She became the first Black woman in South Africa to found a microbrewery and South Africa's first Black woman brewmaster.

A year later, she launched the project of her heart: Brewster's Craft. It was the first Black female–majority owned brewing company in South Africa. But Brewster's Craft wasn't just about making beer. Apiwe created the company to celebrate women in the brewing industry and let them take back their place in it. Brewster's Craft, which is based in Roodepoort, Johannesburg, offers accredited training in the art of brewing along with quality-testing services. The company works to get more women making beer, and once they make it, then to give them the means to make sure the final product is up to industry standards.

Two years later, in 2017, Apiwe sold her shares in Brewhogs and left to focus on Brewster's Craft full-time. The first beer she created there was a sorghum pilsner that had all the traditional taste and feel of umqombothi without the drink's usual thickness. She assembled an all-female brewing team to help her, with a woman named Yamkela Mbakaza as the head brewer. Apiwe is passionate about employing women and breaking the stereotype that brewing is a man's job.

Apiwe didn't stop there. She became the chairperson for both the Africa Section of the Institute of Brewing and Distilling and the Beer Association of South Africa. She somehow found the time to also join the board of directors for the Craft Brewers Association of South Africa. Apiwe utilizes all of these roles to support and encourage Black female brewers across the entire continent.

In 2019, Apiwe ended up combining all of her passions—Africa, science and brewsters—into one very special beer.

Sister Doris Engelhard is part of a German abbey that has been brewing since the twelfth century, when Hildegard von Bingen was writing about hops. Sister Doris came to Mallersdorf Abbey as a young student in 1961, and the nuns took such wonderful care of her that she knew that she wanted to join their ranks someday. But her father really wanted her to find a job where she could work with her hands. Sister Doris herself was interested in agriculture. The nuns figured out how to combine the two for her and asked if she wanted to work in the abbey's brewery. In 1966, Sister Doris began an apprenticeship under the nuns there.

She loved it.

In 1969, she completed a course in brewing at the nearby vocational school. First, she became certified as a master brewer. Then, Sister Doris took her vows, and she became certified as a nun. At seventy-one years old (as of the writing of this book) she is still making beer and is now the last nun in the world who is an active brewmaster. Sister Doris wasn't always the only one but all the others have either retired or had their breweries closed.

Her days usually start at five thirty with choral prayer alongside her fellow nuns. But Sundays are special. On Sunday mornings, Sister Doris rises even earlier—at three—to brew. It's her assigned job at Mallersdorf Abbey. For each season, she crafts a different beer. The batches and recipes change from year to year. Although the abbey's tradition of brewing is medieval, Sister Doris's recipes and machinery are not. It's a fully modern brewery. Her beer tastes nothing like what Hildegard was brewing, but that's a good thing.

Sister Doris's beer is untreated with preservatives, so it's best served as soon as possible. It is only sold locally and is not able to be shipped anywhere. If you want a taste, you'll have to head to Germany. Sister Doris recommends having a glass every day. She herself never misses her daily pint.

Beer is her passion. She loves to make it and loves to drink it. The work of brewing, the smell of the malt and the joy of the people who drink her beer are all a source of great happiness for this brewnun. For Sister Doris, brewing is her way of serving her god.

Just as some women are carrying on centuries-long alcohol traditions, others are creating new ones. Women have never stopped making alcohol, and in the twenty-first century, they finally began to organize and connect on a huge scale.

In 2015, Deborah Brenner author of *Women of the Vine*, a book that profiled twenty women working in the California wine industry, organized the first global symposium of Women of the Vine and Spirits. She wanted to finally get women in the industry together, both to show their numbers to the world and to create an international supportive community. The event was a colossal success.

The symposium turned into an organization for the empowerment and advancement of women in the alcohol industry. It stood in direct contrast to the all-male Greek symposiums of old. Women of the Vine and Spirits is now the leading membership organization worldwide doing this type of work. They provide scholarship, mentorship and education for women, along with developing and promoting diversity initiatives. In 2018, Deborah was named by *Wine Enthusiast* magazine as the Social Visionary of the Year.

It's a good thing for the industry as a whole. According to Women of the Vine and Spirits, ninety percent of women in the United States say they would go out of their way to buy spirits or wine made by women. In most homes (eighty-five percent!) women control all of the alcohol purchases. Alcohol companies are leaving money on the table by not including female distillers, winemakers and brewers.

As wonderful as it is to get more women in the wine industry, it's just as important to make sure that *all* women are included. The wine world is still predominantly white, and Black wine professionals still face racism in the industry. To celebrate Black wine culture and to change the narrative, celebrated sommelier Tahiirah Habibi founded the Hue Society. The organization is dedicated to providing both education and community for Black wine enthusiasts. She was the first Black woman seen on the cover of *Wine Enthusiast*.

In 2020, wine journalist and consultant Julia Coney launched Black Wine Professionals. In an interview with *Imbibe* magazine, Julia said, "Black Wine Professionals is about getting Black people in work, getting them access—and not just for free, but making sure that they get paid, too."

Women in the spirits industry are banding together, as well. In 2018, Dr. Nicola Nice cofounded the Women's Cocktail Collective, a group of leading female spirits producers, who want "to elevate and amplify the voices of all women in the alcohol beverage industry through a belief that we are stronger together."

The group includes Macchu Pisco, a pisco (Peruvian or Chilean grape brandy) company founded in 2006 by sisters Melanie and Lizzie Asher. Melanie and Lizzie support fair trade practices for the female workers in the region of southern Peru where they grow their grapes and ensure fair wages to their female co-op of grape harvesters. Over five hundred years since the clandestinistas worked to make alcohol in secret to resist their Spanish colonizers, women are still using alcohol to both support their families and fight for fairer treatment.

The year before the Women's Cocktail Collective was founded, Dr. Nicola Nice created a brand of cordial-style gin as a homage to all those Victorian home cooks who wrote their own cordial recipes and distilled at home. After years of working in market research and brand consulting for big liquor brands, Dr. Nice got frustrated that female consumers were not being actively targeted, despite their extraordinary spending power. She saw a big opportunity in the problem, and went on to formulate and brand her gin with those female consumers in mind. The year it came out, Pomp and Whimsy won Gold at three spirits competitions in Los Angeles, San Francisco and New York and Double Gold at the Global Spirit Awards.

In 2017, Fawn Weaver became the first Black woman in United States history to own a major liquor brand with her whiskey, Uncle Nearest. The brand was created to honor Nearest Green, the first Black master distiller in America. Born into slavery, he was the man who taught Jack Daniel how to make whiskey. After the Civil War, Nearest became the first master distiller for the newly created Jack Daniel Distillery. Weaver helped unearth his legacy and created the Uncle Nearest Foundation to continue honoring him and the pivotal contribution he made to whiskey history. Uncle Nearest is also the first whiskey brand named after a Black person.

To create the taste of Uncle Nearest, Weaver hired America's first Black female master distiller. Victoria Butler is the great-great-granddaughter of Nearest Green, so you might say she's got whiskey in her blood. Since Uncle Nearest launched in 2017, it has won over fifteen major spirits awards, earning some every single year that it has been out. Weaver has further expansion plans for both the brand and the foundation.

That same year, Michelle di Augustino launched the first Black woman–owned cognac company with Noir King Cognac. The Black community in the United States has long-standing ties with cognac after Black soldiers sent to France in World War II brought home a taste for the drink. In the 1990s and 2000s and into today, the connection was fostered by the rap and hip-hop music community. There are over a thousand songs that feature the words *Hennessey* or *cognac*, including "Cognac Queen," off Megan Thee Stallion's 2018 album *Tina Snow*.

Continuing down the booze supply line, the once all-male bartender's guild finally got its first female president in its over-fifty-year history in 2016 with Pamela Wiznitzer. Ms. Franky Marshall, one of the bartenders who helped open Julie Reiner's Clover Club, has also served as the United States Bartenders' Guild vice president. Thanks to all the activists fighting for women's rights in the 1960s and 70s, now women make up sixty percent of bartenders.

The tiki world is still booming, too. In 2018, rum expert Shannon Mustipher founded Women Who Tiki, a community of bartenders and tiki drink fanatics. Mustipher is passionate about representation behind the bar. In 2019, with the release of her excellent cocktail book, *Tiki: Modern Tropical Cocktails*, she became the first working Black bartender to write a cocktail book released by a major publisher in over one hundred years.[174]

Chockie Tom is one of the cofounders of Doom Tiki, a reg-

---

174 The book before Shannon's was *The Ideal Bartender*, published in 1917 and written by Tom Bullock. Tom was a Black American bartender who worked before Prohibition.

ular pop-up bar in Queens, New York, that works to push racism and cultural appropriation out of the tiki bar. Doom Tiki has featured the work of a number of brilliant Indigenous bartenders and partnered with Mariah Kunkel to raise money for organizations that give back to Pasifika and Indigenous cultures. Kunkel is the cofounder of the Pasifika Project, an organization by and for Oceanic people working in hospitality. With Doom Tiki, Chockie Tom has set out to confront, challenge and eradicate the problems inherent in tiki culture, while still making awesome drinks. She serves them in mugs shaped like pineapples or cats instead of tiki gods.

There are also women working to save the lesbian bar, of which there are now only about fifteen in the United States. In 2020, filmmakers Erica Rose and Elina Street launched the Lesbian Bar Project, whose goals are to "celebrate, support and preserve the remaining lesbian bars that exist in the United States." They want to preserve lesbian bars because, according to their website,

> …Without space, we lose power, validity and communal safety and access to intergenerational dialogue.

Ventures like Doom Tiki and the Lesbian Bar Project show that bars are still a vital part of our many cultures and communities, and that women are a vital part of bars.

Female drinkers have also banded together and created organizations to promote inclusion in the world of booze. In 2011, Peggy Noe Stevens created Bourbon Women, a female-centric bourbon enthusiast group with the aim of changing the perception of bourbon as a grandpa drink. Their mission is to provide education while also encouraging distillers to market to women. The first year, they had over three hundred members, and now Bourbon Women has chapters all over the country.

In 2016, Samara Rivers founded the Black Bourbon Society, which seeks to bridge the gap between the spirits industry and Black consumers. Rivers wanted to show bourbon companies all the customers they were missing out on. Overwhelmed by the response (the Facebook group has over sixteen thousand members), she also launched Diversity Distilled, a consulting organization that helps brands and companies to up the inclusivity of their workforce.

Women's whiskey clubs have popped up all over, in places across Europe, Japan, Venezuela and China. Spirit of Nero is India's first women's whiskey club. It has monthly meetings that feature talks designed to educate and engage women with the industry. Spirit of Nero has no membership fees, and all the food and whiskey at their events are free. India banned alcohol with a total prohibition law in 1997, but the ban only lasted for two years. There are still several states that uphold it, but now the country is one of the fastest growing markets for spirits and especially wine. Wine drinking in India tripled between 2004 and 2020. The fastest growing group in this fastest growing market is women.

And these are only some of the incredible women working to make the drinks industry and community a better place.

Women, women everywhere, and so much booze to drink.

In 2014, the first International Women's Collaboration Brew Day was held. The event was founded by brewer Sophie de Ronde in conjunction with the Pink Boots Society. IWCBD was created to raise awareness about women in the brewing industry, and it coincided with International Women's Day on March 8. The first year, sixty female brewers in five countries participated by all brewing the same type of beer, a pale ale called Unite. The next year, there were eighty brewers in eleven countries. Apiwe Nxusani-Mawela helped organize the first IWCBD in Johannesburg that year.

For 2019's event, South African Breweries wanted to create a special beer, and they tapped Apiwe to lead the brewing process. She wanted both the label and the beer itself to embody the traits of strong, independent women. Apiwe worked with other female brewers to create the recipe for what was eventually called Bold Brew. The beer was designed and crafted entirely by women. On March 8, 2019, Bold Brew was released, with artwork on its label that featured a woman holding up the sun.

Apiwe wanted the commemorative beer to provide inspiration for female brewers and make the industry more appealing to women. She started giving talks at high schools to raise awareness about the opportunities that the industry can hold for young women. Hearing Apiwe speak about her work, it's easy to see how a student would be impressed and inspired by her calm intelligence and confidence. In an interview for the University of South Africa's student magazine, she said that "Our struggles today are paving a path for the next generation of women in our workspace, so they do not have to go through what we went or are going through. One day, having women in male-dominated fields will be the norm."

Later in the year, Brewster's Craft launched their own line of beers and ciders called Tolokazi, the name of Apiwe's clan. For her, the brand celebrates not just her family and the long line of female brewers she comes from but all African brewsters. The ingredients used for all the products are Indigenous African products, and the company plans to take the brand to the global stage.

Apiwe Nxusani-Mawela is a visionary and one of the most important figures in the world of brewing, but she is not a woman ahead of her time. No woman in the alcohol industry has ever been ahead of her time. It started thousands of years ago.

After all these years, women are right back where they started, before patriarchal control and the fear of female independence took their own industry away from them. Advances in women's rights have marched forward, only to be dragged back by governments and systems that were frightened of their power and determined to oppress them. Women are still fighting and winning and losing and fighting again. The one constant is their resilience.

While women are breaking into the alcohol industry in some parts of the world, there are still countries where women are not even allowed to drink. For a woman, having a drink in public is still a test of how society will treat her.

No matter what you're having, you can toast knowing that women had a part in its history. Saying that some types of alcohol are better, more noble, more *masculine* to drink than others is just outright silly. Women can look around a brewery, a vineyard, a distillery, a liquor store, a bar and know that they belong there just as much as anyone.

All drinks are girly drinks.

EPILOGUE

After thousands of years of women's drinking history, what do we do now? Where do we go from here?

Harmony Moon Colangelo answers that question every single day.

Harmony is the head bartender at the Side Quest, a bar in Cleveland, Ohio. The tall, blue-haired cocktail slinger has been there since 2016, but it took some convincing from friends for her to try out bartending. Writing to me in 2020, she said, "I'd almost exclusively worked in retail previously because, being a trans person in Ohio, I didn't trust people to tip me well enough in a service industry job to actually make ends meet. After a couple years of insistence from one of my oldest friends that I would be an amazing bartender, I picked up a job as a barback at two different places she worked and climbed the ladder from there."

Women everywhere know that just because they belong in bars, that doesn't always mean that they are welcome. While more women is always the goal, making sure *all* women are welcome is, too. Many disabled women avoid going to bars because the bathrooms, the bars and the tables are not accessible for those using wheelchairs or other mobility aids. By not lowering the height of tables and seating, adding a lower portion of the bar and creating accessible bathrooms, bars are missing out on a lot of customers. In America alone, the spending power of disabled individuals is estimated to be around $500 billion.

Bars are still important spaces for networking, socializing and community. Having nonalcoholic drinks on the menu is something that is becoming more widespread, but it certainly needs to be normalized. There are so many women in this world who do not drink for a number of reasons—personal, health, religious or just not feeling like it—who want and would benefit from access to these public spaces. They deserve more than just tap water or soda.

In Harmony's years of bartending, she has seen bars becoming more welcoming and inclusive spaces and has worked hard to make sure that her own bar is the same way.

"Following the old punk mindset of creating your own scene if you don't like the ones you're seeing, I pushed for the bar I work in to have more LGBTQIA+ oriented events…. From that point forward, we hosted several queer-focused events every month, including a monthly meetup, complete with pronoun stickers, for people to get out and make friends. This included music exclusively by queer artists to buck the trend of the teen pop–oriented playlists of traditional gay bars, movies and shows on the televisions around the bar, either by or about queer people, and a special drink list featuring exclusive cocktails that I would make for each event."

It was this drink list that led Harmony to make cocktail history.

The LGBTQIA+ events and cocktails that Harmony created were so popular that after the 2020 coronavirus pandemic temporarily shut the bar down, the owners of the Side Quest asked her if she'd want to take all her recipes and put them together

in a book. *A Year of Queer Cocktails* was born, making Harmony
the first trans woman in history to write a cocktail book. She
designed the book to be accessible to everyone, even cocktail
novices. In addition to the recipes, the book also includes snippets of important queer history. The sales of the first edition of
A Year of Queer Cocktails went to provide financial help to all
the out-of-work staff of the Side Quest.

In 2020, Harmony was nominated for and won Best Bartender
in the greater Cleveland area—the only woman nominated.

And what does she normally order at a bar? An old-fashioned.
Women making and drinking booze? About as old-fashioned
as it gets.

As I finish this book, the world is still gripped tight in the
fist of COVID-19. Bars and historic drinking spaces everywhere have closed permanently in its wake, including Audrey
Saunders's legendary Pegu Club. Many liquor companies have
halted production, and the future of the industry (along with
many others) looks uncertain.

Women have always found a way to make and drink alcohol, no matter what they've come up against. Their persistence
gives me hope. Whatever the future holds, one thing we can all
count on is that women will be there. Female distillers, brewers, bartenders and drinkers have survived nearly four thousand
years of oppression and insufferable guys in bars. They can survive anything.

Cheers!

★ ★ ★ ★ ★

ACKNOWLEDGMENTS

Writing a research-intense global history book during an international pandemic really sucks. Thanks to a group of truly amazing people, I was still able to get this book done.

Of course, my agent, Brady McReynolds, who made this whole thing happen.

My editor, Peter Joseph, who made the original idea I had so much better. Peter, I am so, so happy I got to do this book with you.

Grace Towery, for the editorial support and insight.

Laura Gianino, my publicist/superhero. You are the only reason I am still sane. Lia Ferrone, Linette Kim, Eden Church, Vanessa Wells and the entire Hanover Square Press team. You are all absolutely goddamn wonderful.

I could not write books without the support and resources of the Los Angeles Public Library. I wish I could buy every LAPL librarian a bottle of whiskey. Thank you for answering questions and hauling countless boxes of research materials for me.

Jillian Barndt, for the help with the Japanese women's history.

Hyunhee Park, for responding to the woman who emailed you about soju out of the blue.

I am so grateful to all the women who spent time talking to me for this project, especially Apiwe Nxusani Mawela, Dr. Nicola Nice and Harmony Moon Colangelo. Tran Nguyen, thank you for answering my questions about Vietnamese booze.

As soon as travel is safe again, I need to buy drinks for all the friends who supported this book. Grady Hendrix, I owe you a martini. Sean Cook, for answering all my annoying questions about Australia.

Brea Grant, as always, for being an incredible friend, giving me great advice, supporting everything I do and making sure our podcast still happens while I'm on deadline. All the *Reading Glasses* listeners, for being the most supportive, positive and kind bookish community I could ever ask for.

My double set of Barbaras and Joes, both Panepinto and Lambert. I'm unbelievably lucky to have you all in my life. Thank you for always believing in me. My therapist, Chris, thank you for keeping my brain from melting.

Buffalo Trace, my favorite bourbon and trusty companion during many long nights of research and writing. Please hire me to be your writer in residence. You don't have one yet, but we could fix that. Call me.

Jeremy Lambert, for helping me haul endless loads of library books, for taking care of me (and our cats) while I finished this, for listening to me discuss every single fact in this book ad nauseam over dinner, for convincing me that it was good, for making sure that I didn't lose my mind. I don't know how you manage to make me love and appreciate you more every single goddamn day, but you do. I love you more than bourbon.

Finally, Lauren Panepinto, my best friend, first reader and the only reason this book exists to begin with. For telling me to write this book, for constantly giving your advice and expertise on every single aspect of it, for yanking my brain out of the hole it fell into when I thought everything was falling apart, for hunting down the best photos to use. I'd need another book to list the ways you supported both me and this project. I love you so goddamn much. Here's to having cocktails in cool bars all over the world until we're withered crones.

SOURCES

Alexander, John T. *Catherine the Great: Life and Legend*. Oxford University Press, 1989.

"Alfred the Great: Law Code on Anglo-Saxon Women (ca. 893 CE)." *World History: Ancient and Medieval Eras*, ABC-CLIO, 2020.

Ambrose, Hugh, and John Schuttler. *Liberated Spirits: Two Women Who Battled over Prohibition*. Penguin, 2018.

"America's Beer, Wine & Spirits Retailers Create 2.03 Million Jobs & $122.63 Billion in Direct Economic Impact." American Beverage Licensees, October 23, 2018. https://ablusa.org/americas-beer-wine-spirits-retailers-create-2-03-million-jobs-122-63-billion-in-direct-economic-impact/.

Anderson, E. N. *Food and Environment in Early and Medieval China*. Philadelphia: University of Pennsylvania Press, 2014.

Appleby, John C. *Women and English Piracy, 1540-1720: Partners and Victims of Crime*. Boydell & Brewer, 2013.

Bailey, Mark. *Of All the Gin Joints: Stumbling through Hollywood History.* Chapel Hill, NC: Algonquin Books, 2014.

Baker, Phil. *The Book of Absinthe: A Cultural History.* Grove/Atlantic, 2007.

Bardsley, Sandy. "Nuns: Medieval World." *Daily Life through History*, ABC-CLIO, 2020.

Barndt, Jillian Rose. "Women of the Rear Palace: Naishi no kami and the Fujiwara Clan." Master's thesis, University of Alberta (Canada), 2013.

Barnett, Richard. *The Book of Gin: A Spirited History from Alchemists' Stills and Colonial Outposts to Gin Palaces, Bathtub Gin, and Artisanal Cocktails.* Grove/Atlantic, 2012.

Bayles, Jaq. "Profile: Joy Spence." *Drinks International*, July 13, 2012. https://drinksint.com/news/fullstory.php/aid/3121/Profile:_Joy_Spence.html.

Bennett, Judith M. *Ale, Beer, and Brewsters in England: Women's Work in a Changing World, 1300-1600.* New York: Oxford University Press, 1996.

Bennett Peterson, Barbara, ed. *Notable Women of China: Shang Dynasty to the Early Twentieth Century.* London: Taylor & Francis Group, 2000. ProQuest Ebook Central.

Bernstein, Gail Lee, ed. *Recreating Japanese Women, 1600-1945.* University of California Press, 1991.

Berry, Jeff. *Beachbum Berry's Potions of the Caribbean: 500 Years of Tropical Drinks and the People behind Them.* New York: Cocktail Kingdom, 2014.

Blumenthal, Karen. *Bootleg: Murder, Moonshine, and the Lawless Years of Prohibition.* New York: Roaring Brook Press, 2011.

Brennan, Thomas E. *Public Drinking in the Early Modern World: Voices from the Tavern, 1500-1800.* London: Pickering & Chatto, 2011.

Brennan, Thomas E. "Taverns and the Public Sphere in the French Revolution." In *Alcohol: A Social and Cultural History*. Mack Holt, ed. 107-120, Oxford: Berg, 2006. https://doi.org/10.5040/9781350044609-ch-007.

Brooks, Polly Schoyer. *Cleopatra: Goddess of Egypt, Enemy of Rome*. New York: HarperCollins Publishers, 1995.

Brown, Sally, and David R. Brown. *A Biography of Mrs. Marty Mann: The First Lady of Alcoholics Anonymous*. Simon and Schuster, 2011.

Bryceson, Deborah Fahy. "Alcohol." In *Encyclopedia of Western Colonialism since 1450*, edited by Thomas Benjamin, 29–33. Vol. 1. Detroit: Macmillan Reference USA, 2007. Gale in Context: World History.

Burns, Eric. *The Spirits of America: A Social History of Alcohol*. Philadelphia: Temple University Press, 2004.

Buss, Carla Wilson. "Sources: Great Lives from History; Notorious Lives." *Reference & User Services Quarterly* 47, no. 1 (2007). https://doi.org/10.5860/rusq.47n1.85.2.

Carrigan, Matthew A., Oleg Uryasev, Carole B. Frye, Blair L. Eckman, Candace R. Myers, Thomas D. Hurley, and Steven A. Benner. "Hominids Adapted to Metabolize Ethanol Long Before Human-Directed Fermentation." *Proceedings of the National Academy of Sciences* 112, no. 2 (January 13, 2015): 458–63. https://doi.org/10.1073/pnas.1404167111.

"Catherine, II, the Great." In *Historic World Leaders*, edited by Anne Commire. Detroit: Gale, 1994. Gale in Context: World History.

Chang, Kwang-chih. *Food in Chinese Culture: Anthropological and Historical Perspectives*. New Haven: Yale University Press, 1977.

Chartres, J. A. Review of *The English Alehouse: A Social History, 1200–1800*, by Peter Clark. *The Economic History Review*, n.s., 38, no. 3 (August 1985): 449–51. https://doi.org/10.2307/2597002.

Civil, Miguel. "A Hymn to the Beer Goddess and a Drinking Song." In *Studies Presented to A. Leo Oppenheim: June 7, 1964*, edited by R.D. Biggs and J. A. Brinkman. Chicago: Oriental Institute of the University of Chicago, 1964.

Clark, James G., ed. *The Culture of Medieval English Monasticism.* Woodbridge, Suffolk, UK: Boydell & Brewer, 2007.

Conrad, Barnaby, III. *Absinthe: History in a Bottle.* San Francisco: Chronicle Books, 1988.

Cooke, Anthony. *A History of Drinking: The Scottish Pub since 1700.* Edinburgh: Edinburgh University Press, 2015.

Corrigan, Vincent J. "Hildegard of Bingen." In *Icons of the Middle Ages: Rulers, Writers, Rebels, and Saints*, edited by Lister M. Matheson, 1:355. Santa Barbara: Greenwood Publishing Group, 2012.

Costantino, Roselyn. "And She Wears It Well: Feminist and Cultural Debates in the Performance Art of Astrid Hadad." In *Latinas on Stage*, edited by Alicia Arrizón and Lillian Manzor. Berkeley: Third Woman Press, 2000.

Crush, Jonathan, and Charles H. Ambler. *Liquor and Labor in Southern Africa.* Athens: Ohio University Press, 1992.

Daryaee, Touraj. *Sasanian Persia: The Rise and Fall of an Empire.* New York: Bloomsbury Publishing, 2014.

Davis, Angela Y. *Blues Legacies and Black Feminism: Gertrude Ma Rainey, Bessie Smith, and Billie Holiday.* New York: Knopf Doubleday Publishing Group, 2011.

Dietler, Michael. 2006. "Alcohol: Anthropological/Archaeological Perspectives." *Annual Review of Anthropology* 35, no. 1 (2006): 229–49.

Donahue, John F. *Food and Drink in Antiquity: Readings from the Graeco-Roman World; A Sourcebook*. London: Bloomsbury Academic, 2015.

Donovan, Pamela. *Drink Spiking and Predatory Drugging*. New York: Palgrave Macmillan US, 2016.

Dudley, Robert, and Aeon. 2016. "How the Drunken Monkey Hypothesis Explains Our Taste for Liquor." *The Atlantic*, December 19, 2016. https://www.theatlantic.com/science/archive/2016/12/drunken-monkey/511046/.

Duis, Perry. *The Saloon: Public Drinking in Chicago and Boston, 1880-1920*. Champaign: University of Illinois Press, 1999.

Dunbar-Ortiz, Roxanne, and Dina Gilio-Whitaker. *"All the Real Indians Died Off": And 20 Other Myths about Native Americans*. Boston: Beacon Press, 2016.

Duncan, Todd C. "Black Bourbon Society Founder Seeks Diversity in Spirits Industry." *Atlanta Journal-Constitution*, May 12, 2020. https://www.ajc.com/entertainment/personalities/black-bourbon-society-founder-seeks-diversity-spirits-industry/7hsSQjm989gLFL7NSGd6HL/.

Durham, William H., and Jane H. Hill, eds. *Annual Review of Anthropology*. Vol. 35. Palo Alto, CA: Annual Reviews, 2006.

Dyhouse, Carol. *Girl Trouble: Panic and Progress in the History of Young Women*. London: Zed Books, 2014.

Egan, Ronald. *The Burden of Female Talent: The Poet Li Qingzhao and Her History in China*. Cambridge: Harvard University Press, 2014.

Elam, Earl H., and James Haley. 1984. "Apaches: A History and Culture Portrait." *American Indian Quarterly* 8, no. 1 (Winter, 1984): 62–64. https://doi.org/10.2307/1184164.

Elliott, Barbara. 1992. Review of *Constructive Drinking: Perspectives on Drink from Anthropology*, edited by Mary Douglas. *Free Associations* 3, no. 1 (1992): 143–46.

Endolyn, Osayi. "The First Cocktail Book by an African American Bartender in More Than a Century." *Los Angeles Times*, April 2, 2019. https://www.latimes.com/food/la-fo-tiki-modern-tropical-cocktails-20190402-story.html.

Erdoes, Richard. *Saloons of the Old West*. New York: Gramercy Books: 1997.

Ewan, Elizabeth. 1999. "'For Whatever Ales Ye': Women as Consumers and Producers in Late Medieval Scottish Towns." In *Women in Scotland c.1100–c.1750*, edited by Elizabeth Ewan, Maureen M. Meikle, and Evelyn S. Newlyn, 125–37. East Linton, Scotland: Tuckwell Press, 1999.

Ewing, Hope. *Movers & Shakers: Women Making Waves in Spirits, Beer, and Wine*. Los Angeles: Unnamed Press, 2018.

Falkowitz, Max. "Heart & Sool." *Imbibe*, May/June 2019.

Fearn, Esther. "Moll Cutpurse." In *Encyclopedia Britannica*. https://www.britannica.com/biography/Moll-Cutpurse.

Fetter, Bruce. Review of *Potent Brews: A Social History of Alcohol in East Africa, 1850–1999*, by Justin Willis. *African Studies Review* 46, no. 3 (December 2003): 134–35. https://doi.org/10.2307/1515053.

Fetters, Ashley. "The Many Faces of the 'Wine Mom.'" *The Atlantic*, May 23, 2020. https://www.theatlantic.com/family/archive/2020/05/wine-moms-explained/612001/.

Fleming, Alice. *Alcohol: The Delightful Poison*. New York: Delacorte Press, 1975.

Foreman, Amanda, dir. *The Ascent of Woman*. United Kingdom: BBC2, 2016.

Forsyth, Mark. *A Short History of Drunkenness*. London: Viking, 2018.

Fox, Anne, and Mike MacAvoy. *Expressions of Drunkenness (Four Hundred Rabbits)*. New York: Taylor & Francis, 2010.

Fragner, Bert G., Ralph Kauz and Florian Schwarz. *Wine Culture in Iran and Beyond*. Wien: Austrian Academy of Sciences Press, 2014. http://www.jstor.org/stable/j.ctt1vw0ps2.

Garrett, Brianne. "How Black Women in Wine—and Their Allies—Are Banding Together to Achieve Better Representation." *Forbes*, November 6, 2019. https://www.forbes.com/sites/briannegarrett/2019/11/06/how-black-women-in-wineand-their-alliesare-banding-together-to-achieve-better-representation/.

Gately, Iain. *Drink: A Cultural History of Alcohol*. New York: Penguin, 2008.

Gaytán, Marie Sarita. *¡Tequila!: Distilling the Spirit of Mexico*. Stanford: Stanford University Press, 2014.

Gies, Frances, and Joseph Gies. *Daily Life in Medieval Times: A Vivid, Detailed Account of Birth, Marriage and Death; Food, Clothing and Housing; Love and Labor in the Middle Ages*. New York: Barnes & Noble Books, 1990.

Govender, Ishay. "The Underground Spaces Where Drinking While Female Was a Radical Act." *Wine Enthusiast Magazine*, March 8, 2020. https://www.winemag.com/2020/03/08/ladies-drinking-rooms-history/.

Govender-Ypma, Ishay. 2019. "The Singapore Sling: Colonialism, Gender Roles and Pink Drinks for Pale People." *Wine Enthusiast Magazine*, September 7, 2019. https://www.winemag.com/recipe/the-singapore-sling-colonialism-gender-roles-pink-drinks-for-pale-people/.

Graves-Brown, Carolyn. *Dancing for Hathor: Women in Ancient Egypt*. New York: Bloomsbury Publishing, 2010.

Groom, Susanne. *At the King's Table: Royal Dining through the Ages*. London: Merrell, 2013.

Guy, Kolleen M. *When Champagne Became French: Wine and the Making of a National Identity.* Johns Hopkins University Press, 2007.

Hailwood, Mark. *Alehouses and Good Fellowship in Early Modern England.* Boydell & Brewer, 2014.

Hambly, Gavin R. G. Review of *Nur Jahan: Empress of Mughal India,* by Ellison Banks Findly. *American Historical Review* 99, no. 3 (June 1994): 954–55. https://doi.org/10.2307/2167895.

Hamilton, Roy W. *The Art of Rice: Spirit and Sustenance in Asia.* Seattle: University of Washington Press, 2004.

Hamilton, Tracy Brown. "The Meditations of Europe's Last Brewmaster Nun." *The Atlantic,* October 2, 2014. https://web.archive.org/web/20160413031323/http://www.theatlantic.com/international/archive/2014/10/the-meditations-of-europes-last-brewmaster-nun/380967/.

Hayward, Hurricane. "What We Learned at Appleton Master Blender Joy Spence's Rum Tasting at The Mai-Kai." *The Atomic Grog,* August 14, 2019. http://www.slammie.com/atomicgrog/blog/2019/08/14/appleton-master-blender-joy-spence-to-host-rare-rum-tasting-at-the-mai-kai/.

Hebbar, Prajakta. "In High Spirits." *Indian Express,* September 23, 2012.

Herlihy, Patricia. *The Alcoholic Empire: Vodka & Politics in Late Imperial Russia.* Oxford University Press, 2003.

Heron, Craig. *Booze: A Distilled History.* Toronto: Between the Lines, 2003.

Hildegard. *Hildegard Von Bingen's Physica: The Complete English Translation of Her Classic Work on Health and Healing.* Translated by Priscilla Throop. Inner Traditions / Bear, 1998.

Hoalst-Pullen, Nancy, and Mark W. Patterson. *National Geographic Atlas* of Beer: A Globe-Trotting Journey through the World of Beer. Washington, DC: National Geographic Books, 2017.

Hockings, Kimberley, and Robin Dunbar. Alcohol and Humans: A Long and Social Affair. Oxford University Press, 2020.

Höllmann, Thomas Ottfried. The Land of the Five Flavors: A Cultural History of Chinese Cuisine. New York: Columbia University Press, 2014.

Holman, Bianca. "Hennessy's Popularity Is Not Due to Hip Hop. The Story Is Much Deeper Than That." VinePair, September 13, 2016. https://vinepair.com/articles/hennessys-popularity-is-not-due-to-hip-hop-the-story-is-much-deeper-than-that/.

Hoog, Tycho van der. Breweries, Politics and Identity: The History behind Namibian Beer. Basel, Switzerland: Basler Afrika Bibliographien, 2019.

Huggins, Mike. Vice and the Victorians. London: Bloomsbury Publishing, 2015.

Hurt, Jeanette. "A Short History of Women Working Behind the Bar." Thrillist, February 14, 2017. https://www.thrillist.com/culture/women-bartender-history.

Jackson, Lee. Palaces of Pleasure: From Music Halls to the Seaside to Football, How the Victorians Invented Mass Entertainment. Yale University Press, 2019.

James, Margery Kirkbride, and Elspeth M. Veale. Studies in the Medieval Wine Trade. Oxford, Clarendon Press, 1971.

Jeffreys, Henry. "Five Minutes with Joy Spence from Appleton Estate." Master of Malt Blog, June 6, 2019. https://www.masterofmalt.com/blog/post/five-minutes-with-joy-spence-from-appleton-estate.aspx.

Jennings, Justin, and Brenda J. Bowser. Drink, Power, and Society in the Andes. 2009. https://doi.org/10.5744/florida/9780813033068.003.0001.

Jochens, Jenny. Women in Old Norse Society. Ithaca: Cornell University Press, 1998.

Joffe, Alexander H. "Alcohol and Social Complexity in Ancient Western Asia." *Current Anthropology* 39, no. 3 (1998): 297–322. DOI:10.1086/204736

Johnston, Ruth A. "Beverage Production in Medieval Europe." In *World History: Ancient and Medieval Eras*, ABC-CLIO, 2020.

Kia, Mehrdad. *Daily Life in the Ottoman Empire*. Santa Barbara: Greenwood Publishing Group, 2011. ABC-CLIO.

Kladstrup, Don, and Petie Kladstrup. *Champagne: How the World's Most Glamorous Wine Triumphed over War and Hard Times*. New York: Harper-Collins, 2006.

Koehler, Robert. *Korean Wines & Spirits: Drinks That Warm the Soul*. Irvine: Seoul Selection, 2016.

Kondō, Hiroshi. *Saké: A Drinker's Guide*. Tokyo: Kodansha International, 1992.

Krishna, Priya. "The Definitive History of the Cosmopolitan." *PUNCH*, September 11, 2019. https://punchdrink.com/articles/definitive-history-cosmopolitan-cosmo-vodka-cranberry-cocktail/.

Larsen, Jeanne. "Li Qingzhao." In *Asian Poets*, edited by Rosemary M. Canfield Reisman, 53–60. *Critical Survey of Poetry*. Ipswich, MA: Salem Press, 2012. Accessed April 8, 2020. Gale eBooks. https://link.gale.com/apps/doc/CX4000200010/GVRL?u=lapl&sid=GVRL&xid=c4707c16.

Lee, Lily Xiao Hong, and Sue Wiles, eds. *Biographical Dictionary of Chinese Women: Tang through Ming, 618–1644*. Armonk, NY: M. E. Sharpe, 2014. Accessed June 23, 2020. ProQuest Ebook Central.

Lefkowitz, Mary Rosenthal, and Maureen B. Fant. *Women's Life in Greece and Rome: A Source Book in Translation*. Baltimore, MD: Johns Hopkins University Press, 2016.

Legodi, Nancy. "TMALI Alumna Adds Feminine Flair to an Ancient Craft."

Younisa no. 1 (2020): 10–11. https://www.unisa.ac.za/static/corporate_web/Content/News%20&%20Media/Publications/younisa/docs/Younisa%20Issue%201%202020%20web.pdf.

Levin, Carole, Anna Riehl Bertolet, and Jo Eldridge Carney. *A Biographical Encyclopedia of Early Modern Englishwomen: Exemplary Lives and Memorable Acts, 1500–1650.* Taylor & Francis, 2016.

LeWine, Howard. "Drinking a Little Alcohol Early in Pregnancy May Be Okay." *Harvard Health Blog,* January 29, 2020. Accessed March 3, 2021. https://www.health.harvard.edu/blog/study-no-connection-between-drinking-alcohol-early-in-pregnancy-and-birth-problems-201309106667.

Li, Qingzhao [Ch'ing-Chao]. *Li Ch'ing-Chao: Complete Poems.* Translated by Kenneth Rexroth and Ling Chung. New York: New Directions, 1979.

Li, Qingzhao [Ch'ing-Chao]. *The Complete Ci-Poems of Li Qingzhao: A New English Translation.* Translated by Jiaosheng Wang. Philadelphia: Department of Oriental Studies, University of Pennsylvania, 1989.

Lim, Wei-Yen, Chee Weng Fong, Jacqelene Meow Ling Chan, Derrick Heng, Vineta Bhalla, Suok Kai Chew. "Trends in Alcohol Consumption in Singapore 1992–2004." *Alcohol and Alcoholism* 42, no. 4 (July 2007): 354–61. https://doi.org/10.1093/alcalc/agm017.

Lindblom, Jeanette. "Women and Public Space: Social Codes and Female Presence in the Byzantine Urban Society of the 6th to the 8th Centuries." PhD diss., University of Helsinki, 2019. https://helda.helsinki.fi/handle/10138/300676.

Ling, Sally J. *Run the Rum In: South Florida During Prohibition.* Charleston, SC: History Press, 2007.

Locker, Melissa. "The Mixologist Who Shook Up Bartending's Boys' Club." *Brooklyn Based,* December 4, 2019. https://brooklynbased.com/2019/11/15/womenbehindthebarafter3-reiner-clover-club-50-best/.

Lomnitz, Larissa. "Patterns of Alcohol Consumption among the Mapuche." *Human Organization* 28, no. 4 (Winter 1969): 287–96. Accessed December 1, 2020. http://www.jstor.org/stable/44125043.

"Lucha Reyes." Strachwitz Frontera Collection. Accessed December 1, 2020. http://frontera.library.ucla.edu/artists/lucha-reyes.

Lukacs, Paul. *Inventing Wine: A New History of One of the World's Most Ancient Pleasures.* New York: W.W. Norton, 2013.

Lyman, Stephen, and Chris Bunting. *The Complete Guide to Japanese Drinks: Sake, Shochu, Japanese Whisky, Beer, Wine, Cocktails and Other Beverages.* Tuttle Publishing, 2019.

Maddocks, Fiona. *Hildegard of Bingen: The Woman of Her Age.* London: Faber & Faber, 2013.

Mancall, Peter C. *Deadly Medicine: Indians and Alcohol in Early America.* Cornell University Press, 1997.

Mannheimer, Emma. "How 'Sex and the City' Ruined the Cosmo." *Vice*, November 29, 2017. https://www.vice.com/en/article/mb9q58/how-sex-and-the-city-ruined-the-cosmo.

"Maria the Jewess." In *Encyclopedia of World Biography Online.* Vol. 32. Detroit, MI: Gale, 2012. Accessed June 11, 2020. Gale in Context: World History.

Markham, Gervase. *Countrey Contentments, Or, The English Huswife: Containing the Inward and Outward Vertues Which Ought to Be in a Compleate Woman : As Her Skill in Physicke, Surgerie, Extraction of Oyles, Banqueting-Stuffe, Ordering of Great Feasts, Preseruing All Sorts of Wines, Conceited Secrets.* By J.B. for R. Jackson, 1623.

Marre, Oliver. "Girl, Interrupted." *The Guardian*, March 18, 2007. https://www.theguardian.com/uk/2007/mar/18/monarchy.features.

Martell, Nevin. "Skinny Sipping." *FSR*, January 2013. https://www.fsr-magazine.com/skinny-sipping.

Martin, A. Lynn. *Alcohol, Sex and Gender in Late Medieval and Early Modern Europe*. London: Palgrave Macmillan, 2001.

Martin, Pete. "Pago Pago in Hollywood." *Saturday Evening Post*, May 1, 1948.

Martin, Scott C. *Devil of the Domestic Sphere: Temperance, Gender, and Middle-Class Ideology, 1800–1860*. De Kalb: Northern Illinois University Press, 2010.

Masiwa, Duncan. "Master Brewer Sees a Fizzing Future for African Beer." *Food for Mzansi*, February 14, 2020. https://www.foodformzansi.co.za/master-brewer-sees-a-fizzing-future-for-african-beer/.

Mazzeo, Tilar J. *The Widow Clicquot: The Story of a Champagne Empire and the Woman Who Ruled It*. HarperCollins, 2009.

McAvey, Marion S. "Moll Cutpurse." In *Great Lives from History: Notorious Lives*, edited by Carl L. Bankston. Hackensack, NJ: Salem, 2007.

McGovern, Patrick E. *Uncorking the Past: The Quest for Wine, Beer, and Other Alcoholic Beverages*. Berkeley: University of California Press, 2010.

McNamara, John. "Saint Brigid." In *World History: Ancient and Medieval Eras*, ABC-CLIO, 2020. http://ancienthistory.abc-clio.com.ezproxy.lapl.org/Search/Display/593524.

McNie, Maggie. *Champagne*. Faber & Faber, 1999.

Meacham, Sarah Hand. *Every Home a Distillery: Alcohol, Gender, and Technology in the Colonial Chesapeake*. Baltimore: Johns Hopkins University Press, 2009.

Medicine, Beatrice. *Drinking and Sobriety among the Lakota Sioux*. Altamira Press, 2007.

Minnick, Fred. *Whiskey Women: The Untold Story of How Women Saved Bourbon, Scotch, and Irish Whiskey.* Potomac Books, 2013.

Montalbano, Mara. "How Many Calories Do Skinnygirl Cocktails Really Save You?" *VinePair*, April 14, 2015. https://vinepair.com/wine-blog/how-many-calories-do-skinnygirl-cocktails-really-save-you/.

Morales, Mónica P. *Reading Inebriation in Early Colonial Peru.* London: Routledge, 2016. https://doi.org/10.4324/9781315603735.

Mortimer, Ian. *The Time Traveler's Guide to Medieval England: A Handbook for Visitors to the Fourteenth Century.* Simon and Schuster, 2009.

Moss, Gabrielle. "Party Out of Bounds: Booze, the Pleasure Principle, and Party-Girl Pop." *Bitch Media*, May 18, 2011. https://www.bitchmedia.org/article/party-out-of-bounds.

Murdock, Catherine Gilbert. *Domesticating Drink: Women, Men, and Alcohol in America, 1870–1940.* Baltimore: Johns Hopkins University Press, 2002.

Nice, Dr. Nicola. "Episode 398: Wouldn't It Be Nice." Interview by Damon Boelte, Sother Teague, and Greg Benson. *The Speakeasy*, September 24, 2020. Podcast audio. https://heritageradionetwork.org/episode/wouldnt-it-be-nice.

Obayemi, Ade M. U. "Alcohol Usage in an African Society." In *Cross-Cultural Approaches to the Study of Alcohol: An Interdisciplinary Perspective*, edited by Michael W. Everett, Jack O. Waddell, and Dwight B. Heath. Berlin: De Gruyter Mouton, 1976.

O'Brien, Christopher Mark. *Fermenting Revolution: How to Drink Beer and Save the World.* Post Hypnotic Press, 2011.

O'Connor, Kaori. *The Never-Ending Feast: The Anthropology and Archaeology of Feasting.* New York: Bloomsbury, 2015.

Olsson, Sven-Olle R. "Fermented Beverages Other Than Wine and Beer."

In *Encyclopedia of Food and Culture*, edited by Solomon H. Katz, 631–634. Vol. 1. New York: Charles Scribner's Sons, 2003. Gale In Context: World History. https://link.gale.com/apps/doc/CX3403400222/WHIC?u=lapl& sid=WHIC&xid=d65f350.

Opler, Morris Edward. *An Apache Life-Way: The Economic, Social, and Religious Institutions of the Chiricahua Indians.* University of Nebraska Press, 1996.

Osborn, Matthew Warner. *Rum Maniacs: Alcoholic Insanity in the Early American Republic.* University of Chicago Press, 2014.

Pasulka, Nicole. "The History of Lesbian Bars." *Vice*, August 17, 2015. https://www.vice.com/en/article/8x443v/the-history-of-lesbian-bars.

Phillips, Laura L. *Bolsheviks and the Bottle: Drink and Worker Culture in St. Petersburg, 1900–1929.* De Kalb: Northern Illinois University Press, 2000.

Phillips, Rod. *French Wine: A History.* Oakland: University of California Press, 2016.

Phillips, Rod. *A Short History of Wine.* Vancouver: Whitecap Books, 2015.

Pierce, Gretchen, and Áurea Toxqui. *Alcohol in Latin America: A Social and Cultural History.* Tucson: The University of Arizona Press, 2017.

Powers, Madelon. "Women and Public Drinking, 1890–1920." *History Today* 45, no. 2 (February 1995): 46–52.

Prakash, Om. *Foods and Drink in Ancient India: From Earliest Times to C. 1200 A.D.* Munshi Ram Manohar Lal, 1961.

Pyörälä, Eeva. "Comparing Drinking Cultures: Finnish and Spanish Drinking Stories in Interviews with Young Adults." *Acta Sociologica* 38, no. 3 (1995): 217–29. Accessed September 24, 2020. http://www.jstor.org/stable/4200967.

Rageot Maxime, Angela Mötsch, Birgit Schorer, David Bardel, Alexandra

Winkler, et al. "New Insights into Early Celtic Consumption Practices: Organic Residue Analyses of Local and Imported Pottery from Vix-Mont Lassois." *PLOS ONE* 14, no. 6 (June 19, 2019): e0218001. https://doi.org/10.1371/journal.pone.0218001.

Roberts, Benjamin. *Sex and Drugs Before Rock 'n' Roll: Youth Culture and Masculinity During Holland's Golden Age.* Amsterdam: Amsterdam University Press, 2012.

Rorabaugh, W. J. *Prohibition: A Concise History.* New York: Oxford University Press, 2018. https://public.ebookcentral.proquest.com/choice/publicfullrecord.aspx?p=5205547.

Rose, Susan. *The Wine Trade in Medieval Europe 1000–1500.* London: A&C Black, 2011.

Rotskoff, Lori. *Love on the Rocks: Men, Women, and Alcohol in Post-World War II America.* University of North Carolina Press, 2003.

Salinger, Sharon V. *Taverns and Drinking in Early America.* Baltimore: Johns Hopkins University Press, 2004.

Sasges, Gerard. "Drunken Poets and New Women: Consuming Tradition and Modernity in Colonial Vietnam." *Journal of Southeast Asian Studies* 48, no. 1 (2017): 6–30. Gale in Context: World History.

Sasges, Gerard. *Imperial Intoxication: Alcohol and the Making of Colonial Indochina.* Honolulu: University of Hawaii Press, 2017.

Schiff, Stacy. *Cleopatra: A Life.* New York: Little, Brown, 2010.

Schrad, Mark Lawrence. *Vodka Politics: Alcohol, Autocracy, and the Secret History of the Russian State.* New York: Oxford University Press, 2014.

Seltman, Charles Theodore. *Wine in the Ancient World.* London: Routledge & Kegan Paul, 1957.

Sen, Colleen Taylor. *Feasts and Fasts: A History of Food in India.* London: Reaktion Books, 2014.

Serrant, Laura. "The Silences in Our Dance: Black Caribbean Women and Alcohol (Mis)Use." In *Women and Alcohol: Social Perspectives,* edited by Patsy Staddon, Pg. #119-137 . Bristol: Bristol University Press, 2015. https://doi.org/10.2307/j.ctt1t89dmt.13.

Shirley, Glenn. *"Hello, Sucker!": The Story of Texas Guinan.* Austin: Eakin Press, 1989.

Simonson, Robert. *The Old-Fashioned: The Story of the World's First Classic Cocktail, with Recipes and Lore.* Ten Speed Press, 2014.

Simonson, Robert. *A Proper Drink: The Untold Story of How a Band of Bartenders Saved the Civilized Drinking World.* Ten Speed Press, 2016.

Sismondo, Christine. *America Walks into a Bar: A Spirited History of Taverns and Saloons, Speakeasies and Grog Shops.* New York: Oxford University Press, 2011.

Smith, Gregg. *Beer in America: The Early Years, 1587–1840; Beer's Role in the Settling of America and the Birth of a Nation.* Boulder, CO: Siris Books, 1998.

Smith, Lesley, and David Foxcroft. "Drinking in the UK: An Exploration of Trends." https://www.jrf.org.uk/sites/default/files/jrf/migrated/files/UK-alcohol-trends-FULL.pdf.

Smith, Robert J., and Ella Lury Wiswell. *The Women of Suye Mura.* Chicago: University of Chicago Press, 1982.

Snodgrass, Mary Ellen. *Encyclopedia of Kitchen History.* Routledge, 2004.

Snyder, Solomon H., Paul R. Sandberg, Barry L. Jacobs, and Jerome Jaffe. *The Encyclopedia of Psychoactive Drugs.* New York: Chelsea House Publishers, 1992.

"Spirited Women Who've Run the World of Spirits." ASW Distillery, March

8, 2018. https://www.aswdistillery.com/crafted-with-characters/2018/3/8/
spirited-women-whove-run-the-world-of-spirits.

Spude, Catherine Holder. *Saloons, Prostitutes, and Temperance in Alaska Territory*. Norman: University of Oklahoma Press, 2015.

Standage, Tom. *A History of the World in 6 Glasses*. Bloomsbury USA, 2006.

Stegall, Gwendolyn. "A Spatial History of Lesbian Bars in New York City." Master's thesis, Columbia University, 2019. https://doi.org/10.7916/d8-k46h-fa23.

Stuart, Walton. *Out of It: A Cultural History of Intoxication*. Three Rivers Press, 2003.

"Supreme Court Historical Society." The Supreme Court Historical Society. https://supremecourthistory.org/learning-center/text-books-supreme-court-decisions-womens-rights-milestones-to-equality/justice-for-beer-drinkers-craig-v-boren-429-u-s-190-1976/.

Swanson, Sonja. "The Secret History of Makgeolli, the Korean Alcohol with a Yogurt-Tart Taste." *Los Angeles Times*, May 1, 2019. https://www.latimes.com/food/la-fo-homemade-makgeolli-korean-alcohol-20190501-story.html.

Thompkins, Gwen. "Forebears: Bessie Smith, the Empress of the Blues." NPR, January 5, 2018. https://www.npr.org/2018/01/05/575422226/forebears-bessie-smith-the-empress-of-the-blues.

Tlusty, Beverly Ann. "Crossing Gender Boundaries: Women as Drunkards in Early Modern Augsburg." In *Ehrkonzepte in der Frühen Neuzeit*, edited by Sibylle Backmann, 185–98. Berlin: De Gruyter, 2018. https://doi.org/10.1515/9783050073576-011.

Todd, Janet, and Elizabeth Spearing, eds. *Counterfeit Ladies: The Life and Death of Mal Cutpurse; The Case of Mary Carleton*. London: Routledge, 2018. https://doi.org/10.4324/9781315477855.

Toner, Deborah. Review of *Distilling the Influence of Alcohol: Aguardiente in Guatemalan History*, edited by David Jr. Carey. *Hispanic American Historical Review* 94, no. 4 (2014): 709–10. https://doi.org/10.1215/00182168-2802858.

Tracy, Sarah W. *Alcoholism in America: From Reconstruction to Prohibition*. Baltimore: Johns Hopkins University Press, 2009.

Transchel, Kate. *Under the Influence: Working-Class Drinking, Temperance, and Cultural Revolution in Russia, 1895–1932*. Pittsburgh: University of Pittsburgh Press, 2006.

Tsjeng, Zing. *Forgotten Women: The Scientists*. Octopus Publishing Group, 2018.

Tyldesley, Joyce. *Cleopatra: Last Queen of Egypt*. London: Profile, 2011.

Unger, Richard W. *Beer in the Middle Ages and the Renaissance*. Philadelphia: University of Pennsylvania Press, 2004.

Unwin, P. T. H. *Wine and the Vine: An Historical Geography of Viticulture and the Wine Trade*. London: Routledge, 2010.

Vivante, Bella. *Daughters of Gaia: Women in the Ancient Mediterranean World*. Praeger, 2007.

Vivante, Bella, ed. *Women's Roles in Ancient Civilizations: A Reference Guide*. London: Greenwood Press, 1999.

Vora, Shivani. "From Chemist to Cocktails: Meet the Rum Industry's First Female Master Blender." *Fortune*, October 24, 2015. https://fortune.com/2015/10/24/female-master-blender/.

Warner, Jessica. *Craze: Gin and Debauchery in an Age of Reason; Consisting of a Tragicomedy in Three Acts in Which High and Low Are Brought together, Much to Their Mutual Discomfort; Complete with Stories, Some Witty and Some Not,*

Conducive to Meditation on Recent Events. New York: Random House Trade Paperbacks, 2003.

Wolfram, Herwig. *History of the Goths.* Translated by Thomas J. Dunlap. University of California Press, 1990.

Wolputte, Steven van, and Mattia Fumanti. *Beer in Africa: Drinking Spaces, States and Selves.* Münster: LIT Verlag, 2010.

Wondrich, David. *Imbibe! Updated and Revised Edition: From Absinthe Cocktail to Whiskey Smash, a Salute in Stories and Drinks to "Professor" Jerry Thomas, Pioneer of the American Bar.* Penguin Publishing Group, 2015.

Wong, Eugene C., Jean H. Kim, William B. Goggins, Joseph Lau, Samuel Y. S. Wong, and Sian M. Griffiths. "Chinese Women's Drinking Patterns Before and After the Hong Kong Alcohol Policy Changes." *Alcohol and Alcoholism* 53, no. 4 (July 2018): 477–86. https://doi.org/10.1093/alcalc/agy010.

Young, James Harvey. Review of *Brewed in America: A History of Beer and Ale in the United States,* by Stanley Baron. *Journal of American History,* Volume 49, Issue 2, Pages 349–350. September 1962. https://doi.org/10.2307/1888660.

Zharkevich, Ina. *War, Maoism and Everyday Revolution in Nepal.* Cambridge: Cambridge University Press, 2019.

INDEX